3A

FOCUS
ON
GRAMMAR

AN INTEGRATED SKILLS APPROACH

3A

FOCUS ON GRAMMAR

AN INTEGRATED SKILLS APPROACH

THIRD EDITION

MARJORIE FUCHS

MARGARET BONNER

MIRIAM WESTHEIMER

PEARSON
Longman

To the memory of my parents, Edith and Joseph Fuchs—MF
To my parents, Marie and Joseph Maus, and to my son, Luke Frances—MB
To my husband, Joel Einleger, and my children, Ari and Leora—MW

FOCUS ON GRAMMAR 3A: An Integrated Skills Approach, Third Edition

Pearson Education, 10 Bank Street, White Plains, NY 10606

Vice president, multimedia and skills: Sherry Preiss
Executive editor: Laura Le Dréan
Senior development editor: Françoise Leffler
Vice president, director of design and production: Rhea Banker
Director of editorial production: Linda Moser
Production supervisor: Christine Edmonds
Senior production editor: Kathleen Silloway
Art director: Ann France
Senior manufacturing buyer: Nancy Flaggman
Photo research: Aerin Csigay
Cover design: Rhea Banker
Cover images: (background) Comstock Images (#comks76622) RF, (background center) Nick
    Koudis (#AA010649) RF; (center) Harald Sund (#200131667-001) RM
Text design: Quorum Creative Services, Rhea Banker
Text composition: ElectraGraphics, Inc.
Illustrators: Steve Attoe pp. 2, 58, 59, 135, 163, 356; Bumar Technical Corporation p. 172; Moffitt Cecil pp. 19,
    21, 240, 406; Ronald Chironna pp. 28, 419; Chi Chung pp. 249, 250; Chris Gash pp. 8, 9, 212, 217; Brian
    Hughes pp. 16, 139, 210, 229, 230, 281, 285; Jock MacRae pp. 42, 103; Tom Newsom pp. 41, 49, 50, 99,
    100, 208; PC&F pp. 259, 261; Dusan Petrici pp. 17, 65, 149, 150, 256; Steve Schulman pp. 226, 352, 354,
    364, 366, 420 (left); Susan Scott p. 34; Gary Torrisi pp. 199, 201, 295, 420 (right); Meryl Treatner pp. 73, 113.
Text credits: See p. x.
Photo credits: See p. x.

Library of Congress Cataloging-in-Publication Data

Focus on grammar. An integrated skills approach.— 3rd ed.
    p. cm.
  ISBN 0-13-147466-9 (v. 1 : student book : alk. paper) — ISBN 0-13-189971-6 (v. 2 :
student book : alk. paper) — ISBN 0-13-189984-8 (v. 3 : student book : alk. paper) —
ISBN 0-13-190008-0 (v. 4 : student book : alk. paper) — ISBN 0-13-191273-9 (v. 5 :
student book : alk. paper)
  1. English language—Textbooks for foreign speakers. 2. English language—Grammar—
Problems, exercises, etc.
PE1128.F555 2005
428.2'4—dc22

                                                                                        2005007655

ISBNs: 0-13-189993-7 (Student Book A)
        5 6 7 8 9 10—WC—12 11 10 09

        0-13-193925-4 (Student Book A with Audio CD)
        5 6 7 8 9 10—WC—12 11 10 09

Printed in The United States of America

CONTENTS

PART IV   **PRESENT PERFECT**

APPENDICES

ABOUT THE AUTHORS

Marjorie Fuchs has taught ESL at New York City Technical College and LaGuardia Community College of the City University of New York and EFL at the Sprach Studio Lingua Nova in Munich, Germany. She has a master's degree in Applied English Linguistics and a Certificate in TESOL from the University of Wisconsin—Madison. She has authored and co-authored many widely used books and multimedia materials, notably *Crossroads, Top Twenty ESL Word Games: Beginning Vocabulary Development, Families: Ten Card Games for Language Learners, Focus on Grammar 4: An Integrated Skills Approach, Focus on Grammar 3 CD-ROM, Focus on Grammar 4 CD-ROM, Longman English Interactive 3* and *4, Grammar Express Basic, Grammar Express Basic CD-ROM, Grammar Express Intermediate,* and the workbooks to the *Longman Dictionary of American English, the Longman Photo Dictionary, The Oxford Picture Dictionary, Focus on Grammar 3* and *4,* and *Grammar Express Basic.*

Margaret Bonner has taught ESL at Hunter College and the Borough of Manhattan Community College of the City University of New York, at Taiwan National University in Taipei, and at Virginia Commonwealth University in Richmond. She holds a master's degree in Library Science from Columbia University, and she has done work toward a Ph.D. in English Literature at the Graduate Center of the City University of New York. She has authored and co-authored numerous ESL and EFL print and multimedia materials, including textbooks for the national school system of Oman, *Step into Writing: A Basic Writing Text, Focus on Grammar 4: An Integrated Skills Approach, Focus on Grammar 4 Workbook, Grammar Express Basic, Grammar Express Basic CD-ROM, Grammar Express Basic Workbook, Grammar Express Intermediate, Focus on Grammar 3 CD-ROM, Focus on Grammar 4 CD-ROM, Longman English Interactive 4,* and *The Oxford Picture Dictionary Intermediate Workbook.*

Miriam Westheimer taught EFL at all levels of instruction in Haifa, Israel, for a period of six years. She has also taught ESL at Queens College, at LaGuardia Community College, and in the American Language Program of Columbia University. She holds a master's degree in TESOL and a doctorate in Curriculum and Teaching from Teachers College of Columbia University. She is the co-author of a communicative grammar program developed and widely used in Israel.

TEXT AND PHOTO CREDITS

INTRODUCTION

The *Focus on Grammar* series

Written by ELT professionals, *Focus on Grammar: An Integrated Skills Approach* helps students to understand and practice English grammar. The primary aim of the course is for students to gain confidence in their ability to speak and write English accurately and fluently.

The **third edition** retains the series' focus on English grammar through lively listening, speaking, reading, and writing activities. The new *Focus on Grammar* also maintains the same five-level progression as the second edition:

- Level 1 (Beginning, formerly Introductory)
- Level 2 (High-Beginning, formerly Basic)
- Level 3 (Intermediate)
- Level 4 (High-Intermediate)
- Level 5 (Advanced)

What is the *Focus on Grammar* methodology?

Both controlled and communicative practice

While students expect and need to learn the formal rules of a language, it is crucial that they also practice new structures in a variety of contexts in order to internalize and master them. To this end, *Focus on Grammar* provides an abundance of both controlled and communicative exercises so that students can bridge the gap between knowing grammatical structures and using them. The many communicative activities in each Student Book unit provide opportunity for critical thinking while enabling students to personalize what they have learned in order to talk to one another with ease about hundreds of everyday issues.

A unique four-step approach

The series follows a four-step approach:

Step 1: Grammar in Context shows the new structures in natural contexts, such as articles and conversations.

Step 2: Grammar Presentation presents the structures in clear and accessible grammar charts, notes, and examples.

Step 3: Focused Practice of both form and meaning of the new structures is provided in numerous and varied controlled exercises.

Step 4: Communication Practice allows students to use the new structures freely and creatively in motivating, open-ended activities.

Thorough recycling

Underpinning the scope and sequence of the *Focus on Grammar* series is the belief that students need to use target structures many times, in different contexts, and at increasing levels of difficulty. For this reason, new grammar is constantly recycled throughout the book so that students have maximum exposure to the target forms and become comfortable using them in speech and in writing.

A complete classroom text and reference guide

A major goal in the development of *Focus on Grammar* has been to provide students with books that serve not only as vehicles for classroom instruction but also as resources for reference and self-study. In each Student Book, the combination of grammar charts, grammar notes, a glossary of grammar terms, and extensive appendices provides a complete and invaluable reference guide for students.

Ongoing assessment

Review Tests at the end of each part of the Student Book allow for continual self-assessment. In addition, the tests in the new *Focus on Grammar* Assessment Package provide teachers with a valid, reliable, and practical means of determining students' appropriate levels of placement in the course and of assessing students' achievement throughout the course. At Levels 4 (High-Intermediate) and 5 (Advanced), Proficiency Tests give teachers an overview of their students' general grammar knowledge.

What are the components of each level of *Focus on Grammar*?

Student Book

The Student Book is divided into eight or more parts, depending on the level. Each part contains grammatically related units, with each unit focusing on specific grammatical structures; where appropriate, units present contrasting forms. The exercises in each unit are thematically related to one another, and all units have the same clear, easy-to-follow format.

Teacher's Manual

The Teacher's Manual contains a variety of suggestions and information to enrich the material in the Student Book. It includes general teaching suggestions for each section of a typical unit, answers to frequently asked questions, unit-by-unit teaching tips with ideas for further communicative practice, and a supplementary activity section. Answers to the Student Book exercises and audioscripts of the listening activities are found at the back of the Teacher's Manual. Also included in the Teacher's Manual is a CD-ROM of teaching tools, including PowerPoint presentations that offer alternative ways of presenting selected grammar structures.

Workbook

The Workbook accompanying each level of *Focus on Grammar* provides additional exercises appropriate for self-study of the target grammar for each Student Book unit. Tests included in each Workbook provide students with additional opportunities for self-assessment.

Audio Program

All of the listening exercises from the Student Book, as well as the Grammar in Context passages and other appropriate exercises, are included on the program's CDs. In the book, the symbol ⌒ appears next to the listening exercises. Another symbol ⌒, indicating that listening is optional, appears next to the Grammar in Context passages and some exercises. All of these scripts appear in the Teacher's Manual and may be used as an alternative way of presenting the activities.

Some Student Books are packaged with a separate Student Audio CD. This CD includes the listening exercise from each unit.

CD-ROM

The *Focus on Grammar* CD-ROM provides students with individualized practice and immediate feedback. Fully contextualized and interactive, the activities broaden and extend practice of the grammatical structures in the reading, writing, listening, and speaking skills areas. The CD-ROM includes grammar review, review tests, score-based remedial practice, games, and all relevant reference material from the Student Book. It can also be used in conjunction with the *Longman Interactive American Dictionary* CD-ROM.

Assessment Package (NEW)

An extensive, comprehensive Assessment Package has been developed for each level of the third edition of *Focus on Grammar*. The components of the Assessment Package are:

1. Placement, Diagnostic, and Achievement Tests

- a Placement Test to screen students and place them into the correct level
- Diagnostic Tests for each part of the Student Book
- Unit Achievement Tests for each unit of the Student Book
- Part Achievement Tests for each part of the Student Book

2. General Proficiency Tests

- two Proficiency Tests at Level 4 (High-Intermediate)
- two Proficiency Tests at Level 5 (Advanced)

These tests can be administered at any point in the course.

3. Audio CD

The listening portions of the Placement, Diagnostic, and Achievement Tests are recorded on CDs. The scripts appear in the Assessment Package.

4. Test-Generating Software

The test-bank software provides thousands of questions from which teachers can create class-appropriate tests. All items are labeled according to the grammar structure they are testing, so teachers can easily select relevant items; they can also design their own items to add to the tests.

Transparencies (NEW)

Transparencies of all the grammar charts in the Student Book are also available. These transparencies are a classroom visual aid that will help instructors point out important patterns and structures of grammar.

Companion Website

The companion website contains a wealth of information and activities for both teachers and students. In addition to general information about the course pedagogy, the website provides extensive practice exercises for the classroom, a language lab, or at home.

What's new in the third edition of the Student Book?

In response to users' requests, this edition has:

- a new four-color design
- easy-to-read color coding for the four steps
- new and updated reading texts for Grammar in Context
- post-reading activities (in addition to the pre-reading questions)
- more exercise items
- an editing (error analysis) exercise in each unit
- an Internet activity in each unit
- a Glossary of Grammar Terms
- expanded Appendices

References

Alexander, L. G. (1988). *Longman English Grammar*. White Plains: Longman.

Biber, D., S. Conrad, E. Finegan, S. Johansson, and G. Leech (1999). *Longman Grammar of Spoken and Written English*. White Plains: Longman.

Celce-Murcia, M., and D. Freeman (1999). *The Grammar Book*. Boston: Heinle and Heinle.

Celce-Murcia, M., and S. Hilles (1988). *Techniques and Resources in Teaching Grammar*. New York: Oxford University Press.

Firsten, R. (2002). *The ELT Grammar Book*. Burlingame, CA: Alta Book Center Publishers.

Garner, B. (2003). *Garner's Modern American Usage*. New York: Oxford University Press.

Greenbaum, S. (1996). *The Oxford English Grammar*. New York: Oxford University Press.

Leech, G. (2004). *Meaning and the English Verb*. Harlow, UK: Pearson.

Lewis, M. (1997). *Implementing the Lexical Approach*. Hove East Sussex, UK: Language Teaching Publications.

Longman (2002). *Longman Dictionary of English Language and Culture*. Harlow, UK: Longman.

Willis, D. (2003). *Rules, Patterns and Words*. New York: Cambridge University Press.

TOUR OF A UNIT

Each unit in the *Focus on Grammar* Series presents a specific grammar structure (or two, in case of a contrast) and develops a major theme, which is set by the opening text. All units follow the same unique **four-step approach.**

Step 1: Grammar in Context

The **conversation** or **reading** in this section shows the grammar structure in a natural context. The high-interest text presents authentic language in a variety of real-life formats: magazine articles, web pages, questionnaires, and more. Students can listen to the text on an audio CD to get accustomed to the sound of the grammar structure in a natural context.

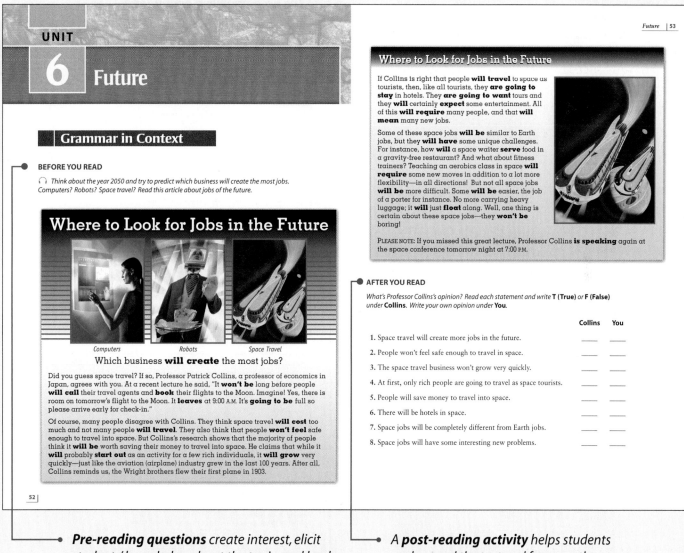

UNIT
6 Future

Grammar in Context

BEFORE YOU READ

Think about the year 2050 and try to predict which business will create the most jobs. Computers? Robots? Space travel? Read this article about jobs of the future.

Where to Look for Jobs in the Future

Computers   Robots   Space Travel

Which business **will create** the most jobs?

Did you guess space travel? If so, Professor Patrick Collins, a professor of economics in Japan, agrees with you. At a recent lecture he said, "It **won't be** long before people **will call** their travel agents and **book** their flights to the Moon. Imagine! Yes, there is room on tomorrow's flight to the Moon. It **leaves** at 9:00 A.M. It's **going to be** full so please arrive early for check-in."

Of course, many people disagree with Collins. They think space travel **will cost** too much and not many people **will travel**. They also think that people **won't feel** safe enough to travel into space. But Collins's research shows that the majority of people think it **will be** worth saving their money to travel into space. He claims that while it **will** probably **start out** as an activity for a few rich individuals, it **will grow** very quickly—just like the aviation (airplane) industry grew in the last 100 years. After all, Collins reminds us, the Wright brothers flew their first plane in 1903.

52

Where to Look for Jobs in the Future

If Collins is right that people **will travel** to space as tourists, then, like all tourists, they **are going to stay** in hotels. They **are going to want** tours and they **will** certainly **expect** some entertainment. All of this **will require** many people, and that **will mean** many new jobs.

Some of these space jobs **will be** similar to Earth jobs, but they **will have** some unique challenges. For instance, how **will** a space waiter **serve** food in a gravity-free restaurant? And what about fitness trainers? Teaching an aerobics class in space **will require** some new moves in addition to a lot more flexibility—in all directions! But not all space jobs **will be** more difficult. Some **will be** easier, the job of a porter for instance. No more carrying heavy luggage; it **will** just **float** along. Well, one thing is certain about these space jobs—they **won't be** boring!

PLEASE NOTE: If you missed this great lecture, Professor Collins **is speaking** again at the space conference tomorrow night at 7:00 P.M.

AFTER YOU READ

What's Professor Collins's opinion? Read each statement and write **T (True)** or **F (False)** under **Collins**. Write your own opinion under **You**.

	Collins	You
1. Space travel will create more jobs in the future.	___	___
2. People won't feel safe enough to travel in space.	___	___
3. The space travel business won't grow very quickly.	___	___
4. At first, only rich people are going to travel as space tourists.	___	___
5. People will save money to travel into space.	___	___
6. There will be hotels in space.	___	___
7. Space jobs will be completely different from Earth jobs.	___	___
8. Space jobs will have some interesting new problems.	___	___

- **Pre-reading questions** *create interest, elicit students' knowledge about the topic, and lead students to make predictions about the text.*

- *A **post-reading activity** helps students understand the text and focus on the grammar structure.*

Step 2: Grammar Presentation

This section is made up of grammar charts, notes, and examples. The **grammar charts** focus on the forms of the grammar structure. The **grammar notes** and **examples** focus on the meanings and uses of the structure.

*Clear and easy-to-read **grammar charts** present the grammar structure in all its forms and combinations.*

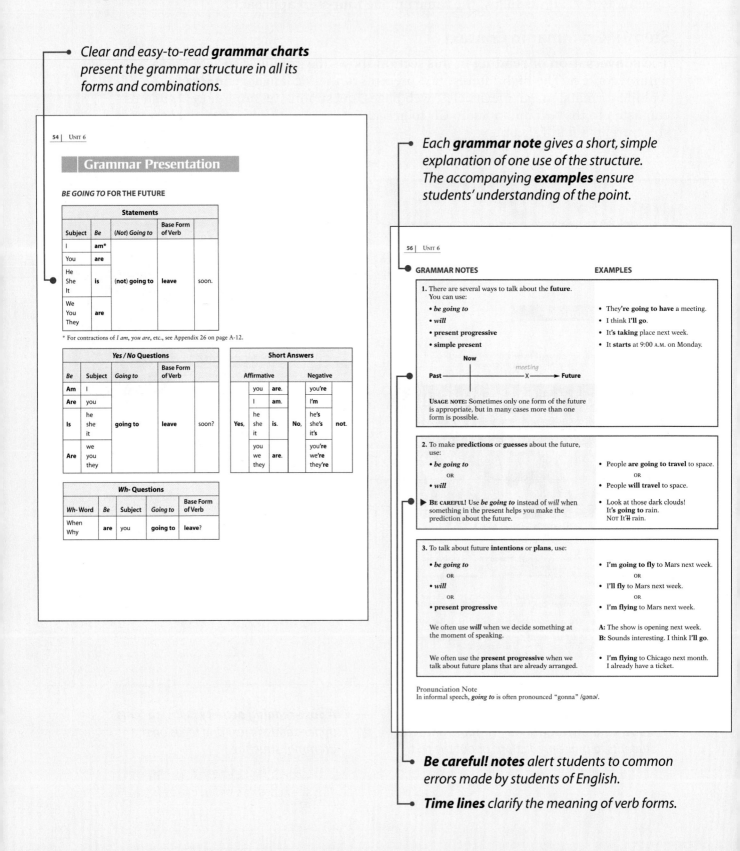

54 | UNIT 6

Grammar Presentation

BE GOING TO FOR THE FUTURE

Statements				
Subject	Be	(Not) Going to	Base Form of Verb	
I	am*			
You	are			
He She It	is	(not) going to	leave	soon.
We You They	are			

* For contractions of *I am*, *you are*, etc., see Appendix 26 on page A-12.

Yes / No Questions				
Be	Subject	Going to	Base Form of Verb	
Am	I			
Are	you			
Is	he she it	going to	leave	soon?
Are	we you they			

Short Answers					
	Affirmative			Negative	
Yes,	you	are.	No,	you're	not.
	I	am.		I'm	
	he she it	is.		he's she's it's	
	you we they	are.		you're we're they're	

Wh- Questions				
Wh- Word	Be	Subject	Going to	Base Form of Verb
When Why	are	you	going to	leave?

*Each **grammar note** gives a short, simple explanation of one use of the structure. The accompanying **examples** ensure students' understanding of the point.*

56 | UNIT 6

GRAMMAR NOTES   **EXAMPLES**

1. There are several ways to talk about the **future**. You can use:
- *be going to*
- *will*
- *present progressive*
- *simple present*

Now

Past ——————|————— *meeting* ——X——→ Future

USAGE NOTE: Sometimes only one form of the future is appropriate, but in many cases more than one form is possible.

- They're **going to have** a meeting.
- I think I'll **go**.
- It's **taking** place next week.
- It **starts** at 9:00 A.M. on Monday.

2. To make **predictions** or **guesses** about the future, use:
- *be going to*
  OR
- *will*

▶ **BE CAREFUL!** Use *be going to* instead of *will* when something in the present helps you make the prediction about the future.

- People **are going to travel** to space.
  OR
- People **will travel** to space.

- Look at those dark clouds! It's **going to** rain.
  NOT It'**ll** rain.

3. To talk about future **intentions** or **plans**, use:
- *be going to*
  OR
- *will*
  OR
- *present progressive*

We often use *will* when we decide something at the moment of speaking.

We often use the **present progressive** when we talk about future plans that are already arranged.

- I'm **going to fly** to Mars next week.
  OR
- I'll **fly** to Mars next week.
  OR
- I'm **flying** to Mars next week.

A: The show is opening next week.
B: Sounds interesting. I think I'll **go**.

- I'm **flying** to Chicago next month. I already have a ticket.

Pronunciation Note
In informal speech, *going to* is often pronounced "gonna" /gənə/.

***Be careful! notes** alert students to common errors made by students of English.*

***Time lines** clarify the meaning of verb forms.*

Step 3: Focused Practice

This section provides students with a variety of contextualized **controlled exercises** to practice both the forms and the uses of the grammar structure.

Focused Practice *always begins with a "for recognition only" exercise called* **Discover the Grammar**.

Focused Practice

1   DISCOVER THE GRAMMAR

Read the question. Then circle the letter of the correct sentence.

1. In which sentence do we know that the diamond necklace is gone?
   a. He was stealing a diamond necklace.
   b. He stole a diamond necklace.

2. Which sentence tells us that the people arrived at the mountains?
   a. They were driving to the mountains.
   b. They drove to the mountains.

3. In which sentence was the action interrupted?
   a. When the phone rang, he answered it.
   b. When the phone rang, he was looking for his bag.

4. Which sentence talks about two actions that were in progress at the same time?
   a. While the officer was questioning Sal, Eve was leaving town.
   b. When the officer questioned Sal, Eve left town.

5. In which sentence did the friends arrive before lunch began?
   a. When our friends arrived, we were eating lunch.
   b. When our friends arrived, we ate lunch.

2   A TRAFFIC ACCIDENT   *Grammar Notes 1–6*

🎧 *Complete the conversation with the past progressive or the simple past form of the verbs in parentheses. Use Appendix 1 on page 000 for help with irregular verbs.*

REPORTER: What was the cause of the accident, Officer?

OFFICER: Well, it looks like there were many causes. First of all, when the accident
_____ , the driver _____ much too fast. The driver
1. (happen)   2. (drive)
is a suspect in a burglary, and she _____ town. While she
3. (leave)
_____ , she _____ to someone on her cell phone.
4. (drive)   5. (speak)
When she _____ the pedestrian, she immediately _____
6. (see)   7. (step)
on the brakes, but it was too late. The victim wasn't paying attention, either. He
_____ the street against a red light when the car _____
8. (cross)   9. (hit)
him. He _____ the approaching car because he _____ to
10. (not see)   11. (talk)

Exercises are **cross-referenced** *to the appropriate grammar notes to provide a quick review.*

A **variety of exercise types** *guide students from recognition to accurate production of the grammar structure.*

4   BLIZZARD   *Grammar Notes 1–6*

Combine the pairs of sentences. Use the past progressive or the simple past form of the verb. Remember to use commas when necessary.

1. The blizzard started. Mr. Ligo attended a party.
   When _the blizzard started, Mr. Ligo was attending a party._

2. The wind began to blow. The electricity went out.
   When _____

3. He drove home. He listened to his car radio.
   While _____

4. He pulled over to the side of the road. He couldn't see anything.
   _____ when _____

5. He listened to the news. He heard about the burglary.
   While _____

6. It stopped snowing. Mr. Ligo went to the police station.
   When _____

5   EDITING

Read this personal journal entry. There are seven mistakes in the use of the past progressive and the simple past. The first mistake is already corrected. Find and correct six more. Remember to look at punctuation!

> What was happening to me this morning was so unbelievable! I walked down the
> street while a woman stopped in front of me and asked me for directions to the
> nearest bank. At that moment, I was seeing my friend Bill across the street.
> I called out to him and asked him to wait for me. Luckily for me, he did. Bill
> saw everything: While I talking to the woman, a pickpocket was put his hand
> into my backpack. Bill started to walk away. I thought he didn't want to wait
> for me, but I was wrong. When Bill saw the pickpocket he went to call the
> police. They were arriving immediately. The police arrested the woman and the
> pickpocket. What an experience!

(correction above "What was happening": happened)

Focused Practice always ends with an **editing** *exercise to teach students to find and correct typical mistakes.*

Step 4: Communication Practice

This section provides open-ended **communicative activities** giving students the opportunity to use the grammar structure appropriately and fluently.

A **listening** activity gives students the opportunity to check their aural comprehension.

A **writing** activity allows students to use the grammar structure in a variety of formats.

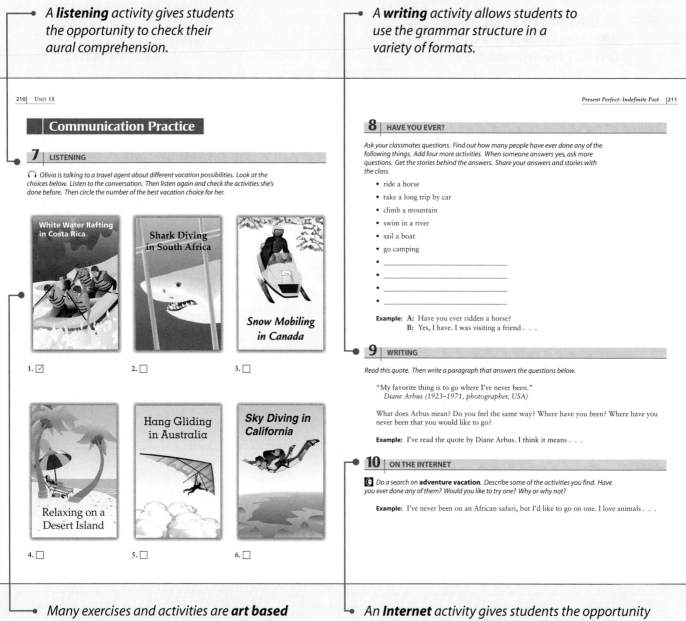

210 | UNIT 18

Communication Practice

7 | LISTENING

🎧 Olivia is talking to a travel agent about different vacation possibilities. Look at the choices below. Listen to the conversation. Then listen again and check the activities she's done before. Then circle the number of the best vacation choice for her.

White Water Rafting in Costa Rica

Shark Diving in South Africa

Snow Mobiling in Canada

1. ☑   2. ☐   3. ☐

Relaxing on a Desert Island

Hang Gliding in Australia

Sky Diving in California

4. ☐   5. ☐   6. ☐

Present Perfect: Indefinite Past | 211

8 | HAVE YOU EVER?

Ask your classmates questions. Find out how many people have ever done any of the following things. Add four more activities. When someone answers yes, ask more questions. Get the stories behind the answers. Share your answers and stories with the class.

- ride a horse
- take a long trip by car
- climb a mountain
- swim in a river
- sail a boat
- go camping
- _____
- _____
- _____
- _____

Example: A: Have you ever ridden a horse?
B: Yes, I have. I was visiting a friend . . .

9 | WRITING

Read this quote. Then write a paragraph that answers the questions below.

"My favorite thing is to go where I've never been."
Diane Arbus (1923–1971, photographer, USA)

What does Arbus mean? Do you feel the same way? Where have you been? Where have you never been that you would like to go?

Example: I've read the quote by Diane Arbus. I think it means . . .

10 | ON THE INTERNET

🌐 Do a search on **adventure vacation**. Describe some of the activities you find. Have you ever done any of them? Would you like to try one? Why or why not?

Example: I've never been on an African safari, but I'd like to go on one. I love animals . . .

Many exercises and activities are **art based** to provide visual cues and an interesting context and springboard for meaningful conversations.

An **Internet** activity gives students the opportunity to expand on the content of the unit and interact with their classmates creatively and fluently.

TOUR BEYOND THE UNIT

In the *Focus on Grammar* series, the grammatically related units are grouped into parts, and each part concludes with a section called **From Grammar to Writing** and a **Review Test** section.

From Grammar to Writing

This section presents a point which applies specifically to writing, for example, using descriptive adjectives to develop a paragraph. Students are guided to practice the point in a **piece of extended writing.**

An **introduction** relates the grammar point to the writing focus.

Students practice **pre-writing strategies** such as word-mapping, tree-diagramming, and outlining.

Writing formats include business letters, personal letters, notes, instructions, paragraphs, reports, and essays.

The section includes **peer review** and **editing** of the students' writing.

Review Test

This review section, covering all the grammar structures presented in the part, can be used as a test. An **Answer Key** is provided at the back of the book.

PART **VI**

Review Test

I *Complete the advertisements by choosing the correct words in parentheses.*

1. FOR RENT. Live _____*comfortably*_____ in this _____ studio
   a. (comfortable / comfortably)   b. (cozy / cozily)
   apartment. _____ rent makes it a _____
   c. (Cheap / Cheaply)   d. (perfect / perfectiy)
   home for one student.

2. FOR SALE. Woman's bicycle. I'm asking the _____ low price of $65
   a. (incredible / incredibly)
   for this _____ five-speed bike. I've _____
   b. (new / newly)   c. (hard / hardly)
   used it at all. Don't miss this _____ bargain.
   d. (terrific / terrifically)

3. FREE to a _____ family. Skipper is a _____
   a. (good / well)   b. (beautiful / beautifully)
   and friendly puppy. He behaves _____ with children, and he is very
   c. (good / well)
   _____. We are moving very soon, so if you want Skipper, please act
   d. (obedient / obediently)
   _____.
   e. (quick / quickly)

II *Circle the letter of the correct answer to complete each sentence.*

1. I passed my driver's test. It seemed much _____ this time.   A (B) C D
   (A) easy   (C) easiest
   (B) easier   (D) easily

2. Our team didn't play _____ I expected. I was disappointed.   A B C D
   (A) as well as   (C) as badly as
   (B) well   (D) better

3. The faster Tranh walks, _____,   A B C D
   (A) more tired   (C) the more tired he gets
   (B) he gets tired   (D) he gets more tired

(continued)

|309|

The Review Tests *include **multiple-choice questions** in standardized test formats, giving students practice in test taking.*

IV **(Unit 21)**
2. enough   8. How many
3. a lot of   9. any
4. How much   10. much
5. a little   11. a lot of
6. a few   12. a few
7. some

III **(Unit 22)**
2. a, a, an   6. the
3. the   7. an
4. The   8. a
5. the, the   9. the, an

IV **(Unit 22)**
3. the   6. The
4. Money   7. Vegetables
5. Travel, Staying

V **(Unit 22)**
1. b. some   2. a. some
   c. a   b. some
   d. an   c. the
   e. The   d. some
   f. The   e. The
                  f. the

VI **(Units 21 and 22)**
2. B   4. A   6. C
3. C   5. A   7. A

PART VI

I **(Unit 23)**
1. b. cozy   3. a. good
   c. Cheap   b. beautiful
   d. perfect   c. well
2. a. incredibly d. obedient
   b. new   e. quickly
   c. hardly
   d. terrific

II **(Units 25 and 26)**
2. A   5. B   8. B   11. D
3. C   6. C   9. A   12. B
4. A   7. D   10. C   13. D

III **(Unit 23)**
2. C   5. C   8. B   11. C
3. D   6. B   9. B   12. B
4. B   7. A   10. C

IV **(Units 25 and 26)**
2. faster, more confused
3. later, sillier
4. harder, more fluently
5. more often, bigger
6. louder, faster
7. more frequently, worse

V **(Units 24 and 26)**
2. is as large as Apartment 22-G.
3. isn't as far (away) as Tony's pizzeria.
4. is as expensive as Tony's pizza.
5. play (OR are playing OR have played) as well as the Shock.
6. doesn't run as fast as (OR isn't as fast as) Jennifer.

VI **(Units 25 and 26)**
1. b. longest   2. a. big
   c. hardest   b. than
   d. the   c. much
   e. of   d. exciting
   f. best   e. Sooner
                     f. as

VII **(Units 23–26)**

    I think today has been the ~~bad~~ *worst* day of my life. My car broke down on the expressway during rush hour this morning—a ~~busiest~~ *the* time of day. I sat there for an hour waiting for a tow truck. The longer I waited, the ~~nervous~~ *more* I became. I was a wreck when I got to work. Of course, this was the day we were closing ~~biggest~~ *the* deal of the year. My boss called me five times about one letter. And ~~more~~ *the* frequently he called, the worse I typed. My next worry is the repair bill for the car. I hope it isn't as high ~~the~~ *as* last time.

    I'm going to try to relax now. There's an ~~interested~~ *interesting* movie on cable TV tonight. Jan saw it last week and says it's the ~~better~~ *best* film she's seen in a long time. After the movie, I'll take a ~~hotter~~ *hot* bath and go to bed. I'm looking forward to tomorrow. It can't be as ~~badly~~ *bad* as today!

RT-4

The Review Tests Answer Key *provides **cross-references** to the appropriate unit(s) for easy review.*

ACKNOWLEDGMENTS

Before acknowledging the many people who have contributed to the third edition of *Focus on Grammar*, we wish to express our gratitude to those who worked on the first and second editions, and whose influence is still present in the new work. Our continuing thanks to:

- Joanne Dresner, who initiated the project and helped conceptualize the general approach of *Focus on Grammar*.

- Nancy Perry, Penny Laporte, Louisa Hellegers, and Joan Saslow, our editors for the first edition, and Françoise Leffler, our editor for the second edition, for helping to bring the books to fruition.

- Sharon Hilles, our grammar consultant, for her insight and advice on the first edition.

In the third edition, *Focus on Grammar* has continued to evolve as we update materials and respond to the valuable feedback from teachers and students who have been using the series. We are grateful to the following editors and colleagues:

- Laura Le Dréan, Executive Editor, for her dedication and commitment. In spite of an incredibly full schedule, she looked at every page of manuscript and offered excellent suggestions. In addition, she was always available and responsive to authors' concerns.

- Françoise Leffler, Senior Development Editor, for her continued dedication to the series and to improving *Focus on Grammar* with each new edition. As in the previous edition, we relied on her unflagging attention to detail and her wonderful sense of style.

- Kathleen Silloway, Senior Production Editor, for piloting the book through its many stages of production and for always giving us a heads up when more *FOG* was about to roll in.

- Irene Schoenberg, for generously sharing her experience in teaching our first two editions and for her enthusiastic support.

Finally, we are grateful, as always, to Rick Smith and Luke Frances, for their helpful input and for standing by and supporting us as we navigated our way through our third *FOG*.

We also wish to acknowledge the many reviewers for reading the manuscript and offering many useful suggestions.

Aileen Allison, Golden Gate Language School, Campbell, CA; **Larisa Álvarez Ávila,** Centro Educativo Renacimiento, Mérida, Yucatán, Mexico; **Jaime Bolaños,** Colegio Ker Liber, Guadalajara, Mexico; **Vahania Carvajal García,** Instituto Cultural Regina Teresiano, Hermosillo, Sonora, Mexico; **Julie Charland,** Ateliers de Langues CSCG, Québec City, Québec, Canada; **Amelia Chávez Ruiz,** Lake Forest School, Mexico State, Mexico; **Elisa Laura Chavira,** Instituto Cumbre del Noroeste, Ciudad

Obregón, Mexico; **Ronald Clark,** Boston University, Boston, MA; **Judy Cleek,** University of Tennessee at Martin, Martin, TN; **Elizabeth Clemente,** Instituto Tecnológico de Estudios Superiores de Monterrey, Atizapan, Mexico State, Mexico; **Sharon Cliff,** Richmond College, Richmond, TX; **Marilyn De Liro Álvarez,** Instituto "Las Brisas," Nuevo León, Mexico; **Susanna Eguren,** Instituto Cultural Peruano Norteamericano, Lima, Peru; **Marcia Gethin-Jones,** University of Connecticut, Stamford, CT; **Monica Hilding,** Central Community School, Salt Lake City, UT; **Sue Hynes,** Daley College, Chicago, IL; **Silvia Icela Espinoza Galvez,** Colegio Lux, Hermosillo, Sonora, Mexico; **Elizabeth Kelley,** University of California, San Diego, CA; **Anik Low,** Collège Jean-de-Brébeuf, Montréal, Québec, Canada; **Hank Mantell,** International Education Programs, University of California, Riverside, CA; **Javier Martínez García,** Instituto Las Américas, Mexico City, D. F., Mexico; **Darlene Mitchell,** International English Center, Boulder, CO; **Norma Morales Sánchez,** Instituto Carlos Gracido, Oaxaca, Mexico; **Robin Persiani,** Sierra College, Grass Valley, CA; **Mary Lou Price,** University of Texas at Austin, Austin, TX; **Mary Kay Purcell,** University of Evansville, Evansville, IN; **Graciela Ramírez Hernández,** Instituto Hispano Inglés de México, Mexico City, Mexico; **Mark Rau,** American River College, Sacramento, CA; **Nicholas Renton,** American Culture and Language Program, Los Angeles, CA; **Ernesto Romo,** Lake Forest School, Mexico State, Mexico; **René Sandoval,** Martin Luther King, Jr. School, Guadalajara, Jalisco, Mexico; **Allen Sellers,** Oregon State University, Corvallis, OR; **Nicola Teague,** San Diego State University, San Diego, CA; **Elena O. Torres González,** Instituto Tecnológico de Estudios Superiores de Monterrey, Atizapan, Mexico State, Mexico; **María Elena Vera de la Rosa,** Lake Forest School, Mexico State, Mexico; **Magneli Villanueva Morales,** Universidad Regiomontana, Monterrey, Nuevo León, Mexico; **Elaine Wilson,** Culture Works, London, Ontario, Canada; **Essio Zamora,** Instituto Carlos Gracido, Oaxaca, Mexico; **Ian Zapp,** Colegio México Irlandés, Guadalajara, Jalisco, Mexico.

PART
I

Present, Past, and Future:
Review and Expansion

Grammar in Context

BEFORE YOU READ

🎧 *Look at the cartoons. What are the people doing? How do they feel? Read this article about cross-cultural communication.*

WHAT'S YOUR CROSS-CULTURAL IQ?

Are you **living** in your native country or in another country? **Do** you ever **travel** abroad? **Do** you **understand** the misunderstandings below?

Why **does** he **look** so surprised? I just **want** to say hello.

What **is** he **doing** here? We **don't have** an appointment.

What**'s** wrong? I**'m** just **saying** hello.

What **is** she **doing**? Why **is** she **kissing** me again?

SITUATION 1

Tomás **is visiting** Claude. Claude **looks** very surprised. In Tomás's culture, people **often visit** without calling first. But in Claude's culture, people **don't do** that. They **always check** with their friends before they **come over**.

SITUATION 2

Nicole and Sheila **are saying** hello and **kissing**. They **are** both **feeling** very uncomfortable. In Nicole's culture, people **usually kiss** twice, once on each cheek. In Sheila's culture, people **don't kiss** more than once.

AFTER YOU READ

Complete each sentence with the correct name.

1. _____ is visiting without calling first.

2. _____ is surprised to have a visitor.

3. _____ is kissing the other woman twice.

4. _____ doesn't expect a second kiss.

Now circle the correct answer for your own culture.

In my culture . . .

5. People usually <u>call / don't call</u> before visiting.

6. When people say hello, they <u>don't kiss / kiss</u>.

Grammar Presentation

PRESENT PROGRESSIVE

Affirmative Statements

Subject	*Be*	Base Form of Verb + *-ing*	
I	**am***		
You	**are**		
He She It	**is**	**traveling**	now.
We You They	**are**		

*For contractions of *I am*, *you are*, etc., see Appendix 26 on page A-12.

Negative Statements

Subject	*Be*	*Not*	Base Form of Verb + *-ing*	
I	**am**			
He	**is**	**not**	**traveling**	now.
We	**are**			

SIMPLE PRESENT

Affirmative Statements

Subject		Verb
I You		**travel**.
He She It	often	**travels**.
We You They		**travel**.

Negative Statements

Subject	*Do*	*Not*	Base Form of Verb	
I	**do**			
He	**does**	**not**	**travel**	often.
We	**do**			

(continued)

Yes / No Questions			
Be	Subject	Base Form of Verb + *-ing*	
Is	he	**traveling**	now?

Yes / No Questions			
Do	Subject	Base Form of Verb	
Does	he	**travel**	often?

Short Answers		
Yes,	he	is.
No,		isn't.

Short Answers		
Yes,	he	does.
No,		doesn't.

Wh- Questions				
Wh- Word	*Be*	Subject	Base Form of Verb + *-ing*	
Where	**are**	you	**traveling**	now?

Wh- Questions				
Wh- Word	*Do*	Subject		Base Form of Verb
Where	**do**	you	usually	**travel**?

GRAMMAR NOTES

EXAMPLES

1. Use the **present progressive** to describe something that is happening <u>right now</u> (for example, *now, at the moment*).

```
              Now
               |
Past ——————————X——————————→ Future
               |
```
He's speaking English.

The present progressive is often used to show that the action is <u>temporary</u>.

- Tomás **is visiting** Claude.
- He**'s speaking** English *right now*.

- I**'m staying** with friends *at the moment*, but I plan to leave soon.

2 . Use the **simple present** to describe what <u>regularly</u> happens (for example, *every day, usually, always*).

```
            Now
             |
Past –X———X———X———X———X—→ Future
```
He speaks Spanish.

Use the simple present to talk about <u>scientific facts</u>.

- Tomás **talks** to Claude *every day*.
- He *usually* **wears** jeans.
- He *always* **speaks** Spanish at home.

- Stress **causes** high blood pressure.
- Water **boils** at 212°F (100°C).

3. Use the **present progressive** to describe something that is happening in the <u>extended present</u> time (for example, *nowadays, these days, this month, this year*), even if it's not happening at the moment of speaking.

- We**'re studying** U.S. customs *this month*.
- Laura**'s studying** in France *this year*.
- **Are** you **studying** hard *these days*?

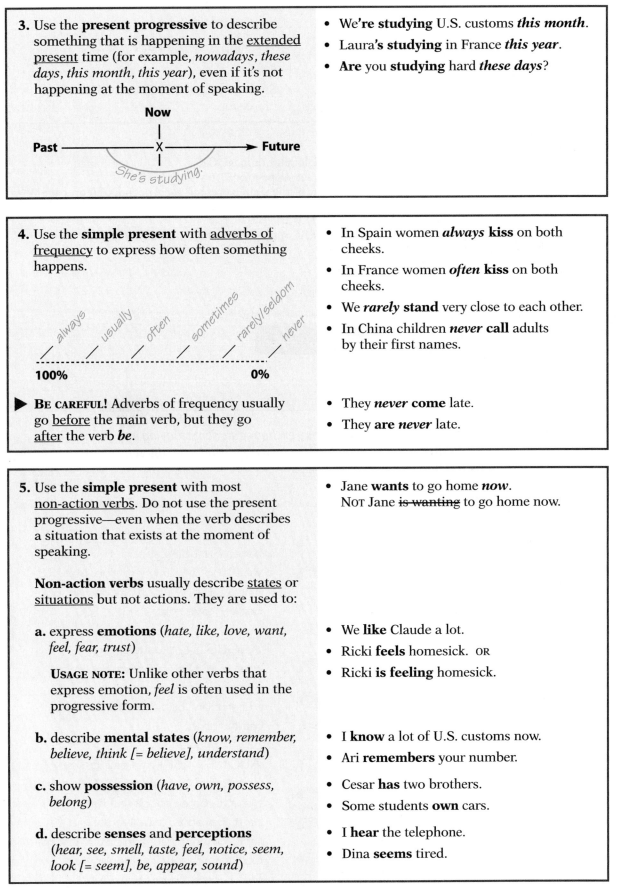

Now

Past ————————X————————> Future

She's studying.

4. Use the **simple present** with <u>adverbs of frequency</u> to express how often something happens.

- In Spain women *always* **kiss** on both cheeks.
- In France women *often* **kiss** on both cheeks.
- We *rarely* **stand** very close to each other.
- In China children *never* **call** adults by their first names.

always   usually   often   sometimes   rarely/seldom   never

100%   **0%**

▶ **BE CAREFUL!** Adverbs of frequency usually go <u>before</u> the main verb, but they go <u>after</u> the verb **be**.

- They *never* **come** late.
- They **are** *never* late.

5. Use the **simple present** with most <u>non-action verbs</u>. Do not use the present progressive—even when the verb describes a situation that exists at the moment of speaking.

- Jane **wants** to go home *now*.
  NOT Jane ~~is wanting~~ to go home now.

Non-action verbs usually describe <u>states</u> or <u>situations</u> but not actions. They are used to:

a. express **emotions** (*hate, like, love, want, feel, fear, trust*)

   USAGE NOTE: Unlike other verbs that express emotion, *feel* is often used in the progressive form.

- We **like** Claude a lot.
- Ricki **feels** homesick. OR
- Ricki **is feeling** homesick.

b. describe **mental states** (*know, remember, believe, think [= believe], understand*)

- I **know** a lot of U.S. customs now.
- Ari **remembers** your number.

c. show **possession** (*have, own, possess, belong*)

- Cesar **has** two brothers.
- Some students **own** cars.

d. describe **senses** and **perceptions** (*hear, see, smell, taste, feel, notice, seem, look [= seem], be, appear, sound*)

- I **hear** the telephone.
- Dina **seems** tired.

(continued)

<table>
<tr><td>

6. BE CAREFUL! Some verbs that describe senses and perceptions such as *taste, smell, feel,* and *look* can have both a non-action and an action meaning.

</td><td>

NON-ACTION

- The soup **tastes** good. Try some.

ACTION

- She**'s tasting** the soup to see if it needs more salt.

</td></tr>
</table>

Reference Notes

For definitions and examples of **grammar terms,** see Glossary on page G-1.

For **spelling rules** on forming the **present progressive,** see Appendix 21 on page A-10.

For **spelling rules** on forming the third person singular of the **simple present,** see Appendix 20 on page A-9.

For **pronunciation rules** for the **simple present,** see Appendix 29 on page A-14.

For a list of **non-action verbs,** see Appendix 2 on page A-2.

For use of the **present progressive** and the **simple present** to talk about the **future,** see Unit 6.

Focused Practice

1 | DISCOVER THE GRAMMAR

Read these journal entries by Brian, a Canadian summer exchange student studying in Argentina. Circle all the verbs that describe what is happening **now***. Underline the verbs that describe what* **regularly** *happens.*

JUNE 28: I'm sitting in a seat 30,000 feet above the Earth en route to Argentina! I usually have dinner at this time, but right now I have an awful headache from all the excitement. My seatmate is eating my food. I guess it's good. She looks happy.

JUNE 30: It's 7:30 P.M. My host parents are still working. Carlos, my father, works at home. My little brother, Ricardo, is cute. He looks (and acts) a lot like Bobby. Right now, he's looking over my shoulder and trying to read my journal.

JULY 4: The weather is cold here. I usually spend the first weekend of July at the beach. Today I'm walking around in a heavy sweater.

AUGUST 6: I usually feel great in the evening because we take long naps in the afternoon, but tonight I feel really tired.

AUGUST 25: I'm feeling very comfortable here now—but it's almost time to go home! My host parents usually cook a light dinner, but tonight they're cooking a special dinner for me. I miss them already!

2 | SCHEDULE CHANGES

Grammar Notes 1–2

Look at Brian's schedule in Argentina. He usually has a regular schedule but today is different. Complete the sentences below. Use the present progressive or the simple present. Choose between affirmative and negative forms.

7:00–8:00	~~run in the park~~	get ready for a field trip
8:30–12:30	~~attend class~~	go on a field trip to the museum
1:00–2:00	eat lunch	
2:00–3:00	~~take a nap~~	work on the family web page
3:00–5:00	work in the cafeteria	
5:00–6:30	~~do homework~~	call home at 5:00 sharp today!
6:30–8:30	~~play tennis~~	watch a video with Eva
8:30	have dinner	
9:30–10:00	~~write letters~~	take a walk with the family
10:00–10:30	~~take a shower~~	do homework

1. Brian always _runs in the park_____ early in the morning,

   but today he _is getting ready for a field trip_____.

2. Brian usually _____ between 8:30 and 12:30,

   but today he _____.

3. He always _____ between 1:00 and 2:00.

4. It's 1:30. He _____.

5. He normally _____ after lunch,

   but today he _____.

6. Every day from 3:00 to 5:00, he _____.

7. It's 5:00, but he _____ now.

   He _____ instead.

8. It's 6:45, but he _____.

   He _____.

9. It's 8:30. Brian _____.

10. He always _____ at 8:30.

11. After dinner, Brian usually _____,

    but tonight he _____.

12. It's 10:15, but he _____.

    He _____.

3 | CULTURAL DIFFERENCES

Some students are talking outside of a classroom. Complete their conversations. Choose between the simple present and the present progressive forms of the verbs in parentheses.

A.   Li-wu: Hi, Paulo. What _____*are you doing*_____?
                1. (do you do / are you doing)

Paulo: Oh, I _____ for class to begin.
                2. (wait / 'm waiting)

Li-wu: How are you? You _____
                3. (seem / 're seeming)

a little down.

Paulo: I'm just tired. I _____ evenings
                4. (work / 'm working)

this semester. Hey, is that your teacher over there?

Li-wu: Yes. She _____ to one of my
                5. (talks / 's talking)

classmates.

Paulo: What's wrong? He _____
                6. (doesn't look / 's not looking)

at her. He _____ uncomfortable.
                7. (seems / 's seeming)

Li-wu: Oh. That _____ anything. In Taiwan it's not respectful to
                8. (doesn't mean / isn't meaning)

look directly at your teacher.

B.   Taro: There's Miguel. He _____ to Luisa.
                1. (talks / 's talking)

Marisa: Yes. They _____ a class together
                2. (take / 're taking)

this semester.

Taro: They _____ very close to each
                3. (stand / 're standing)

other. _____ they
                4. (Do you think / Are you thinking)

_____?
                5. (date / 're dating)

Marisa: No. I _____ it
                6. (don't think / 'm not thinking)

_____ anything special. I
                7. (means / 's meaning)

_____ from Costa Rica, and people
                8. (come / 'm coming)

_____ that close to each other.
                9. (usually stand / are usually standing)

4 | MORE CULTURAL DIFFERENCES

Grammar Notes 1–6

Other students are talking outside of a classroom. Complete their conversations. Use the simple present or the present progressive form of the verbs in parentheses.

A. RASHA: There's Hans. Why ____is____ he ____walking____
1. (walk)

so fast? Class _____ at 9:00.
2. (start)

He still _____ 10 minutes!
3. (have)

CLAUDE: He always _____ fast. I think Swiss
4. (walk)

people often _____ to be in a hurry.
5. (appear)

B. YOKO: Isn't that Sergio and Luis? Why _____

they _____ hands? They already
1. (shake)

_____ each other!
2. (know)

LI-JING: In Brazil, men _____ hands every time
3. (shake)

they _____.
4. (meet)

YOKO: _____ women _____ hands too?
5. (shake)

5 | CULTURE SHOCK!

Grammar Notes 1–6

Complete the following paragraph. Use the correct form of the verbs in the box.

cause	feel	go	live	~~make~~	travel

New food, new customs, new routines—they all ____make____ international travel
1.

interesting. But they also _____ culture shock for many travelers. _____ you
2.

now _____ or _____ in a culture different from your own? If so, why
3.   4.

_____ you _____ so good (or so bad)? Some experts say that we often
5.

_____ through four stages of culture shock:
6.

Honeymoon Stage:	In the first weeks everything seems great.
Rejection Stage:	You have negative feelings about the new culture.
Adjustment Stage:	Things are getting better these days.
Adaptation Stage:	You are finally comfortable in the new culture.

Take the quiz in Exercise 6 and see what stage you are in.

6 | QUIZ

Complete the following statements using the correct form of the verbs in the box. Then check the statements that are true for you **now**.

annoy	feel	improve	live	~~love~~
make	think	treat	understand	want

☐ 1. I _____ *love* _____ it here!

☐ 2. People always _____ me very kindly.

☐ 3. The customs here often _____ me.

☐ 4. I _____ here now, but I _____ I'll stay.

                                                                (negative)

☐ 5. I _____ to go home!

☐ 6. My language skills _____ a lot each month.

☐ 7. I _____ a lot of new friends these days.

☐ 8. I still _____ everything, but I _____ at home here.

              (negative)

To check your Quiz results, go to page 92.

7 | EDITING

Read this student's journal. There are eleven mistakes in the use of the present progressive or simple present. The first mistake is already corrected. Find and correct ten more.

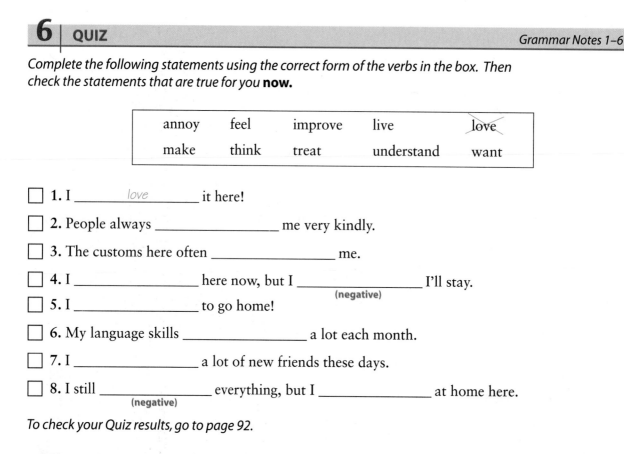

> I'm sitting
>   It's 12:30 and ~~I sit~~ in the library right now. My classmates are eating lunch
> together, but I'm not hungry yet. At home, we eat never this early. Today our journal
> topic is culture shock. It's a good topic for me right now because I'm being pretty
> homesick. I miss my old routine. At home we always are eating a big meal at 2:00 in
> the afternoon. Then we rest. But here in Toronto I'm having a 3:00 conversation class.
> Every day I almost fall asleep in class, and my teacher ask me, "Are you bored?"
> Of course I'm not bored. I just need my afternoon nap! This class always is fun. This
> semester we work on a project with video cameras. My team is filming groups of
> people from different cultures. We are analyze "social distance." That means how close
> to each other these people stand. According to my new watch, it's 12:55, so I leave
> now for my 1:00 class. Teachers here really aren't liking tardiness!

Communication Practice

8 | LISTENING

🎧 *Listen to an interview with a new foreign student. Then listen again and check the things the student usually does and the things she is doing now or these days.*

	Usually	Now or These Days
1. speak English	☐	☑
2. speak Spanish	☐	☐
3. live in a small town	☐	☐
4. live in a big city	☐	☐
5. walk slowly	☐	☐
6. wear a watch	☐	☐
7. study computer science	☐	☐

9 | GETTING TO KNOW YOU

Walk around your classroom. Ask your classmates questions. Find someone who . . .

Name(s)

- likes visiting foreign countries — Hana
- isn't wearing a watch — Hakim
- speaks more than two languages — Majeed
- is studying something besides English — _____
- doesn't watch sports on TV — _____
- is planning to travel this year — Ys
- _____ — _____
  (add your own)

Example: A: Do you like visiting foreign countries?
B: Yes, I do. What about you?

Report back to the class.

Example: Tania and José like visiting foreign countries.

10 | WHAT'S HAPPENING?

Work in pairs. Look at the photographs. Describe them. What's happening? Discuss possible explanations for each situation. Compare your answers with those of your classmates.

Example: A: He's pointing. He looks angry.
B: Maybe he's just explaining something.

11 | QUESTIONABLE QUESTIONS?

Work in small groups. Look at the questions. In your culture, which questions are appropriate to ask someone you just met? Which are not appropriate? Compare your choices with those of your classmates.

- How old are you?
- What do you do?

- How much rent do you pay?
- What are you studying?

- Are you married?
- Where do you live?

12 | WRITING

Write a paragraph about a new experience you are having. Maybe you are living in a new country, taking a new class, or working at a new job. Describe the situation. How is it different from what you usually do? How do you feel in the situation?

Example: I usually live at home with my parents, but this month I'm living with my aunt and uncle. Everything seems different. My aunt . . .

13 | ON THE INTERNET

C *Weather often affects what people in different cultures do. Do a search on* **weather** *for a place you know well. Find out what the weather is now. Then compare it to what the weather usually is this time of year. Tell your classmates about the weather and what people usually do in this weather.*

Example: In Haiti it usually rains this time of year, but today it's not raining. It rains so often in Haiti that people usually ignore it. Children often play outside in the rain.

Imperative

Grammar in Context

BEFORE YOU READ

🎧 *Look at the pictures. What is the woman doing? What do you do to stay fit? Read part of an exercise routine presented in a fitness magazine.*

The Warrior Workout

Having a bad day? **Don't let** it get you down. **Try** our kickboxing workout instead. You'll feel better *and* build your strength. **Do** it three times a week for fast results.

THE JAB

Get into the basic position: **Bend** your knees and **place** your right foot in front. **Raise** your fists with your right hand in front. Now **punch** with your right fist. **Don't stand** straight as you punch. Instead, **lean** forward for more power. **Bring** your fist back immediately. Then **change** sides.

THE POWER KICK

Get into the basic position and **move** your weight onto your right foot. **Bend** your elbows and **bring** your left knee as high as your hip. Then **kick** to the side. **Don't point** your toes as you kick.

AFTER YOU READ

*Read the following instructions. Check **Jab** if it is for the Jab, or **Power Kick** if it is for the Power Kick. Check **Both** if it's for both.*

	Jab	Power Kick	Both
1. Start in the basic position.	☐	☐	☐
2. Punch with one fist.	☐	☐	☐
3. Don't lean back.	☐	☐	☐
4. Bend both elbows.	☐	☐	☐
5. Put your weight on one foot.	☐	☐	☐
6. Don't point your toes.	☐	☐	☐

Grammar Presentation

IMPERATIVE

Affirmative	
Base Form of Verb	
Bend	your knees.
Raise	your fists.

	Negative	
Don't	Base Form of Verb	
Don't	**bend**	your knees.
	raise	your fists.

GRAMMAR NOTES   **EXAMPLES**

1. Use the **imperative** to:

    a. give **directions** and **instructions**

- **Turn** left at the light.
- **Get** into the basic position.

    b. give **orders** or **commands**

- **Get up!**
- **Don't move!**

    c. give **advice** or make **suggestions**

- Always **warm up** first.
- **Don't exercise** when you're sick.

    d. give **warnings**

- **Be** careful!
- **Don't fall!**

2. Use the **imperative** also to:

a. make **requests** (use *please* in addition to the imperative)

- *Please* **read** this article.
- **Read** this article, *please*.

b. make **informal invitations**

- **Have** lunch with us tomorrow.
- **Bring** a friend.

USAGE NOTE: When using the imperative in a formal situation, add *please*.

- *Please* **join** us, Mrs. Rivera.
  NOT ~~Join~~ us, Mrs. Rivera.

3. Note that the **subject** of an imperative statement is *you*. However, do not say or write *you*.

- **Stand up** straight!
  NOT ~~You~~ stand up straight!
- **Don't hold** your breath!
  NOT ~~You~~ don't hold your breath!

▶ **BE CAREFUL!** The imperative form is the same in both the singular and the plural.

- John, **point** your toes.
- John and Susan, **point** your toes.

Focused Practice

1 | DISCOVER THE GRAMMAR

Match an imperative in column A with a situation in column B.

Column A	Column B
_i_ **1.** Don't touch that!	**a.** Someone is visiting a friend.
____ **2.** Buckle your seat belt.	**b.** Someone is going out into the cold.
____ **3.** Look both ways!	**c.** Someone is crossing a street.
____ **4.** Dress warmly!	**d.** Someone is taking an exam.
____ **5.** Don't bend your knees.	**e.** Someone is driving a car.
____ **6.** Mark each answer *true* or *false*.	**f.** Someone is giving directions.
____ **7.** Come in! Make yourself at home.	**g.** Someone is exercising.
____ **8.** Try a little more pepper.	**h.** Someone is tasting some food.
____ **9.** Walk two blocks on First Street.	**i.** Something is hot.

2 | HEALTHY SMOOTHIE

Look at the pictures showing how to make a banana-strawberry smoothie. Match a verb from column A with the appropriate words from column B to give instructions for making the smoothie. Then put the sentences in the correct order.

Column A	**Column B**
_____ Add	the ingredients until smooth.
__1__ Slice	six strawberries.
_____ Cut	a banana.
_____ Wash	orange juice into the blender.
_____ Blend	the strawberries in half.
_____ Pour	the fruit to the orange juice.

Write each sentence under the appropriate picture.

1. _Slice a banana._ _____

2. _____

3. _____

4. _____

5. _____

6. _____

3 | **MARTIAL ARTS**

Complete the advertisement for a martial arts school. Use the affirmative or negative imperative form of the verbs in the box.

become	choose	decrease	increase	learn
miss	register	take	~~think~~	wait

MARTIAL ARTS ACADEMY

_____Don't think_____ that martial arts is only about physical training. A good
    1.
martial arts program offers many other benefits as well.

_____ self-defense and more at the Martial Arts Academy:
    2.

◆ _____ stress. Martial arts training helps you relax.
    3.

◆ _____ concentration. Martial arts students learn to
    4.
focus their attention.

◆ _____ fit. Strength and flexibility improve as you learn.
    5.

We are offering an introductory trial membership. _____ this
    6.
special opportunity. _____ classes with Master Lorenzo
    7.
Gibbons, a ninth-degree Black Belt Master.

_____ classes from our convenient
    8.
schedule. _____!
    9.

_____ now for a two-week trial.
    10.

Only $30. ◆ Uniform included.

4 | EDITING

Read this student's journal entry. There are five mistakes in the use of the imperative. The first mistake is already corrected. Find and correct four more.

For the Black Belt essay, Master Gibbons gave us this assignment:
Write
~~You write~~ about something important to you. My topic was "The Right

Way," the rules of life for the martial arts.

Three of these rules are very important to me:

• First, respects other people—treat them the way you want them to

treat you.

• Second, helped people in need. In other words, use your strength for

others, not use it just for your own good.

• Third, no lie or steal. You can't defend others when you feel guilty.

There are many other rules, but these are the three most important

ones to me.

Communication Practice

5 | LISTENING

🎧 *Listen to a TV chef describing how to make pancakes. Then listen again and number the instructions in the correct order.*

_____ Heat a frying pan and melt a small piece of butter in it.

_1_ Beat two egg whites in a large bowl.

_____ Add one and a quarter cups of whole wheat flour to the egg whites.

_____ Flip the pancakes over.

_____ Blend in some fruit.

_____ Mix thoroughly.

_____ Top them with fruit or yogurt.

_____ Pour some of the pancake mixture into the frying pan.

_____ Add a cup of low-fat milk.

6 | INFORMATION GAP: FIND THE WAY

Work in pairs (A and B). You are both going to give driving directions to places on the map. Student A, follow the instructions on this page. Student B, turn to page 21.

1. Ask your partner for directions to the Martial Arts Academy. Draw the route.

   Example: **A:** I want to go to the Martial Arts Academy. Can you give me directions?
   B: Sure. Start at the corner of Carter and Adams.

2. Draw the route from Carter and Adams to the Sunrise Gym.
   (Be careful! One-way streets are marked →. Don't go the wrong way on a one-way street!)
   Give your partner directions.

   Example: **B:** I want to go to the Sunrise Gym. Can you give me directions?
   A: Sure. Start at the corner of Carter and Adams.

When giving directions, use sentences like these:

Start at the corner of Carter and Adams.	Go straight.	Continue on 9th Street.
(Don't) turn right.	Make a left turn.	Stay on Founders.

When you are finished, compare routes with your partner. Are they the same?

7 | RECIPE EXCHANGE

Work in small groups. Write down one of your favorite recipes. List the ingredients and write the instructions.

Example:

QUICK AND EASY BEAN TACOS
Ingredients: 1 can of beans (black, kidney, or pinto), 4 hard corn taco shells,
         1 tomato, 1 onion, lettuce, salsa, spices (cumin, chili powder)
Instructions: Rinse and drain the beans. Add the spices. Simmer for 10 minutes.
         Chop the tomato and onion. Shred the lettuce. Fill the taco shells
         with the beans, tomato, and onion. Top with the lettuce and salsa.

Read your recipe to your group. Answer your classmates' questions.

Example: A: How long do you rinse the beans?
       B: Until the water looks clear. Use cold water. Don't use hot water.

8 | CALM DOWN!

Work in small groups. Imagine you have been in a traffic jam for an hour. A friend is waiting to meet you on a street corner. What can you say to yourself to calm yourself down? Share your list with the other groups.

Example: A: Take a deep breath.
       B: Don't think about the traffic.
       C: . . .

9 | WRITING

Write directions from your school to another location. It can be your home, a store, the train station, or any place you choose.

Example: To get to my apartment from school, walk two blocks on Oak Street. Turn left on Tenth Avenue. Then take the bus to Main and . . .

10 | ON THE INTERNET

As a class, choose a place that you would like to go to in your area. Then work in small groups. Do a search on **maps and directions** and look up directions to that place. Compare the directions. Are they the same? If not, how are they different? Which directions are the best? Why?

INFORMATION GAP FOR STUDENT B

1. Draw the route from Carter and Adams to the Martial Arts Academy.
   (Be careful! One-way streets are marked →. Don't go the wrong way on a one-way street!)
   Give your partner directions.

   Example: **A:** I want to go to the Martial Arts Academy. Can you give me directions?
   B: Sure. Start at the corner of Carter and Adams.

2. Ask your partner for directions to the Sunrise Gym. Draw the route.

   Example: **B:** I want to go to the Sunrise Gym. Can you give me directions?
   A: Sure. Start at the corner of Carter and Adams.

When giving directions, use sentences like these:

Start at the corner of Carter and Adams.	Go straight.	Continue on 9th Street.
(Don't) turn right.	Make a left turn.	Stay on Founders.

When you are finished, compare routes with your partner. Are they the same?

3 | Simple Past

Grammar in Context

BEFORE YOU READ

🎧 *Look at the picture and the text above it. What did Matsuo Basho do? How long did he live? Read this short biography of Basho.*

Matsuo Basho, 1644–1694

As for that flower
By the road —
My horse ate it!
— Matsuo Basho

Matsuo Basho **wrote** more than 1,000 *haiku* (three-line poems). He **chose** topics from nature, daily life, and human emotions. He **became** one of Japan's most famous poets, and his work **established** haiku as an important art form.

Basho **was** born Matsuo Munefusa near Kyoto in 1644. ("Basho" is the name he later **used** as a poet.) He **did not want** to become a samurai (warrior) like his father. Instead, he **moved** to Edo (present-day Tokyo) and **studied** poetry. Then he **became** a teacher, and by 1681 he **had** many students and admirers.

Basho, however, **was** restless. Starting in 1684, he **traveled** on foot and on horseback all over Japan. Sometimes his friends **joined** him and they **wrote** poetry together. Travel **was** difficult in the 17th century, and Basho often **got** sick. He **died** in 1694, during a journey to Osaka. At that time he **had** 2,000 students.

AFTER YOU READ

*Read the statements. Check **True** or **False**.*

	True	False
1. Basho was born and studied in Japan.	☐	☐
2. Basho only traveled on foot.	☐	☐
3. He wrote poetry with his students.	☐	☐
4. He died at age 50.	☐	☐

Grammar Presentation

SIMPLE PAST: *BE*

Affirmative Statements		
Subject	*Be*	
I	was	
You	were	
He She It	was	famous.
We You They	were	

Negative Statements		
Subject	*Be + Not*	
I	wasn't	
You	weren't	
He She It	wasn't	famous.
We You They	weren't	

Yes / No Questions		
Be	Subject	
Was	I	
Were	you	
Was	he she it	famous?
Were	we you they	

Short Answers							
	Affirmative				Negative		
Yes,		you	were.	No,		you	weren't.
		I	was.			I	wasn't.
		he she it	was.			he she it	wasn't.
		you we they	were.			you we they	weren't.

(continued)

Wh- Questions			
Wh- Word	**Be**	**Subject**	
Where When Why	**was**	I	famous?
	were	you	
	was	he she it	
	were	we you they	

SIMPLE PAST: REGULAR AND IRREGULAR VERBS

Affirmative Statements		
Subject	**Verb**	
I You He She It We You They	**moved traveled**	to Japan.
	came* left*	in 1684.

Negative Statements			
Subject	**Did not**	**Base Form of Verb**	
I You He She It We You They	**didn't**	**move travel**	to Japan.
		come leave	in 1684.

**Come (came)* and *leave (left)* are irregular verbs. See Appendix 1 on page A-1 for a list of irregular verbs.

Yes / No Questions			
Did	**Subject**	**Base Form of Verb**	
Did	I you he she it we you they	**move travel**	to Japan?
		come leave	in 1684?

Short Answers					
Affirmative			**Negative**		
Yes,	you I he she it you we they	**did.**	**No,**	you I he she it you we they	**didn't.**

Wh- Questions				
Wh- Word	*Did*	Subject	Base Form of Verb	
When Why	**did**	I you he she it we you they	**move travel**	to Japan?
			come? leave?	

GRAMMAR NOTES

EXAMPLES

1. Use the **simple past** to talk about actions, states, or situations that are <u>finished</u>.

Past —X————————————→ Future
He was a poet.
(Now)

- Basho **lived** in the 17th century.
- He **was** a poet.
- He **wrote** haiku.
- He **didn't stay** in one place.
- Where **did** he **travel**?

2. You can use the simple past with **time expressions** that refer to the past. Some examples of past time expressions are *by 1681, in the 17th century, 300 years ago, last week.*

- *By 1681* he **had** many students.
- He **lived** *in the 17th century*.
- He **died** more than *300 years ago*.

3. The simple past of **regular** verbs is formed by adding *-d* or *-ed* to the base form of the verb.

▶ **BE CAREFUL!** There are often **spelling changes** when you add *-ed* to the verb.

BASE FORM		SIMPLE PAST
live	→	live**d**
join	→	join**ed**
study	→	stud**ied**
hop	→	hop**ped**
prefer	→	prefer**red**

4. Many common verbs are **irregular**. Their simple past is not formed by adding *-d* or *-ed*.

BASE FORM		SIMPLE PAST
be	→	**was / were**
get	→	**got**
go	→	**went**
have	→	**had**

Reference Notes
For **spelling rules** for the **simple past of regular verbs**, see Appendix 22 on page A-10.
For **pronunciation rules** for the **simple past of regular verbs**, see Appendix 30 on page A-15.
For a list of **irregular verbs**, see Appendix 1 on page A-1.

Focused Practice

1 | DISCOVER THE GRAMMAR

Read more about Basho. Underline all the verbs in the simple past. Then complete the time line on the left.

1644	Basho was born.
1656	Basho's father died.
1664	Published
1666	Todo died
1681	Students built the Basho Hut.
1683	his mother died
1684	began his travel
1689	Basho traveled to northern Honshu.
1693	Basho locked his gate to visitors.
1694	took his final journey and died.

As the son of a samurai, Basho grew up in the household of Todo Yoshitada, a young lord. After his father's death in 1656, Basho stayed in the Yoshitada household. He and Todo wrote poetry together, and in 1664 they published some poems. Two years later, Todo died suddenly. Basho left the area.

Basho moved around for several years. In the 1670s, he went to Edo and stayed there. He found friendship and success once again. Basho judged poetry contests, published his own poetry, and taught students. His students built him a home outside the city in 1681. They planted a banana tree (*basho* in Japanese) in front and called his home "Basho Hut." That is how the poet got his name: Basho.

In spite of this success, Basho became unhappy. He often wrote about loneliness. His mother died in 1683, and he began his travels a year later. His trip to the northern part of Honshu in 1689 was difficult, but his travel diary about this journey, *Narrow Road to the Deep North*, became one of Japan's greatest works of literature.

As a famous poet, Basho had many visitors—too many, in fact. In 1693 he locked his gate for a month, stayed alone, and wrote. The following year he took his final journey, to Osaka. He died there among his friends.

2 | EMILY DICKINSON

Complete this biography of American poet Emily Dickinson. Use the simple past form of the verbs in parentheses. Go to Appendix 1 on page A-1 for help with the irregular verbs.

Emily Dickinson, one of the most popular American poets, ___lived___
                  1. (live)

from 1830 to 1886. She ___wrote___ about love, nature, and time.
               2. (write)

These ___were___ her favorite themes.
          3. (be)

Dickinson ___led___ an unusual life. After just one year
               4. (lead)

of college, she ___became___ a recluse—she almost never
               5. (become)

___left___ her house in Amherst, Massachusetts. At home,
      6. (leave)

she ___didn't have___ visitors, and she only ___wore___
          7. (not have)   **8. (wear)**

white.

3 | MORE ABOUT EMILY DICKINSON

Complete this list of facts about Emily Dickinson. Use the simple past form of the verbs in parentheses. Go to Appendix 1 on page A-1 for help with the irregular verbs.

1. Dickinson ___liked___ science.
         (like)

2. She ___studied___ it in school.
        (study)

3. She ___became___ very interested in chemistry.
        (become)

4. Later she ___read___ about Arctic exploration.
          (read)

5. She ___used___ ideas from science in many of her poems.
        (use)

6. Emily Dickinson ___didn't write___ only poems.
                (not write)

7. She also ___wrote___ letters.
          (write)

8. But she ___didn't address___ the envelopes.
           (not address)

9. Other people always ___did___ that for her.
                (do)

10. During her lifetime, only 7 of her 1,700 poems ___appeared___ in print.
                                   (appear)

11. This ___was___ without her knowledge or permission.
         (be)

4 | A POEM BY EMILY DICKINSON

Grammar Notes 1–4

Now complete these lines from a poem by Emily Dickinson. Use the simple past form of the verbs in the box. Go to Appendix 1 on page A-1 for help with the irregular verbs.

| bite | come | drink | eat | hop | see |

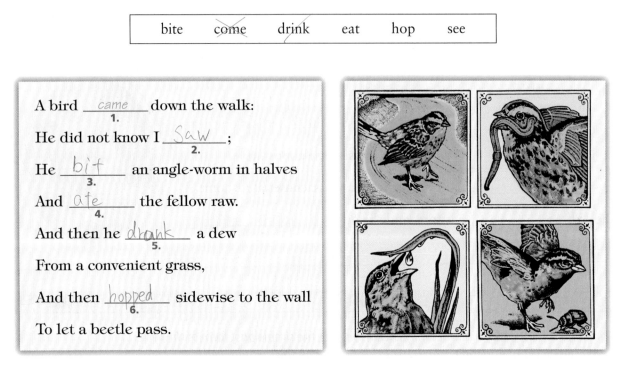

A bird ___came___ down the walk:
1.

He did not know I ___saw___ ;
2.

He ___bit___ an angle-worm in halves
3.

And ___ate___ the fellow raw.
4.

And then he ___drank___ a dew
5.

From a convenient grass,

And then ___hopped___ sidewise to the wall
6.

To let a beetle pass.

5 | BASHO AND DICKINSON

Grammar Notes 1–4

Read these statements about Basho. Then write questions about Emily Dickinson. Write a yes/no question if a verb is underlined , or a wh- question if other words are underlined. Then answer your questions using the information from Exercises 2 and 3.

1. Basho <u>was</u> a poet.

   Q: *Was Dickinson a poet?*

   A: *Yes, she was.*

2. He was born <u>in 1644</u>.

   Q: *When was Dickinson born?*

   A: *She was born in 1830.*

3. He <u>became</u> famous during his lifetime.

   Q: Did she become famous?

   A: Yes, she did,   during her life time

4. Basho <u>received</u> many visitors.

   Q: Did she receive many visitors?

   A: No, she didn't.

5. He <u>traveled</u> a lot.

Q: *Did she travel a lot?*

A: *No, she didn't.*

6. Basho wrote <u>more than 1,000 poems</u>.

Q: *How many poems did she write?*

A: *She wrote ~~only 7 of her~~ 1700 poems.*
        more than

7. He wrote <u>about nature</u>.

Q: *What ~~about~~ did she write?* ↳about

A: *She wrote about love, nature, and time.*

8. He died <u>in 1694</u>.

Q: *When did she die?*

A: *She died in 1886.*

---

6 | ANA CASTILLO
Grammar Notes 1–4

Read this article about a modern writer. Then answer the questions on the next page.

ANA CASTILLO is a modern poet, novelist, short story writer, and teacher. She was born in Chicago in 1953, and she lived there for 32 years. *Otro Canto*, her first book of poetry, appeared in 1977.

In her work, Castillo uses humor and a lively mixture of Spanish and English (Spanglish). She got her special writer's "voice" by living in a neighborhood with many different ethnic groups. She also thanks her father for her writing style. "He had an outgoing and easy personality, and this . . . sense of humor. I got a lot from him . . ."

Castillo attended high school, college, and graduate school in Chicago. In the 1970s, she taught English and Mexican history. She received a Ph.D. in American Studies from Bremen University in Germany in 1992.

(continued)

*Read the statements. Write **That's right** or **That's wrong** and correct the incorrect statements.*

1. Ana Castillo was born in Mexico City.

   That's wrong. She wasn't born in Mexico City. She was born in Chicago.

2. She lived in Chicago until 1977.

   _____

3. Her father was very shy.

   _____

4. She grew up among people of different cultures.

   _____

5. Castillo got most of her education in Chicago.

   _____

6. She taught Spanish in the 1970s.

   _____

7. She went to France for her Ph.D.

   _____

7 | EDITING

Read this student's journal. There are ten mistakes in the use of the simple past. The first mistake is already corrected. Find and correct nine more.

> Today in class we read a poem by American poet Robert Frost. I
> really ~~enjoy~~ *enjoyed* it. It was about a person who choosed between two roads
> in a forest. Many people believed the person were Frost. He thinked
> about his choice for a long time. The two roads didn't looked very
> different. Finally, he didn't took the road most people take. He took
> the one less traveled on. At that time, he didn't thought it was an
> important decision, but his choice change his life.
>
> Sometimes I feel a little like Frost. Two years ago I decide to
> move to a new country. Did I made the right decision?

Communication Practice

8 | LISTENING

 Listen to part of an interview with a poet. Then listen again, and write the years on the time line.

| was born | parents left Turkey | moved to the U.S. | began to write poetry | graduated from college | won a poetry award | became a teacher |

1970

9 | INFORMATION GAP: COMPLETE THE BIOGRAPHY

Work in pairs (A and B). Student A, follow the instructions on this page. Student B, turn to page 33.

1. Read the short biography below. Ask your partner questions to complete the missing information.

Example: A: Where was Vladimir born?
B: He was born in Kiev.

2. Answer your partner's questions.

Example: B: When was he born?
A: He was born on May 6, 1981.

Vladimir Liapunov was born on May 6, 1981, in _____ *Kiev* _____. His mother

was a _____, and his father made shoes.

At home they spoke _____. In 1999

Vlad and his family moved to _____. At

first Vlad felt _____. Then he got a

part-time job as a _____. He worked in

a Russian restaurant. He met _____ at

work, and they got married in 2001. They had a baby in 2002.

_____ ago, Vlad enrolled at the local

community college. His goal is to own his own restaurant someday.

When you are finished, compare the biographies. Are they the same?

10 | DIFFERENT LIVES

Work in pairs. Reread the information about Matsuo Basho (see pages 22 and 26) and Emily Dickinson (see page 27). In what ways were the two poets similar? How were they different? With your partner, write as many ideas as you can. Compare your ideas with those of your classmates.

> **Example:** **A:** Both Basho and Dickinson were poets.
> **B:** Basho lived in the 17th century. Dickinson lived in the 19th century.

11 | RHYMING WORDS

In poetry, the last word of a line sometimes rhymes with the last word of another line. For example, look at these first two lines of a famous poem by Joyce Kilmer. In these lines, **see** *rhymes with* **tree**.

> I think that I shall never **see**
> A poem lovely as a **tree**.

Work with a partner. Write down as many simple past verbs as you can that rhyme with the verbs in the box.

bought	drew	kept	sent	spoke

> **Example:** **Sent** rhymes with **bent, lent, meant, spent,** and **went**.

Compare your lists with those of other students. Who has the most rhyming words?

12 | WRITING

Write a short autobiography. Do not put your name on it. Your teacher will collect all the papers, mix them up, and redistribute them to the class. Read the autobiography your teacher gives you. Then ask your classmates questions to try to find its writer.

> **Example:** Did you come here in 1990? OR When did you come here?

13 | ON THE INTERNET

Look up a poetry website. Find a poem that you like and tell someone about the poem.

> **Example:** I read a / an _____ poem yesterday. It was about . . .
> I really liked / didn't like it because . . .
> When I read the poem, I thought about . . .

INFORMATION GAP FOR STUDENT B

1. Read the short biography below. Answer your partner's questions.

    Example: **A:** Where was Vladimir born?
                B: He was born in Kiev.

2. Ask your partner questions to complete the missing information.

    Example: **B:** When was he born?
                A: He was born on May 6, 1981.

Vladimir Liapunov was born on _____ *May 6, 1981* _____, in Kiev. His mother was a dressmaker, and his father made ___Shoes_____.

At home they spoke Russian. In ___1994_____ Vlad and his family moved to Boston. At first Vlad felt lonely. Then he got a part-time job as a cook. He worked in a ___Russian lestrant_____. He met Elena at work, and they got married in ___2001_____. They had a baby in ___2002_____. A month ago, Vlad enrolled at the local ___Comanuhity college___. His goal is to own his own restaurant someday.

When you are finished, compare the biographies. Are they the same?

Grammar in Context

BEFORE YOU READ

🎧 *Look at the picture. What do you think happened at Ligo Diamonds last Friday night? What was the weather like that night? Read this transcript of a radio play.*

THE ALIBI

[Ding-dong!]

SANDERS: Coming!… Coming!… Oh! Hi, Officer. Sorry I took so long. I **was exercising** in the basement when you **rang**.

OFFICER: Officer Barker, City Police. Are you Sal Sanders?

SANDERS: Yes, I am.

OFFICER: Is your wife home? I'd like to ask her a few questions.

SANDERS: No, Eve is at work. She's a manager at Ligo Diamonds. You know, she **was** very upset when she **heard** about the burglary.

OFFICER: **Was** your wife **working** the night of the burglary?

SANDERS: No, she **wasn't**. We **were staying** at Cypress Ski Lodge when it **happened**. Don't tell me we're suspects!

OFFICER: Just for the record, what **were** you and Mrs. Sanders **doing** between 6:00 P.M. and 9:00 P.M. last Friday?

SANDERS: We **were having** dinner in our room.

OFFICER: **Were** you still **eating** at 7:00?

SANDERS: No. Eve **was making** a call.

OFFICER: What **were** you **doing** while your wife **was talking**?

SANDERS: I **was watching** *Wall Street Watch*.

OFFICER: Hmmm . . . But the electricity **was** out because of the blizzard . . .

AFTER YOU READ

What did Sal Sanders tell the officer? Check the sentences.

☑ **1.** He started to exercise before the doorbell rang.

☐ **2.** He and his wife were home when the burglary happened.

☐ **3.** They were eating dinner at 7:00 P.M. on the night of the burglary.

☑ **4.** He was watching TV at 7:00 P.M. that night.

Grammar Presentation

PAST PROGRESSIVE

Statements				
Subject	**Was / Were**	**(Not)**	**Base Form of Verb + -ing**	
I	**was**			
You	**were**			
He She It	**was**	**(not)**	**eating** **working** **sleeping**	yesterday at 7:00 P.M. when Eve **called**. while Sal **was talking**.
We You They	**were**			

Yes / No Questions			
Was / Were	**Subject**	**Base Form of Verb + -ing**	
Was	I		
Were	you		
Was	he she it	**eating** **working** **sleeping**	yesterday at 7:00 P.M.? when Eve **called**? while Sal **was talking**?
Were	we you they		

Short Answers						
Affirmative			**Negative**		
Yes,	you	**were.**	**No,**	you	**weren't.**
	I	**was.**		I	**wasn't.**
	he she it	**was.**		he she it	**wasn't.**
	you we they	**were.**		you we they	**weren't.**

(continued)

pead

Wh- Questions				
Wh- Word	**Was / Were**	**Subject**	**Base Form of Verb + _ing_**	
Why	**was**	I	**eating** **working** **sleeping**	yesterday at 7:00 P.M.? when Eve **called**? while Sal **was talking**?
	were	you		
	was	he she it		
	were	we you they		

GRAMMAR NOTES

EXAMPLES

1. Use the **past progressive** to describe an action that was <u>in progress</u> at a specific time in the past. The action began before the specific time and may or may not continue after the specific time.

Now

Past ——————X————————→ Future

6:00

were eating

▶ **BE CAREFUL! Non-action verbs** are not usually used in the progressive.

- My wife and I **were eating** at 6:00.
- What **were** you **doing** at 7:00?
- They **weren't working** that night.

- She **heard** about the burglary. NOT She ~~was hearing~~ about the burglary.

2. Use the **past progressive** with the **simple past** to talk about an action that was <u>interrupted</u> by another action. Use the simple past for the interrupting action.

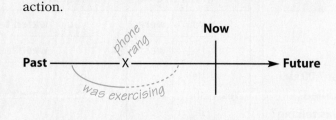

Now

Past ——————X————————→ Future

phone rang

was exercising

- Use **when** to introduce the **simple past** action.
- Use **while** to introduce the **past progressive** action.

- I **was exercising** when he **called**. *(I was exercising. The phone rang and interrupted my exercising.)*

- He was skiing **when** he **fell**.
- **While** he **was skiing**, he fell.

Read

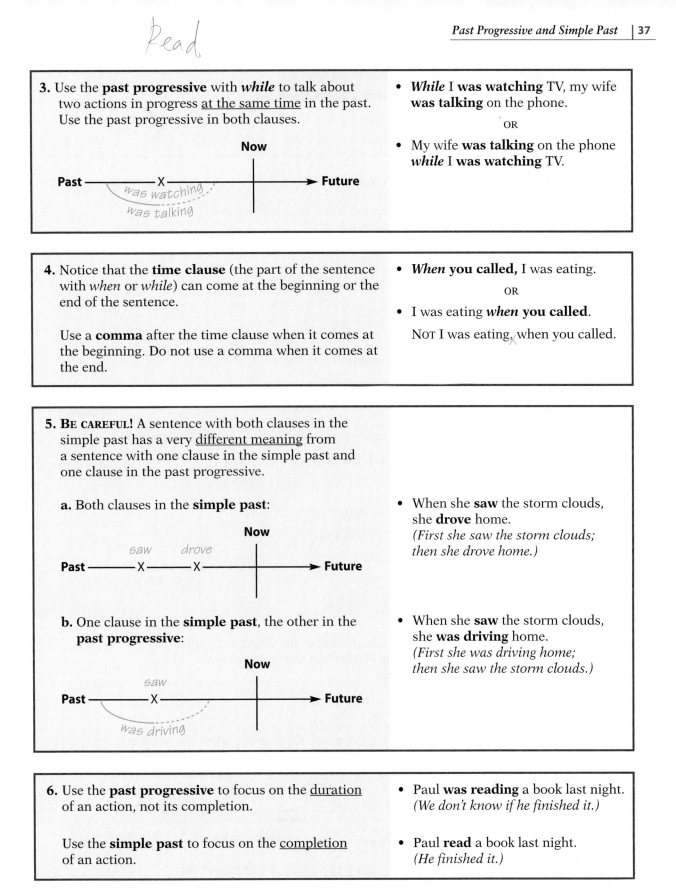

3. Use the **past progressive** with *while* to talk about two actions in progress <u>at the same time</u> in the past. Use the past progressive in both clauses.

- *While* I **was watching** TV, my wife **was talking** on the phone.

  OR

- My wife **was talking** on the phone *while* I **was watching** TV.

4. Notice that the **time clause** (the part of the sentence with *when* or *while*) can come at the beginning or the end of the sentence.

Use a **comma** after the time clause when it comes at the beginning. Do not use a comma when it comes at the end.

- *When* **you called,** I was eating.

  OR

- I was eating *when* **you called**.

  NOT I was eating, when you called.

5. **BE CAREFUL!** A sentence with both clauses in the simple past has a very <u>different meaning</u> from a sentence with one clause in the simple past and one clause in the past progressive.

a. Both clauses in the **simple past**:

- When she **saw** the storm clouds, she **drove** home.
  (First she saw the storm clouds; then she drove home.)

b. One clause in the **simple past**, the other in the **past progressive**:

- When she **saw** the storm clouds, she **was driving** home.
  (First she was driving home; then she saw the storm clouds.)

6. Use the **past progressive** to focus on the <u>duration</u> of an action, not its completion.

- Paul **was reading** a book last night.
  (We don't know if he finished it.)

Use the **simple past** to focus on the <u>completion</u> of an action.

- Paul **read** a book last night.
  (He finished it.)

Reference Note
For a list of **non-action verbs,** see Appendix 2 on page A-2.

Focused Practice

1 | DISCOVER THE GRAMMAR

Read the question. Then circle the letter of the correct sentence.

1. In which sentence do we know that the diamond necklace is gone?
   a. He was stealing a diamond necklace.
   b. He stole a diamond necklace.

2. Which sentence tells us that the people arrived at the mountains?
   a. They were driving to the mountains.
   b. They drove to the mountains.

3. In which sentence was the action interrupted?
   a. When the phone rang, he answered it.
   b. When the phone rang, he was looking for his bag.

4. Which sentence talks about two actions that were in progress at the same time?
   a. While the officer was questioning Sal, Eve was leaving town.
   b. When the officer questioned Sal, Eve left town.

5. In which sentence did the friends arrive before lunch began?
   a. When our friends arrived, we were eating lunch.
   b. When our friends arrived, we ate lunch.

2 | A TRAFFIC ACCIDENT   *Grammar Notes 1–6*

🎧 *Complete the conversation with the past progressive or the simple past form of the verbs in parentheses. Use Appendix 1 on page 000 for help with irregular verbs.*

REPORTER: What was the cause of the accident, Officer?

OFFICER: Well, it looks like there were many causes. First of all, when the accident
_____happened_____, the driver _____was driving_____ much too fast. The driver
　　　　1.(happen)　　　　　　　　　　　2.(drive)

is a suspect in a burglary, and she _was leaving_ town. While she
　　　　　　　　　　　　　　　　　3.(leave)

was driving, she _was speaking_ to someone on her cell phone.
　4.(drive)　　　　　5.(speak)

When she _saw_ the pedestrian, she immediately _stepped_
　　　　6.(see)　　　　　　　　　　　　　　　7.(step)

on the brakes, but it was too late. The victim wasn't paying attention, either. He

was crossing the street against a red light when the car _hit_
　8.(cross)　　　　　　　　　　　　　　　　　　　9.(hit)

him. He _didn't see_ the approaching car because he _was talking_ to
　10.(not see)　　　　　　　　　　　　　　　　　11.(talk)

his friend. The friend ___wasn't paying___ attention, either. He ___was listening___ to
                      12. (not pay)   **13. (listen)**

music with his headphones. When he ___noticed___ the car, he ___tried.___
                                    14. (notice)   **15. (try)**

to push his friend out of the way, but it was too late.

REPORTER: How is the victim doing?

OFFICER: Well, when the ambulance ___arrived,___ , he ___was bleeding___ from a head
                                  16. (arrive)   **17. (bleed)**

wound, but the doctors ___stopped___ the bleeding and they think he'll be OK.
                       18. (stop)

3 | ANSWER CAREFULLY
Grammar Notes 1–6

The police are questioning another suspect in last Friday's burglary. Read this suspect's answers. Use the words in parentheses and the past progressive or simple past to write the police officer's questions.

1. OFFICER: ___What were you doing Friday night?___
   (What / you / do / Friday night)

   SUSPECT: I was visiting a friend.

2. OFFICER: ___Who exactly were you visiting?___
   (Who exactly / you / visit)

   SUSPECT: My girlfriend. I got to her house at 5:30, and then I drove her to work.

3. OFFICER: ___Was she working at 7:00?___
   (she / work / at 7:00)

   SUSPECT: Yes, she was working the late shift.

4. OFFICER: ___Was anyone else working with her?___
   (anyone else / work / with her)

   SUSPECT: No, she was working alone.

5. OFFICER: ___What were you doing while she was working?___
   (What / you / do / while she / work)

   SUSPECT: I was reading the paper in her office.

6. OFFICER: But there was a terrible blizzard Friday night. The lights went out.

   ___What were you doing when the lights go out?___
   (What / you / do / when the lights / go out)

   SUSPECT: I took out my flashlight and looked for my girlfriend.

7. OFFICER: ___what was she doing when you find her?___
   (What / she / do / when you / find her)

   SUSPECT: She was looking for *me*.

8. OFFICER: Then ___what were you doing?___
   (What / you / do)

   SUSPECT: We quickly left the building.

9. OFFICER: ___Why were you running when the police saw you?___
   (Why / run / when the police / see you)

   SUSPECT: We were running because we wanted to get out of the storm.

4 | BLIZZARD

Grammar Notes 1–6

Combine the pairs of sentences. Use the past progressive or the simple past form of the verb. Remember to use commas when necessary.

1. The blizzard started. Mr. Ligo attended a party.

   When *the blizzard started, Mr. Ligo was attending a party.*

2. The wind began to blow. The electricity went out.

   When _____

3. He drove home. He listened to his car radio.

   While _____

4. He pulled over to the side of the road. He couldn't see anything.

   _____ when _____

5. He listened to the news. He heard about the burglary.

   While _____

6. It stopped snowing. Mr. Ligo went to the police station.

   When _____

5 | EDITING

Read this personal journal entry. There are seven mistakes in the use of the past progressive and the simple past. The first mistake is already corrected. Find and correct six more. Remember to look at punctuation!

>   *happened*
> What ~~was happening~~ to me this morning was so unbelievable! I walked down the
> street while a woman stopped in front of me and asked me for directions to the
> nearest bank. At that moment, I was seeing my friend Bill across the street.
> I called out to him and asked him to wait for me. Luckily for me, he did. Bill
> saw everything: while I talking to the woman, a pickpocket was put his hand
> into my backpack. Bill started to walk away. I thought he didn't want to wait
> for me, but I was wrong. When Bill saw the pickpocket he went to call the
> police. They were arriving immediately. The police arrested the woman and the
> pickpocket. What an experience!

Communication Practice

6 | LISTENING

🎧 *Listen to a witness describe a traffic incident. Then listen again. According to the witness, which set of pictures is the most accurate? Circle the number.*

7 | ROLE PLAY: THE REAL STORY

Work in groups of four. Follow these steps:

1. Three students are witnesses; the fourth is a police officer. Look at the pictures in Exercise 6.

2. The police officer asks the witnesses questions about the accident.

3. Each of the witnesses chooses one set of pictures to describe.

Example: **A:** Can you describe the accident?
          B: Yes, two men were crossing the street.

8 | ARE YOU A GOOD WITNESS?

Look at this picture for ten seconds. Then close your book and write down what was happening. See how many details you can remember. What were the people doing? What were they wearing? Was anything unusual going on?

Example: A man and a woman were standing by the fireplace. The woman was wearing . . .

Compare your list with those of your classmates. Who remembered the most?

9 | WRITING

Write a description of an event that you witnessed: an accident, a crime, a reunion, a wedding, or another event. Use the past progressive and the simple past to describe what was happening and what happened during the event.

Example: While I was going to lunch today, I saw a wedding party. People were waiting for the bride and groom outside a temple. When they saw the couple, they . . .

10 | ON THE INTERNET

Do a search for your date of birth. Find out what was happening in the world at that time. Tell your classmates.

Example: I was born on March 1, 1965. At that time, the Beatles were touring the United States. . . .

Used to

BEFORE YOU READ

⌒ *What is a blog or weblog? Look at the pictures. What do you think this blog is about? What toys, TV shows, clothes, and hairstyles do you remember from your childhood? Read Sandra's weblog about the 1980s.*

The Awesome Eighties

Today's blog is a walk down memory lane. Were you a kid in the 1980s? What toys **did** you **use to play** with? What **did** you **use to watch** on TV?

Did you **use to watch** cartoons Saturday mornings? I **used to love** *She-Ra, Princess of Power*. I collected the toys and acted out the stories with my friends. It's hard to believe, but we **didn't use to play** video games then!

A puzzle called the Rubik's cube **used to be** very popular in the 1980s. My older sister Linda carried one in her backpack all the time. She and her friends **used to have** contests. She didn't win very often, but she loved it anyway.

This is my mother, dressed for work. She **used to love** suits with big shoulders. She said they made her feel strong, like She-Ra, Princess of Power. She **used to call** this one her "power suit."

My brother Gary and his friends had a rock band. They **used to practice** in the garage. They **never used to study**. Gary **used to get** some strange haircuts. He's a lawyer now, and he's lost his hair!

AFTER YOU READ

Read the statements. Check **True** *or* **False**.

	True	False
1. Sandra didn't watch TV on Saturdays.	☐	☐
2. She played video games a lot.	☐	☐
3. Her sister Linda played with a Rubik's cube.	☐	☐
4. Her mother wore a suit to work.	☐	☐
5. Her brother's band practiced in the garage.	☐	☐
6. Her brother and his friends studied all the time.	☐	☐
7. Her brother likes strange haircuts now.	☐	☐

Grammar Presentation

USED TO

Statements			
Subject	*Used to*	**Base Form of Verb**	
I You He She It We You They	**used to** **didn't use to**	**be**	popular.

Yes / No Questions				
Did	**Subject**	*Use to*	**Base Form of Verb**	
Did	I you he she it we you they	**use to**	**be**	popular?

Short Answers					
Affirmative			**Negative**		
Yes,	you I he she it you we they	**did.**	**No,**	you I he she it you we they	**didn't.**

Wh- Questions					
Wh- Word	Did	Subject	Use to	Base Form of Verb	
When	**did**	I you he she it we you they	**use to**	**be**	popular?

GRAMMAR NOTES

EXAMPLES

1. Use ***used to* + base form** of the verb to talk about <u>past habits</u> or <u>past situations</u> that no longer exist in the present.

Now

Past ——— X — X — X ————————→ **Future**
used to play

▶ **BE CAREFUL!** *Used to* always refers to the past. There is no present form.

- He **used to play** in a band.
(He played in a band in the past, but he doesn't play in a band now.)

- She **used to love** cartoons.
NOT She ~~uses~~ to love cartoons.

2. Use ***used to*** in sentences that <u>contrast the past and the present</u>. We often use time expressions such as *now, no longer,* and *not anymore* with the present to emphasize the contrast.

- I **used to have** very long hair, but ***now*** my hair is very short.
- We **used to play** with Rubik's cubes, but we do***n't*** like them ***anymore***.

3. Form the **negative** with:
didn't* + *use to

USAGE NOTE: In negative statements, ***never* + *used to*** is more common than *didn't use to*.

- He ***didn't* use to study**.
NOT He didn't ~~used~~ to study.

- He ***never* used to study**.

4. Form **questions** with:
did* + *use to

USAGE NOTE: In questions, the simple past is more common than *did* + *use to*.

- **Did** you **use to have** long hair?
NOT Did you ~~used~~ to have long hair?

- **Did** you **have** long hair when you were younger?

Pronunciation Note
Used to and ***use to*** are pronounced the same: /ˈyustə/.

(continued)

5. BE CAREFUL! Do not confuse **used to + base form** of the verb with the following expressions:

- **be used to + base form + -ing** (be accustomed to)

- **get used to + base form + -ing** (get accustomed to)

- She **used to work**.
  (She doesn't work now.)

- She **is used to working**.
  (She is accustomed to working.)

- She'll **get used to working**.
  (She'll get accustomed to working.)

Focused Practice

1 | DISCOVER THE GRAMMAR

Read these responses to "The Awesome Eighties" blog. Underline the verb forms that refer to past habits.

Remember when Pacman <u>used to be</u> the most popular computer game? A Japanese company brought Pacman to the United States in 1980. In the first 18 months, people spent $1 billion on the game. They used to play it in video arcades, on their computers, and even on special wristwatches!

posted 02.12.06, Comments (14)

We used to listen to music on vinyl records. The quality wasn't always very good, but we were used to it—it never used to bother us. In 1982, CDs appeared. Then we got used to hearing perfect sound. By the end of the 1980s, vinyl records were out, and CDs were in.

posted 02.13.06, Comments (7)

Computers used to be very large and very expensive. In the 1980s they got smaller and cheaper. People got used to working on personal computers in offices and started to buy them for their homes. Now we ask, "What did we use to do before computers?"

posted 02.14.06, Comments (11)

2 | SCHOOL REUNION
Grammar Notes 1–4

Sandra is at her class reunion. Complete the conversations with the correct form of **used to** *and the words in parentheses.*

1. SANDRA: You look familiar. ____*Did*____ you _____*use to be*_____ in the drama club?
   a. (be)

   ROSA: Sandra! It's me—Rosa! I _____ long hair. Remember?
   b. (have)

2. ROSA: There's Glen—all alone. Was he always that shy?

   SANDRA: Glen? He never _____ talking. Let's go say hi to him.
   a. (stop)

3. ROSA: _____ you _____ with Gary's band, the Backyard Boys?
   a. (play)

   GLEN: Sometimes. We _____ in Gary's garage after school.
   b. (practice)

   SANDRA: Tell the truth, Glen. You really _____ to see my sister Linda!
   c. (come)

4. GLEN: There's Jim and Laura. I think they got married a couple of years ago.

   SANDRA: Really? In high school, they _____ each other at all.
   a. (not like)

5. LAURA: I see Sandra! We _____ next to each other in math class.
   a. (sit)

   JIM: She looks so different now. She _____ glasses.
   b. (not wear)

   LAURA: We all look different now. We _____ a lot younger back then.
   c. (be)

3 | LOOKING BACK
Grammar Notes 1–2

Sandra is showing her daughter Megan an old photo album. Complete their conversation. Use **used to** *and the correct verb from the box.*

be	drive	ha̶v̶e̶	love	play	visit	wear

MEGAN: Wow! Uncle Gary ____*used to have*____ a lot of hair!
1.

SANDRA: Not for long. Right after this photo, he shaved his head.

MEGAN: In this picture, were you going to the gym?

SANDRA: No. We _____ exercise clothes everywhere.
2.

MEGAN: You looked cute!

SANDRA: This was your Aunt Linda's car. She _____ her friends to school every
3.

day.

MEGAN: That's not Uncle Fred with her.

SANDRA: No, that's Glen. He _____ her boyfriend before she met Fred.
4.

(continued)

MEGAN: Oh! You had a Barbie doll!

SANDRA: Of course. I _____ with it every day.
  5.

MEGAN: And that's me with Grandma and Grandpa!

SANDRA: Right. You _____ them at the beach every summer.
  6.

  You _____ the water.
  7.

4 | EDITING

*Read this journal entry about a high school reunion in Timmins, Ontario, a small town 500 miles north of Toronto. There are seven mistakes in the use of **used to**. The first mistake is already corrected. Find and correct six more.*

Shania Twain

The high school reunion was great! I talked to
Eileen Edwards. Well, she's the famous Shania Twain
now. In high school, she ~~was~~ used to be just one of us,
and tonight we all called her Eileen. She graduated in
1983, a year before me. Today she lives in a chateau in
Switzerland and models for Revlon, but her life didn't
used to be like that at all! She uses to be very poor,
and her grandma used to made all her clothes because
her family couldn't afford to buy them. She was always a good musician, though. In fact,
she used to earn money for her family that way. She performed with a local rock band,
and my friends and I use to go hear her. She could really sing! Her new name, Shania,
means "on my way" in Ojibwa (her stepfather's Native American language). After she
left Timmins, I got used to think that Timmins wasn't important to her anymore—but I
was wrong. She is always doing good things for our community. And tonight she was just
the way she used be in high school—simple and friendly!

Communication Practice

🎧 *Two friends are talking about their past. Listen to their conversation. Then listen again. Check the things they used to do in the* **past** *and the things they do* **now**.

	Past	Now
1. get up very early without an alarm clock	✓	☐
2. use an alarm clock	☐	☐
3. have a big breakfast	☐	☐
4. have a cup of coffee	☐	☐
5. look at the newspaper	☐	☐
6. have endless energy	☐	☐
7. do aerobics	☐	☐
8. meet at class reunions	☐	☐
9. take car trips on weekends	☐	☐

Work with a partner. Look at the pairs of pictures and talk about how the people have changed. Then write sentences that describe the changes. Compare your sentences with those of your classmates.

THEN

NOW

1. Sharifa _used to be very busy, but now she is more relaxed._

   She used to wear glasses, but now she doesn't.

(continued)

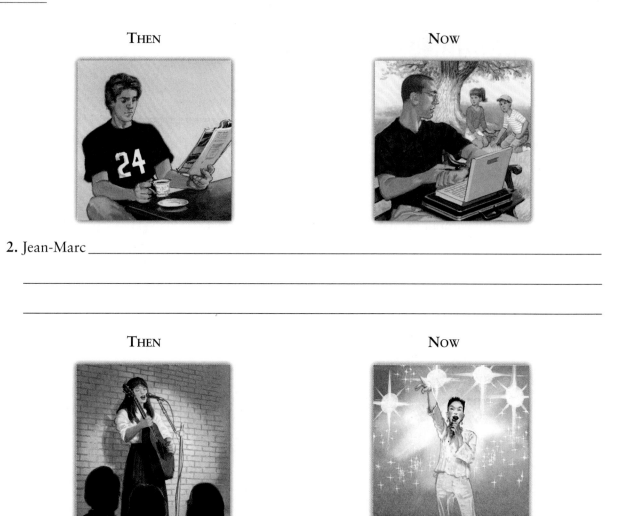

THEN   NOW

2. Jean-Marc _____

_____

_____

THEN   NOW

3. Lyric _____

_____

_____

THEN   NOW

4. Mike _____

_____

_____

7 | THE WAY I USED TO BE

Work in small groups. Bring in a picture of yourself when you were much younger. Talk about the differences in how you used to be and how you are now. What did you use to do? How did you use to dress?

Example: I used to have very long hair. Now I wear my hair short.

8 | WRITING

Write a two-paragraph essay. Contrast your life in the past and your life now. In the first paragraph, describe how your life used to be at some time in the past. In the second paragraph, describe your life today.

Example: I used to live in Russia. I attended St. Petersburg University.
In those days I used to . . .
Today I am living in Florida and attending Miami University . . .

9 | ON THE INTERNET

 Work in small groups. Each group picks a recent decade (ten-year period): 1950s, 1960s, 1970s, 1980s, or 1990s. Each member of the group does a web search on that decade.

1. Look for the fashions, styles, music, or movies of that time.

2. Share the information you find with your group.

3. As a group, share your information with the rest of the class. You can also bring in pictures you find.

Example: Here are some examples of the clothes people used to wear in the 1960s.
Young girls really used to wear their skirts short . . .
And here are some examples of the way people used to wear their hair.
Boys used to let their hair grow very long . . .

Grammar in Context

BEFORE YOU READ

🎧 *Think about the year 2050 and try to predict which business will create the most jobs. Computers? Robots? Space travel? Read this article about jobs of the future.*

Where to Look for Jobs in the Future

Computers   Robots   Space Travel

Which business **will create** the most jobs?

Did you guess space travel? If so, Professor Patrick Collins, a professor of economics in Japan, agrees with you. At a recent lecture he said, "It **won't be** long before people **will call** their travel agents and **book** their flights to the Moon. Imagine! Yes, there is room on tomorrow's flight to the Moon. It **leaves** at 9:00 A.M. It's **going to be** full so please arrive early for check-in."

Of course, many people disagree with Collins. They think space travel **will cost** too much and not many people **will travel**. They also think that people **won't feel** safe enough to travel into space. But Collins's research shows that the majority of people think it **will be** worth saving their money to travel into space. He claims that while it **will** probably **start out** as an activity for a few rich individuals, it **will grow** very quickly—just like the aviation (airplane) industry grew in the last 100 years. After all, Collins reminds us, the Wright brothers flew their first plane in 1903.

Where to Look for Jobs in the Future

If Collins is right that people **will travel** to space as tourists, then, like all tourists, they **are going to stay** in hotels. They **are going to want** tours and they **will** certainly **expect** some entertainment. All of this **will require** many people, and that **will mean** many new jobs.

Some of these space jobs **will be** similar to Earth jobs, but they **will have** some unique challenges. For instance, how **will** a space waiter **serve** food in a gravity-free restaurant? And what about fitness trainers? Teaching an aerobics class in space **will require** some new moves in addition to a lot more flexibility—in all directions! But not all space jobs **will be** more difficult. Some **will be** easier, the job of a porter for instance. No more carrying heavy luggage; it **will** just **float** along. Well, one thing is certain about these space jobs—they **won't be** boring!

PLEASE NOTE: If you missed this great lecture, Professor Collins **is speaking** again at the space conference tomorrow night at 7:00 P.M.

AFTER YOU READ

What's Professor Collins's opinion? Read each statement and write **T (True)** *or* **F (False)** *under* **Collins***. Write your own opinion under* **You***.*

	Collins	You
1. Space travel will create more jobs in the future.	T	T
2. People won't feel safe enough to travel in space.	F ~~T~~	T
3. The space travel business won't grow very quickly.	F ~~T~~	T
4. At first, only rich people are going to travel as space tourists.	T	T
5. People will save money to travel into space.	F	T
6. There will be hotels in space.	T	T
7. Space jobs will be completely different from Earth jobs.	F	F
8. Space jobs will have some interesting new problems.	T	T

Grammar Presentation

BE GOING TO FOR THE FUTURE

Statements				
Subject	*Be*	*(Not) Going to*	**Base Form of Verb**	
I	**am***			
You	**are**			
He She It	**is**	**(not) going to**	**leave**	soon.
We You They	**are**			

* For contractions of *I am*, *you are*, etc., see Appendix 26 on page A-12.

Yes / No Questions				
Be	**Subject**	*Going to*	**Base Form of Verb**	
Am	I			
Are	you			
Is	he she it	**going to**	**leave**	soon?
Are	we you they			

Short Answers						
Affirmative			**Negative**			
Yes,	you	**are.**	**No,**	you**'re**	**not.**	
	I	**am.**		I**'m**		
	he she it	**is.**		he**'s** she**'s** it**'s**		
	you we they	**are.**		you**'re** we**'re** they**'re**		

Wh- Questions				
Wh- Word	*Be*	**Subject**	*Going to*	**Base Form of Verb**
When Why	**are**	you	**going to**	**leave?**

WILL FOR THE FUTURE

Statements			
Subject	***Will*** **(*not*)**	**Base Form of Verb**	
I You He She It We You They	**will** (**not**)*	**leave**	soon.

* For contractions of *I will*, *you will*, etc., see Appendix 26, page A-12.

Yes / No Questions			
Will	**Subject**	**Base Form of Verb**	
Will	I you he she it we you they	**leave**	soon?

Short Answers						
Affirmative			**Negative**			
Yes,	you I he she it you we they	**will.**	**No,**	you I he she it you we they	**won't.**

Wh- Questions			
Wh- **Word**	***Will***	**Subject**	**Base Form of Verb**
When	**will**	you	**leave**?

PRESENT PROGRESSIVE* FOR THE FUTURE

Statements		
Subject + *Be*	**(*Not*) + Base Form + *-ing***	
We**'re**	(**not**) **leaving**	soon.
It**'s**		

SIMPLE PRESENT* FOR THE FUTURE

Statements		
Subject	**Verb**	
We	**leave**	Monday at 6:45 A.M.
It	**leaves**	

*For a complete presentation of present progressive and simple present forms, see Unit 1, page 3.

GRAMMAR NOTES	**EXAMPLES**

1. There are several ways to talk about the **future**. You can use:

- *be going to*
- *will*
- present progressive
- simple present

- They**'re going to have** a meeting.
- I think **I'll go**.
- It**'s taking** place next week.
- It **starts** at 9:00 A.M. on Monday.

USAGE NOTE: Sometimes only one form of the future is appropriate, but in many cases more than one form is possible.

2. To make **predictions** or **guesses** about the future, use:

- *be going to*

  OR

- *will*

▶ **BE CAREFUL!** Use *be going to* instead of *will* when something in the present helps you make the prediction about the future.

- People **are going to travel** to space.

  OR

- People **will travel** to space.

- Look at those dark clouds! It**'s going to** rain.
  NOT It'll rain.

3. To talk about future **intentions** or **plans**, use:

- *be going to*

  OR

- *will*

  OR

- present progressive

We often use *will* when we decide something at the moment of speaking.

We often use the **present progressive** when we talk about future plans that are already arranged.

- **I'm going to fly** to Mars next week.

  OR

- **I'll fly** to Mars next week.

  OR

- **I'm flying** to Mars next week.

A: The show is opening next week.
B: Sounds interesting. I think **I'll go**.

- **I'm flying** to Chicago next month. I already have a ticket.

Pronunciation Note
In informal speech, *going to* is often pronounced "gonna" /gənə/.

4. To talk about **scheduled future events** (timetables, programs, schedules), use the **simple present**. Verbs such as *start*, *leave*, *end*, and *begin* are often used this way.

- The shuttle **leaves** at 9:00 A.M.
- The conference **starts** tomorrow morning.

Reference Note
Will can also be used for **making a request**; see Unit 13 on page 146.

Focused Practice

1 | DISCOVER THE GRAMMAR

Read this transcript of a radio program. The host, Dr. David Livingston, is interviewing Professor Patrick Collins. There are eighteen verb forms that refer to the future. Find and underline them. The first one is already underlined. Find and underline seventeen more.

THE SPACE SHOW

LIVINGSTON: Good evening, everybody, and welcome to my new program, *The Space Show*. I am your host, Dr. David Livingston, and my show <u>will bring</u> you information on anything and everything related to the exploration of space. And today's guest, Professor Patrick Collins, is going to talk about space travel. Professor Collins is speaking to us from Azabu University in Japan. He is an expert on space travel, and he believes that space travel is coming to us sooner than we think. Welcome to the show, Professor. Tell us: Why do you think space travel is going to be so popular and why so soon?

COLLINS: It's simple. Ask most people and they'll tell you they are very curious about outer space. There's already a lot of excitement about space travel.

LIVINGSTON: But how will the average person be able to afford it? It will be very expensive, no?

COLLINS: I know that some people say it'll cost too much. But space travel is also going to create jobs. And with those new jobs, the world's economy will improve. This means that people will have more money to spend, and more people will want to try space travel. And I'd like to add that travel to the Moon is only a start. We won't stop there. Putting people on Mars won't take much longer. We all know this beautiful planet Earth has limited resources. Soon we will have no choice but to look elsewhere, and that means to look into space.

LIVINGSTON: Very interesting. It's time for a short break, but first I want to remind everyone that Professor Collins is speaking at the Annual Space Transportation Conference in Virginia next week. Also, don't forget that *The Space Show* is moving to a new time. Next week's show begins at 8:00 P.M. Pacific Standard Time.

2 | IT'S GOING TO HAPPEN
Grammar Note 2

Look at the pictures. They show events from a day in the life of Professor Starr. Write predictions or guesses. Use the words in the box and a form of **be going to** *or* **not be going to**.

answer the phone	drive	~~get out of bed~~	get very wet	give a speech
go to sleep	have dinner	rain	~~take a trip~~	watch TV

1. _____He's going to take a trip._____

2. _He'sn't going to drive_

3. _It's going to rain_

4. _He'sn't going to get very wet._

5. _He's going to give a speach_

6. _He's going To answer the phone_

7. _He's going To have dinner_

8. _He's going to watch TV_

9. <u>He's'nt going to go to sleep</u>   10. <u>He's going to get out of bed.</u>

3 | PROFESSOR STARR'S SCHEDULE

Grammar Note 3

Write about Professor Starr's plans for next week. Use the information from his calendar and the present progressive.

	Monday	**Tuesday**	**Wednesday**	**Thursday**	**Friday**	**Saturday**
A.M.	Teach my economics class	Take the train to Tokyo	Do the interview for <u>The Space Show</u>	Work on the Space Future website	Go to an exercise class	Answer e-mails from the Space Future website
P.M.		Meet friends from England for dinner	Answer questions from the online chat		Fly to New York for the Space Transportation Conference	Write a speech for the next space travel conference

1. On Monday morning *he's teaching his economics class.*
2. On Tuesday morning he's taking the train to Tokyo.
3. On Tuesday evening he's meeting friends from England for dinner.
4. On Wednesday morning he's doing the interview for The space show.
5. On Wednesday afternoon he's answering questions from the online chat
6. All day Thursday he's working on the Space Future website.
7. On Friday morning he's going to an exercise class.
8. On Friday evening he's Flying to New York for the Space Transportation Conference.
9. On Saturday morning he's answering e-mails from the Space Future website.
10. On Saturday afternoon he's writing a speech for the next space travel Conference

4 | SPACE FUTURE Q & A

Grammar Note 2

*It is the year 2020 and an international group of space tourists are getting ready for their space flight. Part of the preparation includes a Question and Answer (Q & A) session with astronaut William R. Pogue. Complete the questions and answers. Use the verbs in parentheses with **will** or **won't**.*

You'll get used to it!

Q: ___Will___ it ___take___ a long time to get used to zero gravity?
1. (take)

A: No, ___it won't___. Every day you will feel ___more comfortable, and after
2.   3. (feel)

three days you will become ___ used to being in space.
4. (become)

★ ★ ★

Q: will I feel ___ sick?
5. (feel)

A: Yes, you might feel sick for a little while. But it won't last ___ long.
6. (last)

★ ★ ★

Q: I love to read. How will I be able ___ to keep a book open to the right page?
7. (be able)

A: Actually, reading a book in space can be quite a problem. You will need ___ strong
8. (need)

clips to hold the book open. It can be a little frustrating at first, but after a while you

will get ___ used to it.
9. (get)

★ ★ ★

Q: will I look ___ the same?
10. (look)

A: Actually, you won't look ___ the same at all. Your face and eyes will get ___
11. (look)   12. (get)

puffy. The first time you look in a mirror, you probably won't recognize ___ yourself.
13. (recognize)

★ ★ ★

Q: will I float ___ in my sleep?
14. (float)

A: Yes, if you are not tied down. And then you should be careful because you will bump ___
15. (bump)

into things all night long. Trust me. You can get hurt!

★ ★ ★

Q: I like salt and pepper on my food. will I be able ___ to use salt and pepper on
16. (be able)

my food?

A: Yes, you will have ___ salt and pepper, but not like you do on Earth—the grains just
17. (have)

float away in zero gravity. You will use ___ small, squeezable bottles with salt water
18. (use)

and pepper water. You just squeeze it on your food. It tastes great!

5 | MOON SHUTTLE

It is June 2050. You and a friend are planning a trip to the Moon. Your friend just got the schedule, and you are deciding which shuttle to take. Use the words in parentheses to ask questions, and look at the schedule to write the answers. Use the simple present.

2050 SHUTTLE SERVICE TO THE MOON
September–November 2050

All times given in Earth's Eastern Standard Time

SEPTEMBER		OCTOBER		NOVEMBER	
Leave Earth	Arrive Moon	Leave Earth	Arrive Moon	Leave Earth	Arrive Moon
9/4 7:00 A.M.	9/7 6:00 P.M.	10/15 4:00 A.M.	10/18 3:00 P.M.	11/4 1:00 P.M.	11/8 12:00 A.M.
9/20 10:00 A.M.	9/23 9:00 P.M.	10/27 11:00 A.M.	10/30 10:00 P.M.	11/19 6:00 P.M.	11/23 5:00 A.M.

1. (During which months / the shuttle / fly to the Moon this year)

   A: *During which months does the shuttle fly to the Moon this year?*

   B: *It flies to the Moon in September, October, and November.*

2. (How many / shuttle flights / leave this year)

   A: How many shuttle flights do leave this year?

   B: There are six shuttle flights this year.

3. (How often / shuttle / depart for the Moon each month) *does the shuttle*

   A: How often ~~shuttle does~~ depart for the Moon each month?

   B: There are two departs each month. (it depart two times a month)

4. (When / the earliest morning flight / leave Earth)

   A: When does the earliest morning flight leave Earth?

   B: The earliest morning flight is 10/15 4:00 A.M.

5. (At what time / the latest shuttle / leave Earth)

   A: At what time does the latest shuttle leave Earth?

   B: The latest shuttle leave Earth is 11/19 6:00 P.M..

sudden decision → will
certain → be going to

6 | CHOOSE THE FUTURE

Grammar Notes 1–4

🎧 *Two people are traveling to a conference. Read their conversation and circle the most appropriate future forms.*

JASON: I just heard the weather report. It's raining / (It's going to rain) tomorrow.
1.

ARIEL: Oh no. I hate driving in the rain. And it's a long drive to the conference.

JASON: Wait! I have an idea. We'll take / We're going to take the train instead!
2.

ARIEL: Good idea! Do you have a train schedule?

JASON: Yes. Here's one. There's a train that will leave / leaves at 7:00 A.M.
3.

ARIEL: What about lunch? Oh, I know. I'll make / I'm making some sandwiches for us.
4.

JASON: OK. You know, it's a long trip. What are we doing / are we going to do all those hours?
5.

ARIEL: Don't worry. We'll think / We're thinking of something.
6.

JASON: You know, we have to get up really early. I think I'm going / I'll go home now.
7.

ARIEL: OK. I'm seeing you / I'll see you tomorrow. Good night.
8.

7 | EDITING

Read this student's report on space travel. There are eleven mistakes in the use of the future. The first mistake is already corrected. Find and correct ten more.

Both astronauts and space tourists will ~~traveling~~ *travel* in space, but tourists going to have a much different experience. Space tourists is going to travel for fun, not for work. So, they willn't have to worry about many of the technical problems that astronauts worry about. For example, space tourists will need not to figure out how to use a screwdriver without gravity. And they isn't going to try new experiments outside the space shuttle. For the most part, space tourists will just going to see the sights and have a good time.

Still, there will be similarities. Regular activities be the same for astronauts and space tourists. For example, eating, washing, and sleeping will turned into exciting challenges for everyone in space. Everyone is going to doing exercises to stay fit in zero gravity. And both astronauts and space tourists will going to have many new adventures!

Communication Practice

8 | LISTENING

 *Listen to the short conversations. Decide if the people are talking about something happening **Now** or in the **Future**. Then listen again and check the correct column.*

	Now	Future
1.	☐	☑
2.	☐	☐
3.	☐	☐
4.	☐	☐
5.	☐	☐
6.	☐	☐

9 | WHEN ARE YOU FREE?

*Complete your weekend schedule. If you have no plans, write **free**.*

	Friday	Saturday	Sunday
12:00 P.M.			
1:00 P.M.			
2:00 P.M.			
3:00 P.M.			
4:00 P.M.			
5:00 P.M.			
6:00 P.M.			
7:00 P.M.			
8:00 P.M.			
9:00 P.M.			

Now work with a partner. Ask questions to decide on a time when you are both free to do something together.

Example: A: What are you doing Friday afternoon? Do you want to go to the movies?
B: I'm studying at the library. How about Friday night? Are you doing anything?

10 | CHOOSE A TIME

There is a space conference in town this weekend. Work with your partner from Exercise 9. Look at the schedule of events below. Then look at your schedules from Exercise 9. Decide which events to attend and when.

SPACE TOURISM

Friday

8:00 A.M.–4:00 P.M.	Training for Space Travel
10:00 A.M.–12:00 P.M.	Eating in Space
7:00 P.M.	Advertising and Videos of Moon Resorts
8:00 P.M.	Meet Yang Liwei, China's First Astronaut

Saturday

2:00 P.M.–3:00 P.M.	Writing a Résumé for Space Employment
2:00 P.M.–4:00 P.M.	Personal Care in Space, or "How Do I Wash My Hair?"
6:00 P.M.	Advertising and Videos of Moon Resorts
8:00 P.M.	Space Sports

Sunday

8:00 A.M.–4:00 P.M.	Training for Space Travel
12:00 P.M.–2:00 P.M.	Live Taping of *The Space Show*
6:00 P.M.	Lecture: Who Should Invest in Space Tourism?

Example: A: What are you doing Friday? Do you want to go to "Training for Space Travel"?
B: Not really. That will take up the whole day. What else is there on Friday?

11 | WRITING

Imagine you are a travel agent advertising a dream vacation in space. Use your imagination to write about what your clients will do, what they will see, and how they will feel. What will hotel accommodations look like? What kinds of activities are there going to be? What types of food will people eat? Be creative!

Example: This is an experience you will never forget! Come with us to the Moon. We'll show you the sights and what Earth looks like from space . . .

12 | ON THE INTERNET

Do a search on **space sports**. *Read about the possibilities of new games and sports in zero gravity. Describe a game you read about or design your own game. Some websites allow you to submit your new ideas. Try it! Maybe yours will appear on the website too!*

Example: This game is called space water soccer. You will play it in a zero-gravity water room. Large blobs of water will float through the air, and each team will have to move the water blobs to one side of the room . . .

Future Time Clauses

Grammar in Context

BEFORE YOU READ

🎧 *Look at the picture. What is the girl thinking? Read this article about setting goals.*

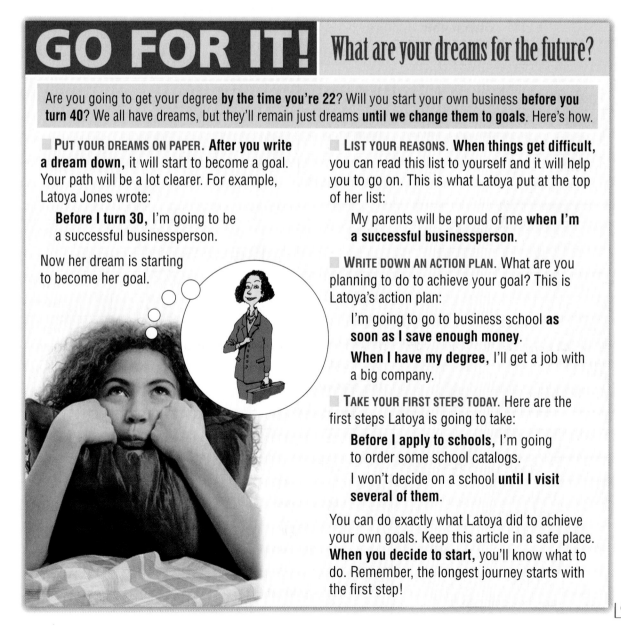

GO FOR IT! What are your dreams for the future?

Are you going to get your degree **by the time you're 22**? Will you start your own business **before you turn 40**? We all have dreams, but they'll remain just dreams **until we change them to goals**. Here's how.

■ **PUT YOUR DREAMS ON PAPER. After you write a dream down,** it will start to become a goal. Your path will be a lot clearer. For example, Latoya Jones wrote:

> **Before I turn 30,** I'm going to be a successful businessperson.

Now her dream is starting to become her goal.

■ **LIST YOUR REASONS. When things get difficult,** you can read this list to yourself and it will help you to go on. This is what Latoya put at the top of her list:

> My parents will be proud of me **when I'm a successful businessperson**.

■ **WRITE DOWN AN ACTION PLAN.** What are you planning to do to achieve your goal? This is Latoya's action plan:

> I'm going to go to business school **as soon as I save enough money**.
>
> **When I have my degree,** I'll get a job with a big company.

■ **TAKE YOUR FIRST STEPS TODAY.** Here are the first steps Latoya is going to take:

> **Before I apply to schools,** I'm going to order some school catalogs.
>
> I won't decide on a school **until I visit several of them**.

You can do exactly what Latoya did to achieve your own goals. Keep this article in a safe place. **When you decide to start,** you'll know what to do. Remember, the longest journey starts with the first step!

AFTER YOU READ

For each pair of sentences (a or b), check the action that comes first.

Latoya's action plan:

1. _____ **a.** She will order school catalogs.   _____ **b.** She will apply to schools.

2. _____ **a.** She will save money.   _____ **b.** She will go to business school.

3. _____ **a.** She will get a job with a big company.   _____ **b.** She will get her degree.

Grammar Presentation

FUTURE TIME CLAUSES

Statements				
Main Clause			**Time Clause**	
I **will** I **am going to**				I **graduate**.
She **will** She **is going to**	**get** a job	**when**	she **graduates**.
They **will** They **are going to**				they **graduate**.

Yes / No Questions				
Main Clause			**Time Clause**	
Will I **Am** I **going to**				I **graduate**?
Will she **Is** she **going to**	**get** a job	**when**	she **graduates**?
Will they **Are** they **going to**				they **graduate**?

Short Answers						
Affirmative				**Negative**		
Yes,	you	will. are.	**No,**	you	won't. aren't.
	she	will. is.		she	won't. isn't.
	they	will. are.		they	won't. aren't.

Wh- Questions					
Main Clause				**Time Clause**	
Where	**will** I **am** I **going to**				I **graduate**?
	will she **is** she **going to**	**get** a job	**when**	she **graduates**?
	will they **are** they **going to**				they **graduate**?

GRAMMAR NOTES

EXAMPLES

1. When a **sentence about future time** has two clauses, the verb in the main clause is often in the future (*will* or *be going to*). But the verb in the **time clause** is often in the **simple present**.

► **BE CAREFUL!** Do not use *will* or *be going to* in a future time clause.

The **time clause** can come at the beginning or at the end of the sentence. The meaning is the same.

Use a **comma** after the time clause when it comes at the beginning. Do not use a comma when it comes at the end.

- main clause   time clause
  She**'ll look** for a job *when* she **graduates**.
- main clause   time clause
  He**'s going to work** *after* he **graduates**.

NOT when she ~~will graduate~~.

NOT after he ~~is going to graduate~~.

- *Before* she applies, she'll visit schools.

  OR

- She'll visit schools *before* she applies.
  NOT She'll visit school‚ before she applies.

2. Here are some common **time expressions** you can use to begin future time clauses.

a. *When*, *after*, *not until*, and *as soon as* often introduce the event that happens <u>first</u>.

b. *Before*, *until*, and *by the time* often introduce the event that happens <u>second</u>.

c. *While* introduces an event that will happen <u>at the same time</u> as another event.

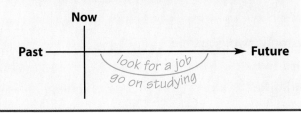

- *When* I graduate, I'll look for a job.
- I'll look for a job *after* I graduate.
- I wo*n't* look for a job *until* I graduate.
- *As soon as* I graduate, I'll look for a job.
  (First I'll graduate. Then I'll look for a job.)

- *Before* I get a job, I'll finish school.
- I'll stay in school *until* I get a job.
- *By the time* I get a job, I'll be out of school.
  (First I'll finish school. Then I'll get a job.)

- *While* I look for a job, I'll go on studying.
  (I will look for a job and study at the same time.)

Focused Practice

1 | DISCOVER THE GRAMMAR

Read the numbered sentence. Then circle the letter of the two sentences that have a similar meaning.

1. Amber will open her own business when she finishes school.

   a. Amber will open her own business. Then she'll finish school.

   (b.) Amber will finish school. Then she'll open her own business.

2. Denzell won't quit until he finds another job.

   (a.) Denzell will find another job. Then he'll quit.

   b. Denzell will quit. Then he'll find another job.

3. Jake will retire as soon as he turns 60.

   a. Jake will retire. Then he'll turn 60.

   (b.) Jake will turn 60. Then he'll retire.

4. After the Morrisons sell their house, they'll move to Florida.

   (a.) The Morrisons will sell their house. Then they'll move to Florida.

   b. The Morrisons will move to Florida. Then they'll sell their house.

5. Marisa will call you when she gets home.

   a. Marisa will call you. Then she'll get home.

   (b.) Marisa will get home. Then she'll call you.

6. Dimitri is going to live with his parents until he gets married.

   a. Dimitri is going to get married. Then he'll live with his parents.

   b. Dimitri will live with his parents. Then he'll get married.

7. While Li-jing is in school, she'll work part-time.

   a. Li-jing will finish school. Then she'll get a part-time job.

   b. Li-jing will go to school. At the same time she'll have a part-time job.

8. By the time Marta gets her diploma, she'll be 21.

   a. Marta will get her diploma. Then she'll turn 21.

   b. Marta will turn 21. Then she'll get her diploma.

9. Adel and Farah won't buy a house until their son is two years old.

   a. They'll buy a house. Then their son will turn two.

   b. Their son will turn two. Then they'll buy a house.

10. Ina will live in Paris while she studies French cooking.

    a. First she'll study French cooking. Then she will move to Paris.

    b. She'll study French cooking. At the same time, she'll live in Paris.

2 | **LOOKING AHEAD**   *Grammar Notes 1–2*

Complete this student's worksheet. Use the correct form of the verbs in parentheses.

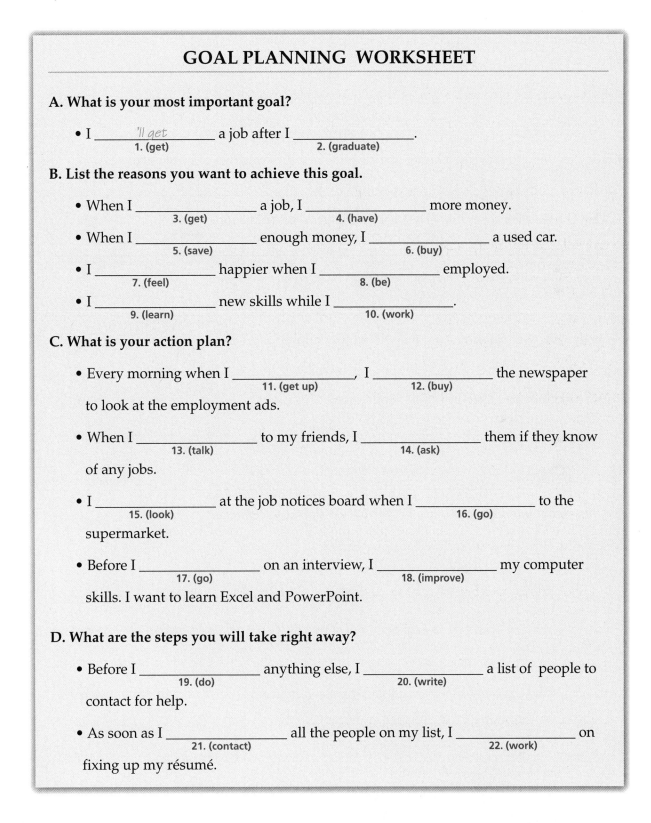

GOAL PLANNING WORKSHEET

A. What is your most important goal?

- I _____*'ll get*_____ a job after I _____.
        1. (get)   **2. (graduate)**

B. List the reasons you want to achieve this goal.

- When I _____ a job, I _____ more money.
          3. (get)   **4. (have)**
- When I _____ enough money, I _____ a used car.
         5. (save)   **6. (buy)**
- I _____ happier when I _____ employed.
     7. (feel)   **8. (be)**
- I _____ new skills while I _____.
     9. (learn)   **10. (work)**

C. What is your action plan?

- Every morning when I _____, I _____ the newspaper
             11. (get up)   **12. (buy)**
  to look at the employment ads.

- When I _____ to my friends, I _____ them if they know
        13. (talk)   **14. (ask)**
  of any jobs.

- I _____ at the job notices board when I _____ to the
     15. (look)   **16. (go)**
  supermarket.

- Before I _____ on an interview, I _____ my computer
        17. (go)   **18. (improve)**
  skills. I want to learn Excel and PowerPoint.

D. What are the steps you will take right away?

- Before I _____ anything else, I _____ a list of people to
        19. (do)   **20. (write)**
  contact for help.

- As soon as I _____ all the people on my list, I _____ on
       21. (contact)   **22. (work)**
  fixing up my résumé.

3 | WHAT'S NEXT?
Grammar Notes 1–2

Combine these pairs of sentences. Use the future or the simple present form of the verb.
Remember to use commas when necessary.

1. Sandy and Jeff will get married. Then Sandy will graduate.

_____Sandy and Jeff will get married_____ before _____Sandy graduates._____

2. Jeff is going to get a raise. Then they are going to move to a larger apartment.

___They are going to move to a ~___ as soon as ___Jeff is going to get a raise___

3. They're going to move to a larger apartment. Then they're going to have a baby.

After ___they move to a larger apartment,___

4. They'll have their first child. Then Sandy will get a part-time job.

___Sandy will get ~___ after ___they have their first child.___

5. Their child will be two. Then Sandy will go back to work full-time.

When _____

6. Sandy will work full-time, and Jeff will go to school.

_____ while _____

7. Jeff will graduate. Then he'll find another job.

_____ when _____

4 | EDITING
Grammar Notes 1–2

Read this journal entry. There are ten mistakes in the use of future time clauses. The first
mistake is already corrected. Find and correct nine more. Remember to look at punctuation!

Graduation is next month! I need to make some plans now because when exams ~~will~~ start, (start)

I don't have any free time. What am I going to do when I will finish school? My roommate

is going to take a vacation before she will look for a job. I can't do that because I need

to earn some money soon. I think that after I will graduate I am going to take a word

processing class. As soon as I learn word processing I look for a job as a bilingual office

assistant. It's hard to find full-time jobs, though. Part-time jobs are easier to find. Maybe

I'll take a part-time job after I find a good full-time one. Or maybe I'll take a workshop in

making decisions, before I do anything!

Communication Practice

5 | LISTENING

🎧 *Listen to a woman calling Jobs Are Us Employment Agency. Read the sentences that follow. Then listen again and number the events in order.*

The woman is going to:

_____ **a.** speak to a job counselor

_____ **b.** have an interview at the agency

__1__ **c.** send a résumé

_____ **d.** receive more job training

_____ **e.** go to companies

_____ **f.** take a skills test

6 | UNTIL WHEN?

Complete these sentences. Then compare your answers with those of your classmates. How many different answers are there? Remember that all sentences refer to future time.

1. I'm going to continue studying English until_____

2. While I'm in this class,_____

3. When I finish this class, _____

4. I'll stay in this country until_____

> **Example:** I'm going to continue studying English until I pass the TOEFL exam.

7 | INTERVIEW

Work with a partner. Interview him or her about some future plans. Ask questions such as:

- What will you do when _____?
- Where will you go after _____?
- Will you _____ while you _____?
- Before you _____, will you _____?

Take notes and then write a short paragraph about your classmate's plans.

> **Example:** Soo Mi is going to get married next year. Before she gets married, she's going to return home to visit her family. While she's away, she'll miss her boyfriend, but she'll e-mail him every day.

8 | WRITING

Complete this worksheet for yourself. Use future time clauses.

GOAL PLANNING WORKSHEET

A. What is your most important goal?

1. _____

B. List the reasons you want to achieve this goal.

1. _____

2. _____

3. _____

4. _____

C. What is your action plan?

1. _____

2. _____

3. _____

4. _____

D. What are the steps you will take right away?

1. _____

2. _____

3. _____

9 | ON THE INTERNET

Choose one personal dream. Write it down to make it a goal. What are the first steps you will take? Do a search to find the information you need. Report to the class on the information you find. Use future time clauses.

Example: GOAL: When I finish this English course, I will go to college.
SEARCH: Look up **colleges**.
REPORT: My goal is that when I finish this English course, I'll go to college. I looked up information about colleges. As soon as I am ready, I will apply to City College.

Wh- Questions: Subject and Object

Grammar in Context

BEFORE YOU READ

🎧 *Look at the drawing by a courtroom artist. A lawyer is questioning a crime witness. What kind of questions do you think the lawyer is asking? Read this excerpt from a court transcript.*

STATE OF ILLINOIS V. HARRY M. ADAMS   MARCH 31, 2006

LAWYER: **What happened on the night of May 12?** Please tell the court.
WITNESS: I went to Al's Grill.
LAWYER: **Who did you see there?**
WITNESS: I saw one of the defendants.
LAWYER: **Which one did you see?**
WITNESS: It was that man.
LAWYER: Let the record show that the witness
          is pointing to the defendant, Harry Adams.
          OK, you saw Mr. Adams. Did he see you?
WITNESS: No, he didn't see me.
LAWYER: But somebody saw you. **Who saw you?**
WITNESS: A woman. He was talking to a woman. She saw me.
LAWYER: OK. **What happened next?**
WITNESS: The woman gave him a box.
LAWYER: A box! **What did it look like?**
WITNESS: It was about this long . . .
LAWYER: So, about a foot and a half. **What did Mr. Adams do then?**
WITNESS: He took the box. He looked frightened.
LAWYER: **Why did he look frightened? What was in the box?**
WITNESS: I don't know. He didn't open it. He just took it and left in a hurry.
LAWYER: **Where did he go?**
WITNESS: Toward the parking lot.
LAWYER: **When did the woman leave?**
WITNESS: She was still there when we heard his car speed away.

AFTER YOU READ

Read the statements. Check **True** *or* **False**.

	True	False
1. The witness saw Harry Adams.	☐	☐
2. Harry Adams saw the witness.	☐	☐
3. The witness saw a woman.	☐	☐
4. The woman saw the witness.	☐	☐

Grammar Presentation

WH- QUESTIONS: SUBJECT AND OBJECT

Questions About the Subject		
Wh- Word Subject	Verb	Object
Who	saw	Harry?
		the box?

Answers		
Subject	Verb	Object
Marta	saw	him.
		it.

Questions About the Object			
*Wh-*Word Object	Auxiliary Verb	Subject	Main Verb
Who(m)	did	Marta	see?
What			

Answers		
Subject	Verb	Object
She	saw	Harry.
		the box.

GRAMMAR NOTES

EXAMPLES

1. Use **wh- questions** (also called *information questions*) to ask for specific information.	**A: Who** did you see at Al's Grill? **B:** Harry Adams.
Wh- questions begin with **wh- words** such as *who, what, where, when, why, which, whose, how, how many, how much,* and *how long*.	**A: When** did you go there? **B:** On May 12. **A: How many** people saw you? **B:** Two.

2. When you are asking about the **subject**, use:

- a *wh-* word in place of the subject, and statement word order: **subject + verb**

For questions beginning with **which**, **whose**, **how much**, and **how many**, we often use **wh- word + noun** in place of the subject.

subject   subject
<u>Someone</u> saw you.   <u>Something</u> happened.
↓   ↓

Who saw you?   **What** happened?

- **Which witness** told the truth?
- **How many people** saw the trial?

---

3. When the verb is a form of *be (am, is, are, was, were)* use:

- *wh-* word + *be*

Harry Adams is the defendant.
↓

- **Who is** the defendant?

Harry Adams is <u>the defendant</u>.

- **Who is** Harry Adams?

---

4. When you are asking about the **object**, use:

- a *wh-* word, and the following word order: **auxiliary verb + subject + main verb**

For questions beginning with **which**, **whose**, **how much**, and **how many**, we often use **wh- word + noun** in place of the object.

REMEMBER: An **auxiliary** verb is a verb such as *do (does, did)*, **have** *(has, had)*, **can**, or **will**. *Be* can be an auxiliary too.

object   object
You saw <u>someone</u>.   He said <u>something</u>.
↓   ↓

Who did you see?   **What** did he say?

- **Which witness** did you believe?
- **How much time** did the jury need?

- **Who does** she defend?
- **Who is** she helping?

---

5. **USAGE NOTE:** In **very formal** English when asking about people as object, **whom** is sometimes used instead of *who*.

▶ **BE CAREFUL!** If the main verb is a form of *be*, you cannot use *whom*.

VERY FORMAL

- **Whom** did you see?

MORE COMMON

- **Who** did you see?

- **Who is** the next witness?
  NOT ~~Whom~~ is the next witness?

---

6. *Wh-* questions with **why**, **when**, or **where** have the following word order:

- **auxiliary verb + subject + main verb**

This is the same word order as in *wh-* questions about the object.

- **Why does** she want to defend him?
- **When did** she arrive?
- **Where will** she go?

Focused Practice

1 | DISCOVER THE GRAMMAR

Match the questions and answers.

__f__ 1. Who did you see?

_____ 2. Who saw you?

_____ 3. What hit her?

_____ 4. What did she hit?

_____ 5. Which man did you give the money to?

_____ 6. Which man gave you the money?

a. His wife saw me.

b. She hit a car.

c. Harry gave me the money.

d. A car hit her.

e. I gave the money to Harry.

f. I saw the defendant.

2 | CROSS-EXAMINATION

Grammar Notes 1–6

Complete the cross-examination. Write the lawyer's questions.

1. LAWYER: *What time did you return home?*
   (**What time / you / return home**)

   WITNESS: I returned home just before midnight.

2. LAWYER: _____
   (**How / you / get home**)

   WITNESS: Someone gave me a ride.

3. LAWYER: _____
   (**Who / give / you / a ride**)

   WITNESS: A friend from work.

4. LAWYER: _____
   (**What / happen / next**)

   WITNESS: I opened my door and saw someone on my living room floor.

5. LAWYER: _____
   (**Who / you / see**)

   WITNESS: Deborah Collins.

6. LAWYER: _____
   (**Who / be / Deborah Collins**)

   WITNESS: She's my wife's boss. I mean, she *was* my wife's boss. She's dead now.

7. LAWYER: _____
   (**What / you / do**)

   WITNESS: I called the police.

8. LAWYER: _____
   (**When / the police / arrive**)

   WITNESS: In about 10 minutes.

9. **LAWYER:** _____
   (What / they / ask you)

   WITNESS: They asked me to describe the crime scene.

10. **LAWYER:** _____
    (How many police officers / come)

    WITNESS: I don't remember. Why?

    LAWYER: I'm asking the questions here. Please just answer.

---

3 | Q & A   *Grammar Notes 1–6*

Read the answers. Then ask questions about the underlined words.

1. Court begins <u>at 9:00 A.M.</u>

   When does court begin?

2. <u>Something horrible</u> happened.

   _____

3. <u>Five</u> witnesses testified.

   _____

4. The witness recognized <u>Harry Adams</u>.

   _____

5. <u>The witness</u> recognized Harry Adams.

   _____

6. The district attorney questioned <u>the restaurant manager</u>.

   _____

7. <u>The judge</u> spoke to the jury.

   _____

8. The verdict was <u>"guilty."</u>

   _____

9. The jury found Adams guilty <u>because he didn't have an alibi</u>.

   _____

10. The trial lasted <u>two weeks</u>.

    _____

11. Adams paid his lawyer <u>$2,000</u>.

    _____

4 | EDITING

Read a reporter's notes. There are eight mistakes in the use of wh- questions. The first
mistake is already corrected. Find and correct seven more.

<u>Questions</u>

did Jones go
Where ~~Jones went~~ on January 15?

Who went with him?

What time he return home?

Who he called?

How much money he had with him?

Whom saw him at the station the next day?

How did he look?

How many suitcases did he have?

When the witness call the police?

What did happen next?

What his alibi was?

Communication Practice

5 | LISTENING

⌒ _You are on the phone with a friend. There is a bad connection. Listen to the following
sentences. Then listen again. Circle the letter of the question you need to ask in order to get
the correct information._

1. **a.** Who did you see at the restaurant?
   b. Who saw you at the restaurant?

2. **a.** Which car did the truck hit?
   b. Which car hit the truck?

3. **a.** When did it happen?
   b. Why did it happen?

4. **a.** Whose mother did you call?
   b. Whose mother called you?

5. **a.** Who did you report it to?
   b. Who reported it?

6. **a.** How many people heard the shouts?
   b. How many shouts did you hear?

7. **a.** Who saw the man?
   b. Who did the man see?

8. **a.** Why do you have to hang up?
   b. When do you have to hang up?

6 | WHAT HAPPENED NEXT?

Work with a partner. Look at the court transcript on page 73 again. Read it aloud. Then continue the lawyer's questioning of the witness. Ask at least six more questions.

Example: LAWYER: When did the woman leave?
WITNESS: She was still there when we heard his car speed away.
LAWYER: What happened next?

7 | INFORMATION GAP: POLICE CRIME INVESTIGATION

Two detectives (Maigret and Poirot) are investigating a case. All the suspects work at the same office. The detectives interviewed Mary Rogers, the office manager. Each detective took notes, but their notes are incomplete. You have to complete them. Work in pairs (A and B). Student A, follow the instructions on this page. Student B, turn to page 81.

1. Read Maigret's notes below.

2. Ask your partner for the information you need to complete Maigret's notes.

Example: **A:** Who did Mary Rogers see at 8:00 P.M.?
B: Rick Simon.

3. Maigret's notes have the information your partner needs to complete Poirot's notes. Answer your partner's questions.

Example: **B:** Where did Mary Rogers see Rick Simon?
A: She saw him at Al's Grill.

INTERVIEW WITH: Mary Rogers		DETECTIVE: Maigret	
SUSPECT (Who?)	**TIME** (When?)	**LOCATION** (Where?)	**OTHER WITNESSES** (Who else?)
Rick Simon	8:00 P.M.	Al's Grill	
Alice May		Fifth Avenue	Bob May
Jake Bordon	6:30 P.M.		the janitor
	7:15 P.M.		some children
John Daniels	7:00 P.M.		

When you are finished, compare Maigret's and Poirot's completed notes. Are they the same?

8 | STAR REPORTERS

Work in small groups. You are going to interview a ten-year-old child genius who is attending law school. You have five minutes to think of as many wh- *questions as you can. One student should write down all the questions.*

Examples: When did you decide to become a lawyer?
Who influenced you to become a lawyer?

You will be allowed to ask only six questions. Choose the six best questions. Now work in pairs. Role-play the interview. Use the six questions your group chose. Then write up the interview for a magazine article.

9 | WRITING

Work with a partner. Think of something exciting or interesting that you once saw. Tell your partner. Then write a list of questions and interview your partner to get more information. Take notes and write up the interview.

Example: A: I once saw a bad car accident.
B: Where did it happen?
A: On the highway.
B: How many cars were in the accident?
A: There was one car and a truck.
B: What did you do?
A: I . . .

10 | ON THE INTERNET

First do an online search for the definitions of these words. Write the definitions.

defense attorney	judge	jury	prosecutor	verdict	victim

The trial in this unit took place in the state of Illinois. Do a search on **criminal trial process in the United States**. *Do a web search or look at an online encyclopedia. Answer these questions:*

- Who does the defense attorney work for?
- Who represents the victim?
- Who chooses the jury?
- How many people sit on the jury?
- What does the judge do?
- Who gives the verdict?

When you are done, compare your answers with those of your classmates.

INFORMATION GAP FOR STUDENT B

1. Read Poirot's notes below.

2. Poirot's notes have the information your partner needs to complete Maigret's notes. Answer your partner's questions.

   Example: **A:** Who did Mary Rogers see at 8:00 P.M.?

   B: Rick Simon.

3. Ask your partner for the information you need to complete Poirot's notes.

   Example: **B:** Where did Mary Rogers see Rick Simon?

   A: She saw him at Al's Grill.

INTERVIEW WITH: Mary Rogers		DETECTIVE: Poirot	
SUSPECT (Who?)	**TIME** (When?)	**LOCATION** (Where?)	**OTHER WITNESSES** (Who else?)
Rick Simon	8:00 P.M.	Al's Grill	the waiter
Alice May	7:30 P.M.		
Jake Bordon	6:30 P.M.	the office	
Lilly Green	7:15 P.M.	in the park	
		Tony's Pizza	two customers

When you are finished, compare Maigret's and Poirot's completed notes. Are they the same?

From Grammar to Writing
Combining Sentences with Time Words

You can often improve your writing by combining two short sentences into one longer sentence that connects the two ideas. The two sentences can be combined by using time words such as *while*, *when*, *as soon as*, *before*, *after*, or *until*. The resulting longer sentence is made up of a main clause and a time clause.

Example: I was shopping. I saw the perfect dress for her. —→

        time clause   main clause

    While I was shopping, I saw the perfect dress for her.

    main clause   time clause

    I saw the perfect dress for her **while** I was shopping.

Notice that the time clause can come first or second. When it comes first, a comma separates the two clauses.

1 Read this paragraph. Underline all the sentences that are combined with a time word. Circle the time words.

>   I always exchange holiday presents with my girlfriend, Shao Fen.
> Last year, (while) I was shopping for her, I saw an umbrella in her
> favorite color. As soon as I saw it, I thought of her. I bought the
> umbrella and a scarf in the same color. When Shao Fen opened the
> present, she looked really upset. She didn't say anything, and she
> didn't look at me. I felt hurt and confused by her reaction. Later
> she explained that in Chinese the word for "umbrella" sounds like the
> word for "separation." When she saw the umbrella, she misunderstood.
> She thought I wanted to end the relationship. After I heard that,
> I was very upset! I decided that next year, before I buy something,
> I'm going to check with her sister!

2 | *Look at this student's paragraph. Combine the pairs of underlined sentences with time words such as* **when**, **while**, **as soon as**, **before**, *and* **after**. *Use your own paper.*

I usually keep my wallet in my back pocket when I go out. Two weeks ago, I was walking on a crowded street. I felt something. I didn't pay any attention to it at the time. I got home. I noticed that my wallet was missing. I was very upset. It didn't have much money in it, but my credit card and my driver's license were there. I was thinking about the situation. My brother came home. He told me to report it to the police. I called the police. They weren't very encouraging. They said that wallets often get "picked" from back pockets. They didn't think I would get it back. Tomorrow, I'm going to the movies. I'll keep my new wallet in my front pocket.

Example: Two weeks ago, **while** I was walking on a crowded street, I felt something.

3 | *Before you write . . .*

1. We often say, "Learn from your mistakes." Think about a misunderstanding or a mistake that you experienced or observed. How did your behavior or thinking change because of your experience?

2. Describe the experience to a partner. Listen to your partner's experience.

3. Ask and answer questions about your experiences, for example: *When did it happen? Why did you . . . ? Where were you when . . . ? What will you do . . . ?*

4 | *Write a draft of your story. Follow the model below. Remember to use some of these time words and include information that your partner asked about.*

as soon as	before	until	when	while

I (OR My friend) always / often / usually / never _____

_____

_____

Last week / Yesterday / In 2003, _____

_____

_____

_____

_____

In the future / Next time, _____

_____

5 | *Exchange stories with a different partner. Complete the chart.*

1. The writer used time words to connect ideas.   **Yes** _____ **No** _____

2. What I liked in the story:

   _____

   _____

   _____

3. Questions I'd like the writer to answer about the story:

   Who _____?

   What _____?

   When _____?

   Where _____?

   How _____?

   (Other) _____?

6 | *Work with your partner. Discuss each other's chart from Exercise 5. Then rewrite your own paragraph and make any necessary changes.*

Review Test

I *Complete each sentence with the simple present or present progressive form of the verb in parentheses.*

1. You _____ *'re breathing* _____ hard. Sit down and rest for a while.
   (breathe / are breathing)

2. Dolphins are mammals. They have lungs and they _____ air.
   (breathe / are breathing)

3. Fred just left. He _____ to his biology class right now.
   (goes / is going)

4. He _____ to biology class twice a week.
   (goes / is going)

5. In our area, it _____ a lot in March.
   (rains / is raining)

6. It _____ right now, and I don't have my umbrella.
   (rains / is raining)

7. We _____. Is the music too loud for you?
   (dance / are dancing)

8. We _____ every day. It's good exercise.
   (dance / are dancing)

II *Complete the conversations with the simple present or present progressive of the verbs in parentheses. Write short answers when necessary.*

1. **A:** _____ *Are* _____ you _____ *getting* _____ ready for school? It's 7:45.
   a. (get)

   B: Yes, I _____ *am* _____. I _____ my teeth right now.
   b.   c. (brush)

   A: How about Sue? _____ she _____ dressed?
   d. (get)

   B: I _____ so. She _____ for her shoes.
   e. (think)   f. (look)

2. **A:** Something _____ good. What _____ you _____?
   a. (smell)   b. (cook)

   B: Pancakes. Hey, _____ you _____ your book bag?
   c. (have)

   A: No, I _____. _____ you _____ where it is?
   d.   e. (know)

   B: You _____ it in your room these days, right?
   f. (keep)

   A: I _____ in my room right now, but I _____ it.
   g. (stand)   h. (not see)

(continued)

3. A: Yuck. This milk _____ awful. I'm going to have juice instead.

a. (taste)

   B: Look, I _____ one sandwich for lunch. _____ that enough?

b. (pack)   c. (be)

   A: I _____ any lunch. I _____ hungry today.

d. (not want)   e. (not be)

   B: You _____ pale. _____ you _____ OK?

f. (look)   g. (feel)

   A: Yes, I _____. I'm just a little nervous about my spelling test.

h.

   B: Oh no! Look at the time. I think I _____ the school bus.

i. (hear)

   A: Don't worry. We _____ right now. Bye!

j. (leave)

III   *Complete each sentence with an affirmative or negative imperative. Use the verbs in the box. Use some verbs more than once.*

call	enjoy	forget	have	lock	put	walk

1. Please _____*walk*_____ the dog in the morning and afternoon.

2. But _____ her near the Wongs' house. She chases their cat.

3. Please _____ the back door before you go out. The key is in the door.

4. Also, _____ to turn out the lights. We have high electric bills.

5. _____ the newspapers in the garbage. They go in a separate recycling bin.

6. _____ the garbage cans on the sidewalk on Tuesday morning.

7. _____ me if you have any problems.

8. But _____ after 11:00. We go to bed early when we're on vacation.

9. _____ fun, and _____ the house.

IV   *Complete the conversation with the simple past form of the verbs in parentheses. Write short answers when necessary.*

A: Are you from Baltimore?

B: No, I'm not. I _____*was born*_____ in China, but I _____ here 10 years ago.

1. (be born)   2. (move)

A: Where _____ you _____ in China?

3. (live)

B: In Shanghai.

A: Oh really? I _____ in Shanghai last year. I _____ English there
4. (be)   5. (teach)

for three years.

B: That's interesting. _____ you _____ it?
6. (like)

A: Yes, I _____. Very much.
7.

B: _____ the United States _____ strange to you after China?
8. (appear)

A: Yes, it _____. I _____ comfortable in Baltimore for months.
9.   10. (not be)

For one thing, my students here _____ very polite.
11. (not seem)

B: I think it's called "reverse culture shock". I _____ uncomfortable when
12. (be)

I _____ back to China a few years ago.
13. (go)

A: _____ you uncomfortable for a long time?
14. (be)

B: No, I _____. Things _____ to feel normal again after a
15.   16. (begin)

few weeks.

A: _____ you _____ to feel culture shock in your own culture?
17. (expect)

B: No, I _____! But I'll be prepared the next time I visit!
18.

V *Circle the correct verbs to complete the conversation.*

A: When you were young, did you use to ate /(eat) in restaurants a lot?
1.

B: No, not that often. We used to cooking / cook dinner at home.
2.

A: How about prices? Were / Did they lower when you were a kid?
3.

B: They sure were. Here's an example. A movie got used to / used to cost a dollar.
4.

A: Wow! Did you go / went to the movies a lot?
5.

B: Yes. We were going / went every Saturday afternoon. Hey, how about eating that
6.

hamburger?

A: OK—but one last question. Did / Are you like everything better in those days?
7.

B: Nope. In those days, I wasn't having / didn't have you to talk to. I like things much
8.

better now.

VI *Complete the telephone conversation with the simple past or past progressive form of the verbs in parentheses.*

A: Hi, I'm glad you're home! No one _____*answered*_____ a few minutes ago.
1. (answer)

B: I _____ the lawn when the phone _____. What's up?
2. (mow)   3. (ring)

A: I _____ a little accident with the car. Nothing serious—no injuries.
4. (have)

B: Oh, that's good. How about the car?

A: It's OK. There _____ much damage. I _____ fast when
5. (not be)   6. (not drive)

I _____ the bus.
7. (hit)

B: The bus! How _____ you _____ that?
8. (do)

A: I _____ to find a special radio station, so I _____ attention.
9. (try)   10. (not pay)

B: _____ you _____ the police?
11. (call)

A: No. It _____ in front of a police station. An officer _____
12. (happen)   13. (appear)

before I even _____ out of the car. After the officer _____,
14. (get)   15. (leave)

I _____ the insurance company.
16. (call)

B: Well, I'm just glad you're OK.

VII *Circle the correct verb to complete each conversation.*

1. **A:** Do you and Nora have plans for the weekend?
   B: Yes, we (**'re going**)/ 'll go to a concert on Saturday. I just bought the tickets.

2. **A:** I can't believe I got into medical school.
   B: You are / **'ll be** a doctor in just a few years!

3. **A:** Oh no! I forgot to deposit my paycheck yesterday.
   B: I **'ll** / 'm going to deposit it for you. It's on my way.

4. **A:** I'm taking the train to Boston tomorrow.
   B: Oh. What time **does** / did it leave?

5. A: Take your umbrella. It<u>'s going to / 'll</u> rain.

   B: Thanks. I didn't listen to the weather report this morning.

6. A: My son is really interested in science fiction.

   B: Maybe he <u>has / 'll have</u> a career in space exploration when he grows up.

7. A: Look at Rachel's face. I think she<u>'s going to / 'll</u> cry.

   B: Poor kid. She really wants to come with us today.

8. A: It's almost June. What <u>are we going to / do we</u> do for the summer?

   B: How about summer school?

9. A: <u>Will / Does</u> Mahmoud call back this afternoon?

   B: He promised to call, but he's usually in class all afternoon.

10. A: Should I make a reservation at Dino's for tonight?

    B: It's already arranged. We <u>are / were</u> meeting there at 6:00.

VIII *Complete the sentences with the correct forms of the verbs in parentheses. Use* **will** *in one clause of each sentence.*

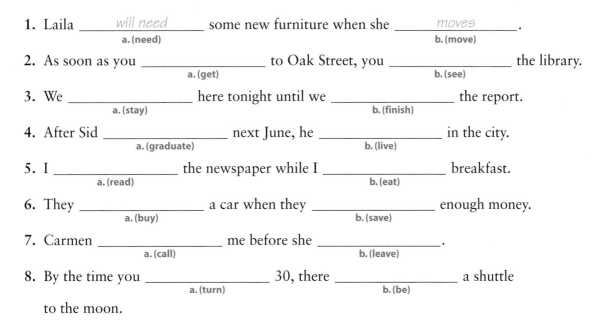

1. Laila _____*will need*_____ some new furniture when she _____*moves*_____ .

a. (need)   b. (move)

2. As soon as you _____ to Oak Street, you _____ the library.

a. (get)   b. (see)

3. We _____ here tonight until we _____ the report.

a. (stay)   b. (finish)

4. After Sid _____ next June, he _____ in the city.

a. (graduate)   b. (live)

5. I _____ the newspaper while I _____ breakfast.

a. (read)   b. (eat)

6. They _____ a car when they _____ enough money.

a. (buy)   b. (save)

7. Carmen _____ me before she _____ .

a. (call)   b. (leave)

8. By the time you _____ 30, there _____ a shuttle

a. (turn)   b. (be)

   to the moon.

IX *Complete the conversations with* **wh-** *questions.*

1. **A:** <u>_Where did you go_ _____</u> last night?
   a.

   B: I went to the movies.

   A: Really? _____ with you?
   b.

   B: Mona did. She goes every weekend.

   A: _____?
   c.

   B: We saw *Earthquake.*

2. **A:** You look upset. _____?
   a.

   B: Nothing happened. I'm just tired.

   A: _____ on the math test?
   b.

   B: I got an A.

   A: Wow! Big improvement. _____ with?
   c.

   B: I studied with Ana. It really helped.

X *Circle the letter of the correct answer to complete each sentence.*

1. What _____? You look fascinated.   (**A**) **B C D**
   (**A**) are you reading   (**C**) will you read
   (**B**) do you read   (**D**) did you read

2. I'm reading about the Internet. Did you know it _____   **A B C D**
   in the 1960s?
   (**A**) begins   (**C**) began
   (**B**) 's going to begin   (**D**) is beginning

3. Jill, please _____ me your e-mail address again. I lost it.   **A B C D**
   (**A**) gives   (**C**) give
   (**B**) is giving   (**D**) gave

4. My e-mail address is jillski4@data.com. _____ it again!   **A B C D**
   (**A**) Not lose   (**C**) Aren't losing
   (**B**) Won't lose   (**D**) Don't lose

5. How are you, Naruyo? You _____ a little tired these days.   **A B C D**
   - (**A**) 'll seem
   - (**B**) seem
   - (**C**) were seeming
   - (**D**) seemed

6. I _____ some evening classes this semester, and I have a lot of homework.   **A B C D**
   - (**A**) 'm taking
   - (**B**) take
   - (**C**) 'm going to take
   - (**D**) was taking

7. I remember you. You _____ to go to school here.   **A B C D**
   - (**A**) used
   - (**B**) were used
   - (**C**) using
   - (**D**) use

8. You have a good memory. I _____ here for only a month.   **A B C D**
   - (**A**) go
   - (**B**) went
   - (**C**) was going to go
   - (**D**) 'm going

9. Will you buy an electric car when they _____ cheaper?   **A B C D**
   - (**A**) will become
   - (**B**) are becoming
   - (**C**) became
   - (**D**) become

10. I think I _____ until electric cars are really cheap.   **A B C D**
    - (**A**) waited
    - (**B**) 'll wait
    - (**C**) wait
    - (**D**) was waiting

11. _____ when it started to rain?   **A B C D**
    - (**A**) Were you driving
    - (**B**) Are you driving
    - (**C**) Do you drive
    - (**D**) Will you drive

12. We were having dinner while it _____.   **A B C D**
    - (**A**) rains
    - (**B**) 's going to rain
    - (**C**) raining
    - (**D**) was raining

13. He _____ a good job when he graduates next year.   **A B C D**
    - (**A**) finds
    - (**B**) 'll find
    - (**C**) 's finding
    - (**D**) found

14. What classes _____ taking now?   **A B C D**
    - (**A**) do you
    - (**B**) were you
    - (**C**) are you
    - (**D**) you are

XI *Each sentence has four underlined words or phrases. The four underlined parts of the sentence are marked A, B, C, or D. Circle the letter of the one underlined word or phrase that is NOT CORRECT.*

1. <u>Before</u> I <u>moved</u> to Chicago, I <u>use to</u> <u>live</u> in the country.   **A**   **B**   **Ⓒ**   **D**
     A   B   C   D

2. We <u>are going to</u> <u>study</u> tonight <u>until</u> we <u>finished</u> the chapter.   **A**   **B**   **C**   **D**
         A   B   C   D

3. It<u>'s</u> a one-way street, <u>so</u> <u>no</u> <u>turn</u> left here.   **A**   **B**   **C**   **D**
    A   B C D

4. <u>When</u> Sid <u>will graduate</u> next June<u>,</u> he <u>will live</u> in the city.   **A**   **B**   **C**   **D**
      A   B   C   D

5. <u>Where</u> <u>you went</u> <u>after</u> you <u>left</u> last night?   **A**   **B**   **C**   **D**
      A   B   C   D

6. Who <u>did</u> <u>saw</u> you <u>while</u> you <u>were leaving</u> the bank?   **A**   **B**   **C**   **D**
        A B   C   D

7. It <u>usually</u> <u>is raining</u> a lot here every winter, <u>but</u> last year it <u>didn't</u>.   **A**   **B**   **C**   **D**
       A   B   C   D

8. <u>Were</u> you <u>watching</u> TV <u>when</u> I <u>call</u> you last night?   **A**   **B**   **C**   **D**
     A   B   C D

9. You<u>'ll see</u> the bank<u>,</u> <u>when</u> you <u>get</u> to Main Street.   **A**   **B**   **C**   **D**
      A   B C   D

10. We <u>didn't hear</u> the doorbell <u>when</u> he <u>arrived</u> because we <u>ate</u>.   **A**   **B**   **C**   **D**
        A   B   C   D

11. Years <u>ago</u>, I didn't <u>used to</u> like rock music, <u>but</u> now I <u>love</u> it.   **A**   **B**   **C**   **D**
         A   B   C   D

12. The movie <u>starts</u> <u>at</u> 7:30, so I <u>think</u> I <u>go</u>.   **A**   **B**   **C**   **D**
          A B   C D

13. <u>Are you wanting</u> to <u>go</u> with me, or <u>are you</u> <u>studying</u> tonight?   **A**   **B**   **C**   **D**
        A   B   C   D

▶ *To check your answers, go to the Answer Key on page RT-1.*

QUIZ RESULTS FOR UNIT 1, EXERCISE 6

If you checked . . .   *you are in the . . .*

1 and 2	Honeymoon Stage
3 and 4 and 5	Rejection Stage
6 and 7	Adjustment Stage
8	Adaptation Stage

PART II

Pronouns and Phrasal Verbs

Grammar in Context

BEFORE YOU READ

🎧 *What do you think* self-talk *is? Look at the examples of self-talk in the photos. Which are positive? Which are negative? Read this article from a psychology magazine.*

SELF-TALK

> It was all my fault.

> I'll never find another job.

> I'm the best worker they had.

> I'll find a better job soon.

Self-talk is the way we explain a problem to **ourselves**. It can affect how we feel and how we act. Take the case of Tom and Sara. They both got laid off from their jobs at the same company, but their reactions were totally different. Sara frequently talked on the phone with her friends, continued her free-time activities, and kept **herself** fit. Tom, on the other hand, spent all of his time **by himself**, didn't allow **himself** to have a good time, and gained 10 pounds.

Why were their reactions so very different from **one another**? They both lost their jobs, so the situation **itself** can't explain Tom's problems. The main difference was the way Tom and Sara explained the problem to **themselves**. Sara told **herself** that the problem was temporary and that she **herself** could change it. Tom saw **himself** as helpless and likely to be unemployed forever.

Tom and Sara both got their jobs back. Their reactions when they talked to **each other** were, again, very different. For his part, Tom grumbled, "Oh, I guess they were really desperate." Sara, on the other hand, smiled and said, "Well! They finally realized that they need me!"

AFTER YOU READ

Who did the following things? Check the correct answers.

	Tom	Sara	Tom and Sara
1. Stayed in good physical condition	☐	☑	☐
2. Spent a lot of time alone	☑	☐	☐
3. Thought the problem was temporary	☐	☑	☐
4. Felt helpless	☑	☐	☐
5. Had a conversation back at work	☐	☐	☑

Grammar Presentation

REFLEXIVE AND RECIPROCAL PRONOUNS

Reflexive Pronouns			
Subject Pronoun		**Reflexive Pronoun**	
I		**myself**	
You		**yourself**	
He		**himself**	
She	looked at	**herself**	in the mirror.
It		**itself**	
We		**ourselves**	
You		**yourselves**	
They		**themselves**	

Reciprocal Pronouns		
Subject Pronoun		**Reciprocal Pronoun**
We You They	looked at	**each other**. **one another**.

GRAMMAR NOTES

1. Use a **reflexive pronoun** when the subject and object of a sentence refer to the same people or things.

EXAMPLES

subject = object
- **Sara** looked at **herself** in the mirror.
  (Sara looked at her own face.)

subject = object
- **They** felt proud of **themselves**.
  (They were proud of their own actions.)

subject = object
- My **office light** turns **itself** off.
  (It turns off automatically.)

(continued)

2. In **imperative sentences** with reflexive pronouns, use:

- *yourself* when the subject is <u>singular</u>

- *yourselves* when the subject is <u>plural</u>

REMEMBER: In imperative sentences, the subject is *you*, and *you* can be either singular or plural.

- "Don't push **yourself** so hard, **Tom**," Sara said. *(talking to one friend)*

- "Don't push **yourselves** so hard, **guys**," Sara said. *(talking to several friends)*

3. Use a reflexive pronoun to **emphasize a noun**. In this case, the reflexive pronoun usually follows the noun directly.

- Tom was upset when he lost his job. The **job itself** wasn't important to him, but he needed the money.

4. *By* + **a reflexive pronoun** means *alone* or *without any help*.

- Sara lives **by herself**. *(Sara lives alone.)*

- We finished the job **by ourselves**. *(No one helped us.)*

Be + **a reflexive pronoun** means *act in the usual way*.

- Just **be yourself** at your interview.

5. Use a **reciprocal pronoun** when the subject and object of a sentence refer to the same people, and these people have a two-way relationship.

- Use *each other* for <u>two</u> people.

- Use *one another* for <u>more than two</u> people.

USAGE NOTE: Many people use *each other* and *one another* in the same way.

▶ **BE CAREFUL!** Reciprocal pronouns and plural reflexive pronouns have **different meanings**.

subject = object
- **Tom and Sara** met **each other** at work. *(Tom met Sara, and Sara met Tom.)*

subject = object
- **We all** told **one another** about our jobs. *(Each person exchanged news with every other person.)*

- **Sara and Tom** talked to **each other**. OR
- **Sara and Tom** talked to **one another**.

- Fred and Jane blamed **each other**. *(Fred blamed Jane, and Jane blamed Fred.)*

- Fred and Jane blamed **themselves**. *(Fred blamed himself, and Jane blamed herself.)*

6. Reciprocal pronouns have **possessive forms**: *each other's, one another's*.

- Tom and Sara took **each other's** number. *(Tom took Sara's number, and Sara took Tom's.)*

Reference Note
For a list of **verbs and expressions that often take reflexive pronouns**, see Appendix 3 on page A-2.

Focused Practice

1 | DISCOVER THE GRAMMAR

Read the rest of the article about self-talk. Underline the reflexive pronouns once and the reciprocal pronouns twice. Draw an arrow to the words that these pronouns refer to.

SELF-TALK *(continued)*

Positive self-talk can make the difference between winning and losing. Top athletes not only compete against <u>one another</u>, they also compete against <u>themselves</u> when they try to improve their performances. Many athletes use self-talk to help <u>themselves</u> reach new goals. For example, golf pro Jack Nicklaus used to imagine <u>himself</u> making a winning shot just before he played. Olympic swimmer Summer Sanders prepares <u>herself</u> for a race by smiling.

One sports psychologist believes that Olympic athletes are not very different from <u>one another</u>— they are all the best in their sports. When two top athletes compete against <u>each other</u>, the winner is the one with the most powerful positive "mental movies."

Psychologists say that ordinary people <u>themselves</u> can use these techniques as well. We can create "mental movies" to help <u>ourselves</u> succeed in difficult situations.

2 | THE OFFICE PARTY

Grammar Notes 1–2, 4–5

🎧 *Tom and Sara's company had an office party. Choose the correct reflexive or reciprocal pronouns to complete the conversations.*

1. **A:** Listen, guys! The food and drinks are over here. Please come and help ____*yourselves*____.
   (yourselves / themselves)

   B: Thanks. We will.

2. **A:** Isn't that the new head of the accounting department over there?

   B: I think so. Let's go over and introduce ____*ourselves*____.
   (himself / ourselves)

3. **A:** I'm really nervous about my date with Nicole after the party. I cut ____*myself*____
   (herself / myself)

   twice while shaving, and then I lost my car keys.

   B: Come on. This is a party. Just relax and be ____*yourself*____. You'll do fine.
   (yourself / yourselves)

4. **A:** What are you giving your boss for the holidays this year?

   B: We always give ____*each other*____ the same holiday gifts.
   (ourselves / each other)

   Every year I give him a book, and he gives me a box of candy.

(continued)

5. **A:** What do you think of the new computer program?

   B: I'm not sure. In our department, we're still teaching _ourselves_ how to use it.
   (ourselves / themselves)

6. **A:** Jessica looks upset. Didn't she get a promotion?

   B: No, and she keeps blaming _herself_. I'll lend her that article about self-talk.
   (herself / himself)

7. **A:** The Aguayos are going to Japan on vacation this year.

   B: Are they going by _themselves_ or with a tour group?
   (each other / themselves)

8. **A:** This was a great party.

   B: Yeah. We really enjoyed _ourselves_.
   (ourselves / myself)

3 | WE LEARN FROM ONE ANOTHER   *Grammar Notes 1–6*

Read this interview with George Prudeau, a high school French teacher. Complete the interview with the correct reflexive or reciprocal pronouns.

INTERVIEWER: How did you become a teacher?

GEORGE: When I got laid off from my 9:00–5:00 job, I told _myself_ "Here's my
1.
chance to do what I really want." One of the great things about teaching is the

freedom I have. I run the class by _myself_—just the way I want to.
2.

I also like the way my students and I learn from _ourselves_. My students
3.
One another/each other / ourselves.

teach me a lot.

INTERVIEWER: What about discipline? Is that a problem?

GEORGE: We have just a few rules. I tell my students, "Keep _yourself_ busy.
Your Selves   4.

Discuss the lessons, but don't interfere with _yourself_'s work."
5.
One another

INTERVIEWER: What do you like to teach best?

GEORGE: I love French, but the subject _itself_ really isn't all that important. A
6.

good teacher helps students learn by _themselves_ and encourages them not
7.

to give up when they have problems. For instance, John, one of my students, just

taught _himself_ how to bake French bread. The first few loaves were
8.

failures. I encouraged him to use positive self-talk, and in the end he succeeded.

INTERVIEWER: What teaching materials do you use?

GEORGE: Very simple ones. I pride __my self__ on the fact that I can teach anywhere,
9.

even on a street corner.

INTERVIEWER: What do you like least about your job?

GEORGE: The salary. I teach French culture, but I can't afford to travel to France.

I have to satisfy __my self__ with trips to French restaurants!
10.

4 | GOING TO THE PARTY

Grammar Notes 1, 4–5

Sara and Tom went to an office party. Look at each picture and write a sentence describing what happened. Use a verb from the box with a reflexive or reciprocal pronoun. You will use one verb more than once.

| buy | cut | drive | greet | introduce to | smile at | talk to |

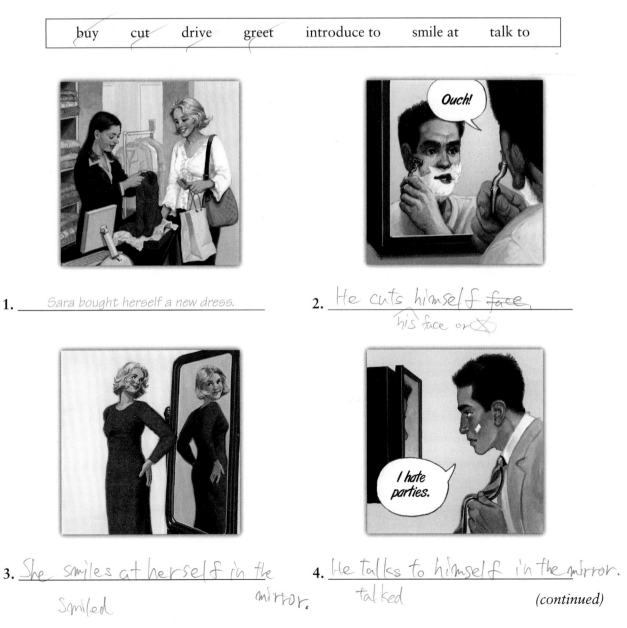

1. _Sara bought herself a new dress._

2. He cuts himself ~~face~~.
   his face or

3. She smiles at herself in the mirror.
   Smiled

4. He talks to himself in the mirror.
   talked

(continued)

5. <u>They talk to each other on the phone.</u>   6. <u>She drives herself.</u>
       talked   drove

7. <u>They greet each other.</u>   8. <u>They introduce to each other.</u>
    greeted.   introduced themselves.

5 | EDITING

Read this woman's diary. There are seven mistakes in the use of reflexive and reciprocal pronouns. The first mistake is already corrected. Find and correct six more.

>   *myself*
> Jan's birthday was Wednesday, and I forgot to call him. I reminded me all day, and then I forgot anyway! I felt terrible. My sister Anna said, "Don't be so hard on yourselves," but I didn't believe her. She prides herself on remembering everything. Then I remembered the article on self-talk. It said that people can change the way they explain problems to theirselves. Well, I listened to the way I talked to me, and it sounded really insulting— like the way our high school math teacher used to talk to us. I thought, Jan and I are good friends, and we treat each others well. In fact, he forgave myself for my mistake right away. And I forgave him for forgetting our dinner date two weeks ago. Friends can forgive themselves, so I guess I can forgive myself.

Communication Practice

6 | LISTENING

🎧 *Listen to the conversations at an office party. Then listen again and circle the pronouns that you hear.*

1. **A:** The guys in Mark's department did a great job this year.

   B: I know. They should be really proud of <u>themselves</u> / <u>each other</u>.

2. **A:** What's wrong? You look upset.

   B: I just heard Ed and Jeff talking. You know Ed blames <u>him / himself</u> for everything.

3. **A:** I hear you're going to Japan on vacation this year. Are you going by <u>yourself / yourselves</u> or with a tour?

   B: Oh, with a tour.

4. **A:** Jennifer looks happy tonight. Did Megan give her the promotion?

   B: No, not yet. Megan keeps asking <u>herself / her</u> if she can do the job.

5. **A:** How do you like the new computer system?

   B: I'm not sure. In our department, we're still teaching <u>each other / ourselves</u> how to use it.

6. **A:** So long, now. Thanks for coming. It was good to see you.

   B: Oh, it was a great party.

   A: I'm glad you enjoyed <u>yourself / yourselves</u>.

7 | CHEER YOURSELF UP!

What do you tell yourself in a difficult situation? Work with a partner and discuss each other's self-talk in the situations below. Then report to the class.

- You're going to take a big test.
- You're stuck in traffic.
- You have a roommate you don't like.
- You're going to compete in a sports event.
- You're having an argument with a friend or relative.
- You forgot something important.

Example: **A:** What do you tell yourself when you're going to take a big test?
   B: I tell myself that I prepared myself well and that I'll do fine.

8 | THE OPTIMIST TEST

Test yourself by completing this questionnaire.

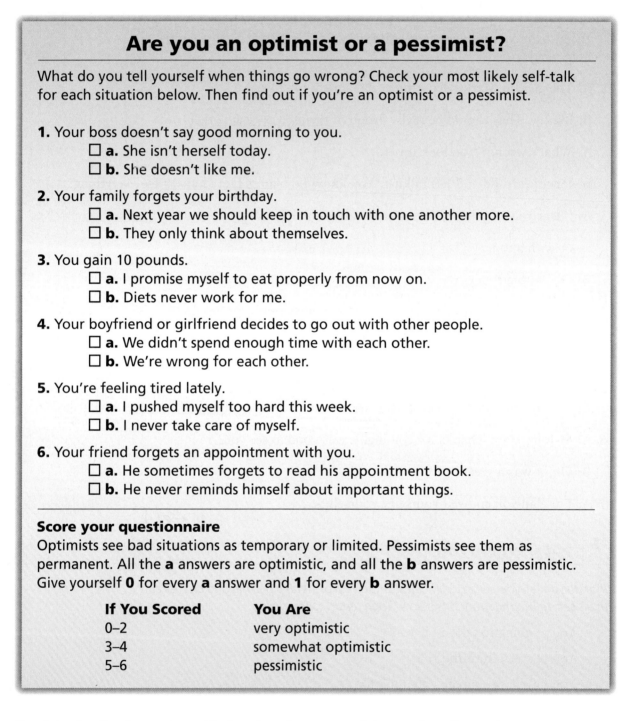

Are you an optimist or a pessimist?

What do you tell yourself when things go wrong? Check your most likely self-talk for each situation below. Then find out if you're an optimist or a pessimist.

1. Your boss doesn't say good morning to you.
- ☐ **a.** She isn't herself today.
- ☐ **b.** She doesn't like me.

2. Your family forgets your birthday.
- ☐ **a.** Next year we should keep in touch with one another more.
- ☐ **b.** They only think about themselves.

3. You gain 10 pounds.
- ☐ **a.** I promise myself to eat properly from now on.
- ☐ **b.** Diets never work for me.

4. Your boyfriend or girlfriend decides to go out with other people.
- ☐ **a.** We didn't spend enough time with each other.
- ☐ **b.** We're wrong for each other.

5. You're feeling tired lately.
- ☐ **a.** I pushed myself too hard this week.
- ☐ **b.** I never take care of myself.

6. Your friend forgets an appointment with you.
- ☐ **a.** He sometimes forgets to read his appointment book.
- ☐ **b.** He never reminds himself about important things.

Score your questionnaire
Optimists see bad situations as temporary or limited. Pessimists see them as permanent. All the **a** answers are optimistic, and all the **b** answers are pessimistic. Give yourself **0** for every **a** answer and **1** for every **b** answer.

If You Scored	You Are
0–2	very optimistic
3–4	somewhat optimistic
5–6	pessimistic

Now interview five classmates and find out how they answered the questions. Report the results to another group.

Example: For question 1, three people checked: "She isn't herself today."
Two people checked: "She doesn't like me."

9 | THE MEMORY GAME

Work with a partner. First look at the picture carefully for 30 seconds. Then shut your books and do the following.

1. Write down as many things as you can remember about what the people in the picture are doing.

2. Then compare your notes. Use reciprocal and reflexive pronouns in your description.

   Example: A: Two men are waving at each other.

   B: No, I think the people waving at each other are women.

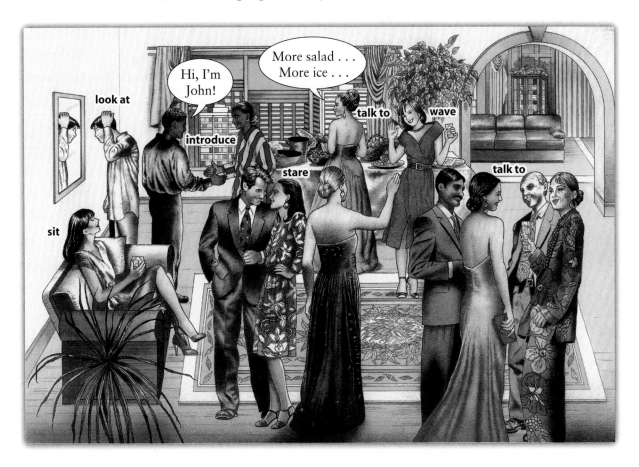

When you are finished, open your books and check your answers. Who remembered the most? What did you leave out?

10 | WHAT ARE THEY THINKING?

With your partner, imagine the self-talk of some of the people at the party.

Examples: The man at the mirror: "I'll never give myself a haircut again."

The woman on the couch: "I don't know many people here. Should I introduce myself?"

11 | WRITING

Imagine you receive an e-mail from a friend who attends school in another city. Your friend is not doing well at school and is having problems with a boyfriend or girlfriend. Write your friend an e-mail. Explain the kind of self-talk you use when things are not going well.

Example: Annette, I'm sorry you are having problems in school. Here's what I tell myself when I have problems . . .

12 | ON THE INTERNET

*Do a search on **self-help**. Find different websites that show people how to help themselves. Choose one that you find interesting and bring information about it to class.*

Example: I found a website on teaching yourself how to meditate. They suggest working with a partner so that you can help each other . . .

Phrasal Verbs

Grammar in Context

BEFORE YOU READ

🎧 *Look at the photograph. What kind of work do you think the man does? Read this article about Dr. Eloy Rodriguez.*

Planting Ideas

As a child, Eloy Rodriguez picked cotton to help support his family. He also **picked up** an interest in plants. Dr. Rodriguez is now a famous scientist, but he is still interested in plants. Every summer he **takes off** his lab coat, **puts on** his mosquito repellent, and travels to the Amazon region of Venezuela with his students. There, they search for medicinal plants.

Dr. Rodriguez **grew up** in Texas. The adults in his very large family (67 cousins lived nearby) **brought** their children **up** to be honest, fair, and *vivo*, or quick-thinking. Rodriguez did well in high school, especially in chemistry, and he **went on** to college. He took a job there cleaning a laboratory. He became a science major and then **went on** to graduate school. Soon he was managing the lab.

Eloy Rodriguez and anthropologist Richard Wrangham once noticed that sick animals often **pick out** certain plants to eat. They **turned** their observations **into** a new area of science—zoopharmacognosy (the study of how animals use plants as medicine). Today Rodriguez is one of the most brilliant scientists in the United States. Rodriguez thanks his family. He **points out** that 64 of his cousins graduated from college, 11 with advanced degrees. "Although poverty was there, family was what helped us **get by** in life."

AFTER YOU READ

Find a phrasal verb from the article that means . . .

1. became an adult _____

2. continued _____

3. survive _____

4. raised _____

5. select _____

6. removes _____

7. developed _____

8. covers himself with _____

Grammar Presentation

PHRASAL VERBS

Transitive Phrasal Verbs			
Subject	**Verb**	**Particle**	**Object (Noun)**
He	**put**	**on**	his lab coat.
	helped	**out**	his students.

Subject	Verb	Object (Noun / Pronoun)	Particle
He	**put**	his lab coat	**on**.
		it	
	helped	his students	**out**.
		them	

Intransitive Phrasal Verbs			
Subject	**Verb**	**Particle**	
She	**started**	**over**.	
He	**grew**	**up**	in Texas.
They	**got**	**back**	early.

GRAMMAR NOTES	EXAMPLES

1. **Phrasal verbs** (also called *two-word verbs*) are made up of a **verb + particle**.

On, off, up, down, in, and *out* are common particles.

Particles and prepositions look the same. However, particles are part of the verb phrase, and they often <u>change the meaning</u> of the verb.

- verb + particle
  He **put on** his lab coat.

- verb + particle
  She **pointed out** a problem.

- verb + preposition
  She's **looking up** at the sky.
  (*She's looking in the direction of the sky.*)

- verb + particle
  She's **looking up** the word.
  (*She's searching for the word in the dictionary.*)

---

2. **USAGE NOTE:** Many **phrasal verbs** and one-word verbs have similar meanings. Phrasal verbs are often <u>less formal</u>, and they are more common in everyday speech.

PHRASAL VERB (LESS FORMAL)	ONE-WORD VERB (MORE FORMAL)
bring up	raise
figure out	solve
go on	continue
pick out	select
take off	remove
wake up	awaken

---

3. Phrasal verbs can be transitive or intransitive. **Transitive phrasal verbs** have <u>objects</u>.

Most transitive phrasal verbs are **separable**. This means that the object can come:

- <u>after</u> the verb + particle

  OR

- <u>between</u> the verb and its particle

▶ **BE CAREFUL!** When the object is a **pronoun**, it must come <u>between</u> the verb and the particle.

- phrasal verb + object
  He **set up** *an experiment*.

- phrasal verb + object
  They **figured out** *the problems*.

- verb + particle + object
  We **dropped off** *the students*.

  OR

- verb + object + particle
  We **dropped** *the students* **off**.

- object
  We **dropped** *them* **off**.
  NOT We ~~dropped off them~~.

---

4. Some phrasal verbs are intransitive. **Intransitive phrasal verbs** do not have objects.

- Dr. Rodriguez **grew up** in Texas.
- He **got back** late.

Reference Notes
For a list of **transitive phrasal verbs** and their meanings, see Appendix 4 on page A-3.
For a list of **intransitive phrasal verbs** and their meanings, see Appendix 5 on page A-4.

Focused Practice

1 | DISCOVER THE GRAMMAR

Read the article. Underline the phrasal verbs. Circle the objects of the transitive phrasal verbs.

In Eloy Rodriguez's elementary school in Edinburg, Texas, teachers <u>passed</u> (Chicano* students) <u>over</u> for special honors classes. They also punished them for speaking Spanish. When Rodriguez became the first U.S.-born Chicano biology instructor at his university, he worked 18 hours a day and slept in his lab. "I was very aware that I was the first this, and the first that, and I knew that some people were waiting for me to slip up." Rodriguez didn't slip up. However, he knows that when students feel teachers don't treat them fairly, it turns them off education. Many of them just give up.

Today, Dr. Rodriguez is passing his own success on. When he became a professor at Cornell University, he set out to find Latino** graduate students. He takes these students with him on many of his trips and works hard to turn them into top scientists. In 1990 he set up KIDS (Kids Investigating and Discovering Science)—a science program for minority elementary school children. They put on white lab coats and investigate science with university teachers who treat them like research scientists. They observe nature and figure out problems. In interviews, Rodriguez always brings up role models. "I saw my first snowflake before I saw my first Chicano scientist," he says. Because of Rodriguez's efforts, many students will not face the same problem.

* Chicano—Mexican-American
** Latino—from a Spanish-speaking country in Central or South America

*Read these sentences and decide if they are **True (T)** or **False (F)**.*

__F__ **1.** In Rodriguez's elementary school, teachers chose Chicano students for honors classes.

_____ **2.** When Rodriguez became a biology instructor, some people expected him to fail.

_____ **3.** Unfair treatment makes students less interested in education.

_____ **4.** Today, Rodriguez wants to forget his own success.

_____ **5.** He searches for Latino graduate students for his program at Cornell.

_____ **6.** In 1990 Rodriguez visited a program called KIDS.

_____ **7.** Children in KIDS wear the same lab clothes as the scientists.

_____ **8.** Rodriguez rarely mentions role models.

2 | COME ALONG!

Complete this advertisement for a field trip to the Amazon. Choose the phrasal verb from the box that is closest in meaning to the verb in parentheses. Use the correct form of the phrasal verb. Use Appendices 4 and 5 on pages A-3 and A-4 for help.

fill out	find out	get up	hand in	keep on	pass up
pick up	set up	sign up	talk over	try out	work out

Two Weeks in the Amazon! ___Sign up___ *Now!*
1. (register)

The Biology Department is now ___set up___ [*setting up*] its summer field trip to the
2. (preparing)

Amazonian rain forest in Venezuela. ___pick up___ your application from the
3. (get)

Department Office (Room 215), and ___fill___ it ___out___ right
4. (complete)

away. ___hand___ it ___in___ by May 1.
5. (submit)

Last summer we collected plants and identified them. This summer we plan to talk to local people and ___find out___
6. (discover)
how they use plants in traditional medicine. This trip is challenging. We travel to our camp by canoe. When there are problems, we

___work___ them ___out___ by ourselves. We ___get up___
7. (solve) **8. (arise)**

very early, and we ___keep on___ working until dark. There is also some danger, so
9. (continue)

___talk___ the trip ___over___ with your families before you
10. (discuss)

decide. This is a chance to ___try out___ your research skills and make a real
11. (use)

contribution. We hope you won't ___pass up___ this opportunity to do important
12. (reject)

"hands-on" science.

3 | FOOD FOR THOUGHT
Grammar Notes 1–2

Circle the correct particle to complete each phrasal verb. Use Appendices 4 and 5 on pages A-3 and A-4 for help.

EAT SOME LEAVES AND CALL ME IN THE MORNING

In 1972, Richard Wrangham of Harvard University set **out** / up to study chimpanzees in Tanzania. He
1.
observed that these chimps get by / **up** at dawn
2.
to eat the leaves of *Aspilia*. They clearly hate the taste. This brought back / **up** a question: Why do
3.
chimpanzees pick **out** / over this plant but pass
4.
out / **up** delicious fruit nearby? Wrangham thought
5.
this question **over** / up for several years. He then asked Eloy Rodriguez to help him
6.
in / **out** with the analysis. Together, they worked over / **out** the puzzle: *Aspilia*
7.   **8.**
contains an antibiotic. Zoopharmacognosy—the study of how animals "doctor" themselves with plants—was born.

4 | IN THE FIELD
Grammar Note 3

Complete the conversations. Use phrasal verbs and pronouns.

1. **A:** Don't forget to put on your mosquito repellent!

   B: Don't worry! I _____ *put it on* _____ as soon as we got here.

2. **A:** Can we take off our hats? It's really hot.

   B: Don't _take these off_ (them). They protect you from the sun.

3. **A:** How do you turn on the generator?

   B: It's easy. You _turn it on_ with this switch.

4. **A:** Did you cover up the leftover food? We don't want the ants to get at it.

   B: Don't worry. We'll _cover it up_ cover food up

5. **A:** Is Dr. Rodriguez going to call off the field trip tomorrow?

   B: He'll only _call it off_ if someone gets sick.

6. **A:** Good night. Oh, can someone wake Mike up tomorrow morning?

   B: No problem. I'll _wake up him_
   wake him up

Pronoun is can't use another type answer

5 | IN THE LAB

Unscramble the words to make sentences. If more than one answer is possible, give both answers.

1. on / Put / your lab coats — Put your lab coats on. OR Put on your lab coats.
2. the experiment / Set / up — Set the experiment up or Set up the experiment
3. out / it / Carry — Carry it out or Carry out it
4. down / Sit / when you're done — Sit down when you're done
5. to page 26 / on / Go — Go on to page 26.
6. up / your reports / Write — Write your reports up or write up ~
7. in / them / Hand — Hand them in or Hand in them
8. off / Take / your lab coats — Take your lab coats off or Take off ~
9. them / Put / away — Put them away or Put away them
10. the lab / Clean / up — Clean the lab up or Clean up the lab

6 | EDITING

Read this student's journal notes. There are nine mistakes in the use of phrasal verbs. The first mistake is already corrected. Find and correct eight more.

I just got from Venezuela back! I spent two weeks in the Amazon rain forest with Dr. Rodriguez's research group. We carried out research there on plants that the Piaroa people use as medicine. We made down a list of these plants, and we're going to analyze them when we get back to school next week.

We set down camp near the Orinoco River, hundreds of miles from any major city. Life there is hard. You get very early up every morning. You must always watch up and never touch a new insect or plant. If you pick up it, you can get a bad skin rash. But plants can also cure. One day, I felt sick. One of the Piaroa gave me the stem of a certain plant to chew. It worked! Later I found at that the same plant helps cure insect bites. And believe me, insects are a big problem in the rain forest. I used up many bottles of repellent. But even when I put on it, it didn't totally keep the insects away.

This trip changed my life! I'm now thinking about switching my major to pharmacology. I want to find over more about how people can use the same plants that animals use as medicine.

Communication Practice

7 | LISTENING

🎧 *Some college students are taking a science class. Listen to these conversations. Circle the phrasal verbs that you hear. Then listen again and check your answers.*

1. **A:** What's Terry doing?

   B: She's <u>handing in</u> / <u>handing out</u> some lab reports.

2. **A:** Are you done with your report, Rea?

   B: Almost. I just have to <u>look up</u> / <u>look over</u> some information.

3. **A:** Hey, guys. That music is disturbing us.

   B: Sorry. We'll <u>turn it down</u> / <u>turn it off</u>.

4. **A:** Jason is discouraged.

   B: I know. He says he can't <u>keep on</u> / <u>keep up</u> with the class.

5. **A:** Did you hear about Lila?

   B: Yes, we were all surprised when she <u>dropped in</u> / <u>dropped out</u> yesterday.

6. **A:** OK, class. It's time to <u>take back</u> / <u>take off</u> your lab coats.

   B: Oh, could we have a few more minutes? We're almost done.

7. **A:** Hi. Can I help you?

   B: Yes, thanks. I need to <u>pick up</u> / <u>pick out</u> a book for my biology report.

8. **A:** Did you see Professor Diaz in lab today?

   B: Yes. He <u>brought up</u> / <u>brought back</u> those plants from the field trip. Very interesting.

*Now look at your completed sentences. Decide if the statements below are **True (T)** or **False (F)**.*

___F___ 9. Terry is giving some reports to the teacher.

_____ 10. Rea is going to look for some information in a reference book.

_____ 11. They're going to make the music lower.

_____ 12. Jason feels that the class is going too fast for him.

_____ 13. Lila visited the class yesterday.

_____ 14. It's time to return the lab coats.

_____ 15. She needs to choose a book for her report.

_____ 16. Professor Diaz returned the plants.

8 | LET'S TALK IT OVER

Work in groups. Imagine that you are going to take a class field trip. Decide where to go—for example, the zoo, a museum, a park. Then assign tasks and make a list. Try to include some of the phrasal verbs from the box. You can also use Appendices 4 and 5 on pages A-3 and A-4 for help.

call up	clean up	figure out	hand out	look over	look up
make up	pass out	pick out	pick up	talk over	write down

Example: **A:** I'll write down the To Do list.
B: Good idea. I'll call up to find out the hours.
C: I can pick up a bus schedule.

9 | A NEW LEAF

Discuss the pictures with a partner. Who are the people, and what are they doing in each picture? Make up a story about the pictures, and write a number under each picture to show the sequence. Then write your story. Compare your story to those of your classmates. Talk over any differences. There is more than one way to tell a story!

Example: In this picture, one of the men is looking up information about a plant . . .

a. _____   b. _____   c. _____

d. _____   e. _____   f. _____

10 | WRITING

Dr. Eloy Rodriguez is a role model to his students. Who was your most important role model when you were growing up? Why did you pick this person? What problems did your role model help you out with? What ideas and actions did you pick up from this person? Write a paragraph. Use phrasal verbs.

Example: When I was growing up, my role model was my high school chemistry teacher. I picked Ms. Suarez because she was a good teacher. She helped me out when I didn't understand the lesson, and she . . .

11 | ON THE INTERNET

*Do a search on **science lab safety rules**. Find rules that use phrasal verbs. Write them down. Share the rules with the rest of your class. Create one list to put up on the board.*

Example: Always clean up spills immediately.

From **Grammar** to **Writing**
Using Pronouns for Coherence

When you write a paragraph, it is usually better to use pronouns than to repeat the same noun. Pronouns can make your writing smoother and more connected.

> **Example:** My **apartment** is pretty cozy. I hope you enjoy staying in **my apartment**. ⟶
> My **apartment** is pretty cozy. I hope you enjoy staying in **it**.

1 | *Read this note from Ted, thanking Felicia in advance for house-sitting. Circle all the pronouns. Above each pronoun, write the noun that it refers to.*

Dear Felicia,

Thanks for staying in my apartment next weekend and taking care of the

dog. Help *(Felicia)* yourself to the food in the fridge —you can use it all up if you want.

I rented some videos for you. They're on top of the TV. I picked out some action

movies. I hope you like them. The VCR is easy to use, but remember to turn it

down at 11:00 P.M. My upstairs neighbor is very touchy about noise. There are

just a few other things to remember. Red's friendly, but please keep her away

from my neighbor's poodle. They don't like each other. Her bowl is on the kitchen

counter. Fill it up once a day with dry food. Please walk her twice a day. When

you go out, remember to turn on the answering machine. It's in the living room.

The Sunday newspaper arrives at about 8:00 A.M. Pick it up early —sometimes

it disappears! When you leave for work Monday, just leave the keys with

Mrs. Delgado next door. I'll get them from her when I get back.

Thanks again!

Ted

---

2 Read this note. Change the nouns to pronouns when you can. With phrasal verbs, remember to put the pronoun between the main verb and the particle.

Dear Dara,

Welcome! I hope you enjoy staying here this week. Here are a few things to keep in mind:

- The mail is delivered every day around noon. You'll find ~~the mail~~ *it* in the mailbox in front of the building. Please pick up the mail and put the mail on the dining room table.

- Feel free to use the air conditioner, but please turn off the air conditioner when you leave the house.

- There's plenty of food in the refrigerator! Please feel free to use up the food.

- I'm expecting a few phone calls. If you're home, could you please take a message? Just write down the message on the yellow pad in the top left desk drawer.

I think you'll find that the apartment is pretty comfortable. I hope you enjoy staying in the apartment. Make yourself at home!

See you in a week.

Rachel

---

3 Before you write . . .

1. Imagine that a friend is going to take care of your home while you are away. What will your friend's responsibilities be? What special things do you need to tell him or her about your home or neighborhood? Make a list.

2. Exchange lists with a partner. Ask questions about your partner's list. Answer your partner's questions.

    Example: **A:** How often should I take out the garbage?
    B: Oh, you can take it out every other day.
    Where do you keep the dog food?
    A: It's in the cupboard under the kitchen sink.

4 | *Write a note to your friend. Use your own paper. Give instructions about taking care of your home. Include answers to your partner's questions in Exercise 3. Use pronouns and phrasal verbs.*

5 | *Exchange notes with a different partner. Complete the chart.*

---

1. Did the writer use pronouns where necessary?   **Yes** _____   **No** _____

2. Put a question mark *(?)* over each pronoun you think is in the wrong place.

3. Complete this chart of daily tasks with information from your partner's note. If you have a question, ask your partner, and write the answer on the chart.

Examples: Sunday: water the plants, feed the pets, pick up the newspaper
Monday: feed the pets, pick up the mail and put it on the hall table

Day	Tasks
_____	_____
_____	_____
_____	_____
_____	_____
_____	_____
_____	_____
_____	_____

---

6 | *Work with your partner. Discuss each other's editing questions from Exercise 5. Then rewrite your note. Make any necessary changes in your use of pronouns. Add information that your partner requested.*

II

Review Test

I *Circle the correct pronouns to complete the article.*

When Marta's company laid (her) / herself off, she told her / herself it was time to start her own

1.
2.

business. Like Marta, a lot of people dream about starting their / one another's own businesses

3.

and working for them / themselves. Unfortunately, very few succeed. Are you a self-starter? Read

4.

about the qualities of successful business owners and decide for you / yourself.

5.

- Do you have a lot of energy? Self-starters have lots of energy. They push itself / themselves

6.

  very hard, and their families often have to force them / itself to take a break.

7.

- Can you lead others? Good team members work well with one another / themselves, but

8.

  self-starters must lead them / themselves.

9.

- Do you like to challenge you / yourself? Self-starters get bored when things are too easy.

10.

- Are you self-confident? Self-starters have lots of self-confidence. You need to believe in

  herself / yourself even when nobody else believes in you / yourself.

11.
12.

- Do you have social support? Self-starters need good friends and family, so don't forget

  themselves / them when you get busy. Even independent people listen to each other's / his

13.
14.

  problems.

II *Complete the article. Choose the phrasal verb from the box that is closest in
meaning to the words in parentheses. Use the correct form of the phrasal verb.*

find out	get back	get by	go on	~~grow up~~	hand over
help out	look up	pass over	pick out	set up	turn into

When you were _____*growing up*_____, did you think that tomatoes grew in

1. (becoming an adult)

supermarkets? Did you realize that cotton was a plant before it _____

2. (became)

your new gym socks? New Yorker Wendy Dubit _____ that a lot of city
                                           3. (learned)

kids don't know anything about farms. She used her own money to _____
                                                                    4. (establish)

Farm Hands/City Hands. This organization buses city people to small farms. Children and adults

from all social classes _____ on family farms and receive room and food
                        5. (assist)

in exchange. They also learn things you can't _____. One lawyer noted,
                                              6. (try to find in a book)

"I worked with the tomatoes for weeks. Now I can _____ the perfectly
                                                  7. (choose)

ripe ones and _____ the ones that need a few more days on the vine."
              8. (decide not to use)

Many people start small gardens of their own when they _____ to the city.
                                                        9. (return)

After the success of Farm Hands/City Hands, Dubit _____ to invent
                                                   10. (continued)

Project Ongoing to train homeless people in farm work and food services. The project has been so

successful that participants _____ on the food that they grow. They sell
                             11. (survive)

any extra. They _____ the profits _____ to the
                                                      12. (give)

program.

III   *Complete each conversation with a phrasal verb and a pronoun.*

1. **A:** This field trip will be difficult. Please think over your decision carefully.

   B: OK. I'll _____ *think it over* _____ this weekend and let you know on Monday.

2. **A:** Did you write down the flight number for our trip?

   B: Yes, I _____ on an envelope. Now where did I put the envelope?

3. **A:** Are we going to pick up Pam on the way to the airport?

   B: No. We don't have to _____. She has a ride.

4. **A:** Don't forget to put on your hat. That sun is hot.

   B: I'll _____ before I leave.

5. **A:** Someone please help out Ramón. That pack's too heavy for one person.

   B: OK. I'll _____. We can carry it together.

6. **A:** Why did you pick out cat's claw to study? It's such a common plant.

   B: I _____ because people use it for a lot of different things.

7. **A:** When are you going to write up your notes?

   B: I'll _____ as soon as we get back.

IV *Circle the letter of the correct answer to complete each sentence.*

1. Maria often goes to the movies by _____.

    (**A**) themselves   (**C**) alone

    (**B**) her   (**D**) herself   A B C (D)

2. Paul set _____ his own business in 1999.

    (**A**) out   (**C**) down

    (**B**) up   (**D**) at   A B C D

3. That frog is poisonous. Don't _____!

    (**A**) pick it up   (**C**) pick up

    (**B**) pick up it   (**D**) pick it   A B C D

4. Sharon didn't want to study, but she talked _____ into it.

    (**A**) each other   (**C**) them

    (**B**) himself   (**D**) herself   A B C D

5. We're going your way. Do you want us to _____ at home?

    (**A**) drop you off   (**C**) drop you down

    (**B**) dropping you off (**D**) drop off you   A B C D

6. When Brad and I study together, we help _____ a lot.

    (**A**) us   (**C**) each other

    (**B**) them   (**D**) her   A B C D

7. After I graduated from high school, I went _____ to college.

    (**A**) over   (**C**) on

    (**B**) herself   (**D**) himself   A B C D

8. He borrowed two books from me; he hasn't given _____ yet.

    (**A**) them back   (**C**) back them

    (**B**) it back   (**D**) back it   A B C D

9. Could you turn _____ the music so we can sleep?

    (**A**) down   (**C**) over

    (**B**) away   (**D**) up   A B C D

10. We'll turn _____ and go to sleep too.

    (**A**) it off   (**C**) it away

    (**B**) off it   (**D**) away it   A B C D

V *Read this student's essay. There are eight mistakes in the use of phrasal verbs and pronouns. The first mistake is already corrected. Find and correct seven more.*

> I have three older brothers, but my role model is my next oldest
> brother, Orlando. Orlando was always there for ~~myself~~ *me* when we were
> growing up. I was very small, and he always kept the bullies away.
> When I couldn't figure up homework problems by myself, he helped out
> me. Orlando never gave up when he had problems. Once in high school,
> my baseball team passed myself up for pitcher. I wanted to quit the
> team, but he talked me over playing. In fact, he woke early every
> morning up to practice with me. When they chose me for pitcher the
> following year, we were really proud of ourselves—he was proud of me for
> succeeding, and I was proud of himself for being such a great coach.

▶ *To check your answers, go to the Answer Key on page RT-2.*

Modals and Similar Expressions

Grammar in Context

BEFORE YOU READ

🎧 *What are the people in the photo doing? Look at the title of the article. Guess the main point. Read the article.*

Born to Dance

by V. Gupta

"**W**ho made up the rule that you **can** only **dance** on your two feet?" asks Mary Verdi-Fletcher, president and founding director of Dancing Wheels. She is also one of its main dancers. Verdi-Fletcher was born with a medical condition that affects the nervous system. By the age of 12, she **wasn't able to stand** or **walk**. But that didn't stop her from dancing. People said, "You **can't walk**; how **can** you **be** a dancer?" Verdi-Fletcher, however, *knew* it was possible to dance in a wheelchair because, as she says, "Dance is an emotion that comes from within."

When she entered her first dance competition, the audience was confused. "She's in a wheelchair. How **can** she **dance**?" But at the end of the performance, they stood and applauded. Not only **could** she **dance**, but she **could hypnotize** an audience with her talent. When the artistic director of the Cleveland Ballet first saw her, he thought, "*That* is a dancer. . . . You **can't take** your eyes off her."

Dancing Wheels has both "sitdown dancers" and "standup dancers." The group offers a new definition of dance. It also changes the perception of what people **can** or **cannot do**. "Through our dance," says Verdi-Fletcher, "we want to show that anything is possible and achievable. . . . People need to see they **can achieve** their dreams and aspirations—but not without a lot of hard work and dedication."

AFTER YOU READ

Read the statements. Check **True**, **False**, *or* **Don't Know**.

	True	False	Don't Know
1. Verdi-Fletcher is a professional dancer.	☐	☐	☐
2. She's also a singer.	☐	☐	☐
3. The audience loves her performance.	☐	☐	☐
4. The director of the Cleveland Ballet didn't like her work.	☐	☐	☐
5. Verdi-Fletcher has changed ideas about people's abilities.	☐	☐	☐

Grammar Presentation

ABILITY: *CAN* AND *COULD*

Statements			
Subject	***Can / Could*** **(not)**	**Base Form of Verb**	
I You He She We You They	**can** (**not**)	**dance**	now.
	could (**not**)		last year.

Contractions		
cannot can not	=	**can't**
could not	=	**couldn't**

Yes / No Questions		
Can / Could	**Subject**	**Base Form of Verb**
Can	I you he she we you they	**dance**?
Could		

Short Answers					
Affirmative			**Negative**		
Yes,	you I he	**can**.	**No,**	you I he	**can't**.
	she you we they	**could**.		she you we they	**couldn't**.

Wh- Questions			
***Wh-* Word**	***Can / Could***	**Subject**	**Base Form of Verb**
How well	**can** **could**	she you	**dance**?

(continued)

Cannot (no space) → never can

Can not (have space) → perhaps can

ABILITY: *BE ABLE TO*

Statements			
Subject	***Be***	***(Not) Able to***	**Base Form of Verb**
I	**am**	**(not) able to**	**practice.**
You	**are**		
He She	**is**		
We You They	**are**		

Yes / No Questions			
Be	**Subject**	***Able to***	**Base Form of Verb**
Is	she	**able to**	**practice?**
Are	you		

Short Answers					
Affirmative			**Negative**		
Yes,	she	**is.**	**No,**	she	**isn't.**
	I	**am.**		I'm	**not.**

Wh- Questions				
***Wh-* Word**	***Be***	**Subject**	***Able to***	**Base Form of Verb**
When	**is**	she	**able to**	**practice?**
How often	**are**	you		

GRAMMAR NOTES

1. *Can* and *could* are **modals**. Like all modals:

- They are followed by the base form of a verb.

- They have the same form for all subjects.
  (They do not use *-s* for the third-person singular.)

- They form the negative with *not*.
  (They do not use *do*.)

- They go before the subject in questions.
  (They do not use *do*.)

The expression ***be able to*** has the same meaning of ability as *can* and *could*. This meaning makes it similar to a modal. Notice that unlike real modals, it has different forms (*am, is, are*; *was, were*; *will be*).

EXAMPLES

- Mary **can dance**.

- I **can** dance, and she **can** dance too.
  Not She ~~cans~~ dance.

- She ca**n't** sing.
  Not She ~~doesn't~~ can sing.

- **Can** Antonio dance too?
  Not ~~Does~~ can Antonio dance too?

- **Are** they **able to** dance?
  (Can they dance?)

- She **wasn't able to** dance then.
  (She couldn't dance then.)

Could you mind the cafe →
Would you mind, Could you mind → Yes 尾
否定になる

---

2. Use *can*, *can't*, *could*, *couldn't*, or a form of *be able to* to express **ability**.

- She **can dance**, but she **can't sing**.
- We **could ride** bikes then, but we **couldn't drive** cars.
- Next year you**'ll be able to write** to me in English.

---

3. Use *can* or *can't* for **present ability**.

- She **can speak** English, but she **can't speak** French.

---

4. Use *can* for **future ability** when you are talking about plans or arrangements.

▶ **BE CAREFUL!** Don't use *can* for future ability when you are talking about things you learn. Use **will be able to**.

learn something)

- I **can buy** tickets on the way home *tomorrow*.

- When I finish this course, **I'll be able to speak** French well. NOT When I finish this course, I ~~can~~ speak French well.

---

5. Use *could* or *couldn't* for **past ability**.

▶ **BE CAREFUL!** Don't use *could* in affirmative 肯定の、断定的な statements for a single event in the past. Use **was / were able to**.

却方、言明

- A: **Could** he **dance** as a child?
- B: No, he **couldn't dance** then.

- In 2002 they **were able to win** first prize in the dance competition. NOT In 2002 they ~~could~~ win . . .

---

6. You can use a form of *be able to* for **present**, **future**, or **past ability**.

Be able to can also be a **gerund** or **infinitive**.

動名詞   不定詞

USAGE NOTE: *Can* is much more common than *be able to* in everyday speech about the present.

PRESENT:	**Are** you **able to drive** this car?
FUTURE:	We**'ll be able to do** that dance soon.
PAST:	Li **wasn't able to win** first prize last year.
GERUND:	**Being able to dance** is important to him.
INFINITIVE:	I want **to be able to drive** by June.
MORE COMMON:	**Can** you dance?
LESS COMMON:	**Are** you **able to** dance?

Reference Notes

Can and *could* are also used to ask and give **permission** (see Unit 12) and make **requests** (see Unit 13).
Can't and *could* are also used to draw **conclusions** (see Unit 37).
Could is also used to make **suggestions** (see Unit 15) and express **future possibility** (see Unit 36).
For a list of **modals and their functions**, see Appendix 19 on page A-8.

Could you mind looking my homework assignment?

Not at all! ← Yes meen   *I'm okay ← no*

Focused Practice

1 | DISCOVER THE GRAMMAR

*Look at this information about Mary Verdi-Fletcher. Then decide whether the statements below are **True (T)** or **False (F)**. Put a question mark **(?)** if there isn't enough information.*

Mary Verdi-Fletcher

1955	born in Ohio
1975	graduated from high school got job as keypunch operator
1978	learned to drive
1979	entered Dance Fever Competition
1980	began Dancing Wheels enrolled in Lakeland Community College, Ohio took course in public speaking
1980–1988	worked for Independent Living Center
1984	married Robert Fletcher
1989–1990	tour director for Cleveland Ballet
1990–present	founding director and dancer, Dancing Wheels teaches dance to people with and without disabilities
Awards	Outstanding Young Clevelander Award (1990) Oracle Merit Award (1991) Invacare Award of Excellence in the Arts (1994) Governor's Award for Outreach (1998)
Other Interests	watching football and soccer games

___T___ **1.** Verdi-Fletcher was able to get a job after high school.

_____ **2.** She can't drive a car.

_____ **3.** She couldn't participate in dance competitions.

_____ **4.** She can speak foreign languages.

_____ **5.** She was able to start a dance company.

_____ **6.** She couldn't finish college.

_____ **7.** She can probably speak well in front of large groups of people.

_____ **8.** She'll be able to help people with disabilities learn to dance.

_____ **9.** She can play the piano.

_____ **10.** She's so busy she can't have other interests.

2 | NOW I CAN

Complete the paragraphs with **can**, **can't**, **could**, *or* **couldn't**.

1. For a long time, Jim and Marie _____*couldn't*_____ agree on a family sport. Jim loves tennis,

   a.

   and Marie takes lessons, but she still _____*Can't*_____ play. Marie _____*Can*_____

   b.   c.

   swim, but Jim hates the water. They recently took up dancing. Now, they _____*Can*_____

   d.

   do the swing *and* spend time together.

2. Stefan has made a lot of progress in English. Last semester he _____*Could* *Couldn't*_____ order a

   a.

   meal in a restaurant or talk on the telephone. His friends helped him do everything. Now he

   _____*Can*_____ speak English in a lot of situations.

   b.

3. Bill almost _____*Couldn't*_____ make his class presentation last semester because he was so

   a.

   nervous. He _____*Could* *Can*_____ communicate well in small groups, but not in big ones. He

   b.

   plans to take a course in public speaking. He _____*Can*_____ register online next week.

   c.

4. Last year I _____*Could* *Couldn't*_____ dance at all, but when I met Stan, I signed up for a class right

   a.

   away. He _____*Can* *Could*_____ really dance, and I wanted to dance with him. Now I

   b.

   _____*Can*_____ do the basic steps. I _____*Can't*_____ do the waltz yet, but we're

   c.   d.

   planning to waltz at our wedding next month.

3 | AT THE DANCE STUDIO

Complete each conversation with the correct form of **be able to** *and the verb in
parentheses. Choose between affirmative and negative.*

1. **A:** I heard your sister wanted to take lessons. _____*Was*_____ she _____*able to start*_____?

   a. (start)

   B: Yes, she was. She started last month. She can do the fox-trot now, but she still

   _____*isn't* ~~*was*~~ *able to do*_____ the waltz.

   b. (do)

2. **A:** Why are you taking dance lessons?

   B: I want to _____*be able to dance*_____ at my wedding!

   a. (dance)

3. **A:** ~~*Are*~~ *were* you _____*able to find*_____ Mrs. Suraikin at the studio yesterday?

   a. (find)

   B: Yes. She told me I _____*will be* ~~*was*~~ *able to compete*_____ in the tango contest next month!

   b. (compete)

   A: Great! I know that's really important to you.

   B: Yes. _____*Be able to do*_____ the tango in a contest means a lot to me.

   Being.   c. (do)

(continued)

4. A: ~~Are~~ *[were]* you _able to speak_ Russian as a child, Mrs. Suraikin?
   a. (speak)

   B: Yes, I was. We spoke it at home, so I ~~am~~ *[was]* _able to spoke_ it fluently.
   b. (speak)

   A: ~~Were~~ *[Are]* your children _able to speak_ Russian too?
   c. (speak)

   B: No, unfortunately my children never learned Russian. They only speak English.

5. A: I ~~am~~ *[wasn't]* _able to practiced_ the waltz last weekend because I hurt my ankle.
   a. (practice)

   B: That's too bad. ~~Are~~ *[Will]* you _able to practice_ *[be]* next week?
   b. (practice)

---

4 | AT THE THEATER

Grammar Notes 2–6

Two friends are at a dance performance. Complete their conversations with **can, could,** *or* **be able to** *and the correct verb from the box. You will use some of these verbs more than once. Use* **can** *or* **could** *when possible. Choose between affirmative and negative.*

dance	do	get	lend	pay	pronounce	see

1. NINA: ___Can___ you ___see___ the stage OK?
   a.

   LEÓN: Yes, I _Can see_ it fine. What about you?
   b.

   NINA: No. I _Can't see_ it very well at all. The man in front of me is too tall.
   c.

   LEÓN: Change seats with me. You ~~Can see~~ *[will be able to see]* it better then.
   d.

2. LEÓN: Wow! This performance is great. This group _[Can] dance_ really beautifully!
   a.

   NINA: I know. I'm glad I _was able to ~~pay~~ get_ tickets. Last year I ~~was able to see~~ *[Couldn't get]* any.
   b. **c.**

   They were sold out.

   LEÓN: What's their name?

   NINA: I'll spell it for you. It's P-i-l-o-b-o-l-u-s. I'm not sure I _[Can] pronounce_ it correctly!
   d.

3. LEÓN: It's intermission. Would you like to get something to eat?

   NINA: Oh, I'm afraid I ~~Can lend~~ *[Can't get]* anything. I left my wallet at home by mistake.
   a.

   LEÓN: No problem. I _can lend_ you some money.
   b.

   NINA: Thanks. I ~~will be able to pay~~ *[Can pay]* you back tomorrow.
   c.

4. NINA: ___Can___ you ___dance___ the tango?
   a.

   LEÓN: Not yet! But I'm taking dance lessons, so I'_ll be able to ~~do~~ [dance]_ it soon!
   b.

5 | EDITING

Read this review of a dance performance. There are ten mistakes in the use of **can**, **could**,
and **be able to***. The first mistake is already corrected. Find and correct nine more.*

The Dance Desk

How ~~They Can~~ Do That?
Can They

By Jennifer Andrews

Pilobolus Dance Theatre, photo by John Kane

Last night was the first time I saw the group
Pilobolus perform. And what a performance it
was! I would like to can tell you that I fully
understood the performance, but I can't.
I *can* to say, however, that the experience was
completely wonderful.

Pilobolus is a very unusual group. The
performers have no background in dance. When they began, they thought,
"Maybe we can't dancing, so why try?" So they just made interesting shapes
with their bodies. Well, this group certainly cans dance, and they are able to
do much more. The six dancers in the group are athletic, artistic, and very
talented. They are able do amazing things with their bodies. In many dances,
they move together as a single unit.

My theater companion and I had great seats. We could saw the entire stage
(not always true in some theaters). The sound system, though, had a few
problems, and we didn't able to hear the music clearly all the time.

Some people in the audience asked: "Is it dance or is it gymnastics?" You
can decide for yourself. Many people weren't able to got tickets for the first
two performances of this series, but you can still buy tickets for next week.
This is the type of dance performance everyone can enjoys.

Highly recommended.

Communication Practice

6 | LISTENING

🎧 *Karl is interviewing for the job of office manager at Carmen's Dance Studio. Listen to the conversation. Then listen again and check all the things that Karl can do now.*

☑ 1. answer the phones   ☐ 5. design a monthly newsletter

☐ 2. speak another language   ☐ 6. schedule appointments

☐ 3. use a computer   ☐ 7. drive

☐ 4. type 50 words per minute   ☐ 8. dance

7 | INFORMATION GAP: CAN THEY DO THE TANGO?

Students at Carmen's Dance Studio are preparing for a dance recital in June. It is now the end of April. Can students do all the dances featured in the recital at this time? Work in pairs (A and B). Student A, follow the instructions on this page. Student B, turn to page 134 and follow the instructions there.

1. Ask your partner for the information you need to complete the schedule below.

   Example: **A:** Can the students do the Argentine tango?
   B: No, they can't. But they'll be able to do it by the end of May.

2. Your schedule has the information your partner needs to complete his or her schedule. Answer your partner's questions.

   Example: **B:** Can they do the cha-cha?
   A: Yes, they can. They could do it in March.

CARMEN'S DANCE STUDIO
Schedule of Dance Classes

Dances	March	April	May
Argentine tango			✔
Cha-cha	✔		
Fox-trot			
Hip-hop		✔	
Hustle			✔
Mambo			
Merengue	✔		
Salsa			✔
Swing			
Tango		✔	
Waltz			

When you are finished, compare schedules. Are they the same?

8 | CLASS PRESENTATION

Work in small groups. Imagine you are planning a class presentation. Look at the list of skills and tell each other what you **can** *and* **can't** *do. Add to the list.*

- do research online
- create a website
- make charts and graphs
- do a spreadsheet
- photocopy handouts
- take photographs
- videotape the presentation
- interview people
- give a PowerPoint presentation
- _____
- _____

Example: **A:** Can you do research online?
  B: Sure. But I can't create a website yet.

9 | ON THE INTERNET

Many people have disabilities. Research one of the famous people listed below. Tell the class about that person. Who is / was the person? What is / was the person's disability? What are / were some of the person's accomplishments?

Ludwig van Beethoven

Andrea Bocelli

Stephen Hawking

Frida Kahlo

Marlee Matlin

Christopher Reeve

Auguste Renoir

Marla Runyan

Example: Ludwig van Beethoven was one of the most famous composers in the world. As the result of an illness toward the end of his life, he lost the ability to hear. Even though he couldn't hear at all, he was able to continue to compose beautiful music that people still listen to today.

10 | WRITING

Write one or two paragraphs about a person who has succeeded in spite of some kind of disability or problem. Use one of the people from Exercise 9, or choose another person.

Example: My aunt had a difficult childhood. She grew up in a poor family. When she was 16, she quit school because she had to stay home and help her mother take care of her younger brothers and sisters. She made all the meals, and by the time she was 18, she could cook and bake very well. She was even able to win a local baking contest. People began ordering cakes from her, and before long she was able to save enough money to start her own small business . . .

INFORMATION GAP FOR STUDENT B

1. The schedule below has the information your partner needs to complete his or her schedule. Answer your partner's questions.

   Example: **A:** Can the students do the Argentine tango?
   B: No, they can't. But they'll be able to do it by the end of May.

2. Ask your partner for the information you need to complete your schedule.

   Example: **B:** Can they do the cha-cha?
   A: Yes, they can. They could do it in March.

CARMEN'S DANCE STUDIO
Schedule of Dance Classes

Dances	March	April	May
Argentine tango			✓
Cha-cha	✓		
Fox-trot		✓	
Hip-hop			
Hustle			
Mambo		✓	
Merengue			
Salsa			
Swing	✓		
Tango			
Waltz	✓		

When you are finished, compare schedules. Are they the same?

Permission: *Can, Could, May, Do you mind if*

Grammar in Context

BEFORE YOU READ

🎧 *Look at the cartoons. Where are these people? What is their relationship? What do two of the people want? How do the others feel about it? Read the article.*

Oh, you're awake! **Can** I **wear** your new jacket today?

Could my friend **stay** here for a few weeks?

Always Ask First

Heather immediately liked Tara, her neat, non-smoking roommate. Their first week together was great. The second week, the cookies from Heather's mom disappeared. Tara didn't ask Heather, "**Could** I **have** one?" Tara's friends always shared food without asking permission. The third week, Tara looked annoyed whenever Heather's friends stopped by to visit. Heather never asked Tara, "Hey, **do you mind if** they **hang out** here for a while?" At home, Heather's friends were always welcome. By October, Heather and Tara weren't speaking to each other.

Luckily, their dorm counselor was able to help them fix their relationship with three simple rules.

1. Always ask permission before you touch your roommate's stuff. Say: "My computer isn't working. **May** I **use** yours for a few hours?"

2. Set times when it's OK to have visitors. If it's not "visiting hours," ask your roommate's permission: "**Can** Luis and Ming-Hwa **work** here tonight? We're doing a presentation in class tomorrow."

3. Try to solve problems. Say: "Your music is too loud, but you **can borrow** my headphones."

Follow these guidelines, and who knows? You may gain a happier roommate *and* a good friend.

135

AFTER YOU READ

Read the statements. Check **True** *or* **False**.

	True	False
1. Some roommates don't know when to ask permission.	☐	☐
2. Tara gave Heather permission to eat her cookies.	☐	☐
3. Heather didn't ask for permission to have visitors.	☐	☐
4. It's very important to ask for permission to borrow things.	☐	☐

Grammar Presentation

PERMISSION: *CAN, COULD, MAY, DO YOU MIND IF*

Questions: *Can / Could / May*			
Can / Could / May*	Subject	Base Form of Verb	
Can **Could** **May**	I he she we they	**stay**	here?

**Can, could,* and *may* are modals. Modals have only one form. They do not have *-s* in the third-person singular.

Short Answers						
Affirmative				Negative		
Yes,	you he she you they	**can.** **may.**		**No**,	you he she you they	**can't.** **may not.**

NOTE: *May not* is not contracted.

Statements: *Can / May*			
Subject	*Can / May (not)*	Base Form of Verb	
You He They	**can (not)** **may (not)**	**stay**	here.

Questions: *Do you mind if*			
Do you mind if	Subject	Verb	
Do you mind if	I we they	**stay**	here?
	he she it	**stays**	

Short Answers	
Affirmative	Negative
Not at all. **No**, I **don't**. Go right ahead.	**Yes**, I **do**.

NOTE: See Grammar Note 4 for a full explanation.

Coald you mind, would you mind
→ Yes ~ ← 反彩にある

GRAMMAR NOTES   **EXAMPLES**

1. Use the modals *can*, *could*, and *may* to **ask permission**.	less formal • **Can** I **borrow** your book?
Notice that when you use *could* for permission, it is not the past.	• **Could** he **come** tomorrow?
USAGE NOTE: *May* is more formal than *can* and *could*.	• **May** I **leave** now, Dr. Lee? more formal

2. We often say *please* when we ask permission. Note the word order.	• **May** I **ask** a question, *please*? OR • **May** I *please* **ask** a question?

3. Use *can* or *may* in **answers**. Don't use *could*.	A: **Could** I borrow this pencil? B: **Yes**, of course you **can**. NOT Yes, you ~~could~~.
▶ **BE CAREFUL!** Do not contract *may not*.	C: **No**, you **may not**. NOT No, you ~~mayn't~~.
USAGE NOTES: In conversation, we usually use <u>informal expressions</u> instead of modals in answers.	A: **Could** I close the window? B: *Sure*. OR *Certainly*. OR *Go ahead*. C: *No, please don't*. It's hot in here.
When people **refuse permission**, they usually apologize and give an explanation.	A: **Can** I please use your computer? B: *I'm sorry*, *but I need it today*.

4. Use *Do you mind if* to ask permission when your action may <u>annoy or inconvenience</u> someone.	A: **Do you mind if I clean up** later? B: Yes, actually, I do. I hate to see a mess in the kitchen.
▶ **BE CAREFUL!** When we answer with *Not at all* or *No, I don't*, we're really saying: *It's OK*. We're giving permission.	A: **Do you mind if I eat** these tacos? B: *Not at all*. OR *No, I don't*. *(It's OK for you to eat these tacos.)*
And when we answer with *Yes, I do*, we're really saying: *It's NOT OK*. We're refusing permission.	C: *Yes, I do*. I bought them for Kyle. *(It's NOT OK for you to eat the tacos.)*

Reference Notes

For general information on **modals**, see Unit 11, Grammar Note 1, on page 126.
Can and *could* are also used to talk about **ability** (see Unit 11) and make **requests** (see Unit 13).
Could and *may* are also used to express **future possibility** (see Unit 36) and to draw **conclusions** (see Unit 37).
For a list of **modals and their functions**, see Appendix 19 on page A-8.

I'm okay ← no の意
Not at all! ← Yes.

Focused Practice

1 | DISCOVER THE GRAMMAR

Read this quiz. Underline all the modals and expressions for permission. Then if you'd like to, you can take the quiz. The answers are below.

Are You a Good Roommate?

Take this short quiz and find out.

1. You want to use your roommate's computer.
   You say:
   ○ **a.** I may use your computer tonight.
   ○ **b.** <u>May I use</u> your computer tonight?
   ○ **c.** I'm using your computer tonight.

2. You don't have any food in the house.
   You say:
   ○ **a.** Can you make dinner for me?
   ○ **b.** I don't mind eating some of your food.
   ⊘ **c.** Do you mind if I have some of your food?

3. You may not have time to wash the dishes tonight.
   You say:
   ○ **a.** Could you wash the dishes?
   ○ **b.** I can't wash the dishes.
   ⊘ **c.** Can I wash the dishes tomorrow?

4. Your roommate asks you: "Could my best friend stay overnight?"
   You answer:
   ○ **a.** Can she stay in a hotel instead?
   ⊘ **b.** Sure.
   ○ **c.** I'm sure she could, but I don't want her to!

5. You can find nothing to wear to the party next Friday.
   You say:
   ⊘ **a.** May I please borrow your new sweater?
   ○ **b.** I may borrow your new sweater.
   ○ **c.** You could lend me your new sweater.

6. You and your roommate need the dorm counselor's permission to have a party in your room.
   You say:
   ⊘ **a.** Could we have a party in our room on Saturday?
   ○ **b.** Maybe we could have a party in our room on Saturday.
   ○ **c.** Could you have a party in your room on Saturday?

ANSWERS: 1. b, 2. c, 3. c, 4. b, 5. a, 6. a

2 | RULES AND REGULATIONS

Look at the signs. Complete each conversation with the words in parentheses and the correct pronouns. Write appropriate short answers.

1. (do you mind if)

JEAN-PIERRE: _____*Do you mind if*_____ I _____*eat*_____
a. (eat)
my lunch here while I get on the Internet?

LAB ASSISTANT: _____*Sorry, but I do*_____. Look at the sign.
b.

Computer Lab

2. (can)

EMIL: Wow! Those guys next door sure are making a lot of noise!

TORY: Well, they _____*Can't play*_____ music now. It's
a. (play)
8:00 A.M.

EMIL: I know. _*Can*_ I _____*borrow*_____
b. (borrow)
your earplugs? I have to study for my English test.

Quiet Hours
11:00 p.m. - 7:00 a.m.
Sunday - Saturday

3. (may)

CARMEN: _*May*_ we _____*ride*_____ our
a. (ride)
bikes here?

GUARD: ~~Sure~~ *Yes, you may*.
b.

4. (could)

DONOVAN: _*Could*_ I _____*bring*_____ my
a. (bring)
dog next semester? My roommate doesn't mind.

COUNSELOR: *No, you ~~couldn't~~* Can't. But some of the other
b.
dorms allow pets. *answers could は答えあり!*

Kent Hall

5. (may)

GABRIELLE: _*May*_ I _____*use*_____ my cell
a. (use)
phone in here?

LIBRARIAN: *No, you may not*.
b.

3 | PARTY TIME

Heather and her roommate Tara are planning a party in Kent Hall. Use the words in parentheses to ask for permission. Answer the questions.

1. Tara's friend Troy is in town. She wants him to come to the party.

    TARA: _Do you mind if Troy comes to the party?_
    (Do you mind if)

    HEATHER: _Not at all._ I'd love to meet him.

2. Heather wants to borrow her roommate's black sweater.

    HEATHER: I have nothing to wear. _Can I borrow your black sweater?_
    (Can)

    TARA: _(No, you can't) I'm sorry_ I'm planning to wear it myself!

3. Tara's sister is coming from out of town. Tara wants her to stay in their room.

    TARA: _Do you mind if my sister stay in this room?_
    (Do you mind if)

    HEATHER: _(No, I don't) Not at all_ She can sleep on the couch.

4. Heather and Tara would like to have the party in the dormitory lounge. Heather asks her

    dormitory counselor for permission.

    HEATHER: _May we please have the party in the dormitory lounge?_
    (May / please)

    COUNSELOR: _Yes, you may_ It's available next Friday.

5. Heather and Tara would like to hang decorations from the ceiling of the lounge.

    HEATHER: _May we please hang decorations from the ceiling of the lounge?_
    (May / please)

    COUNSELOR: _Yes, you may_ Fire regulations won't allow it.

6. Heather and Tara want to party until midnight.

    HEATHER: _Could we please do the party until midnight?_
    (Could / please)

    COUNSELOR: _(No, you couldn't) I'm sorry_ Quiet hours start at 11:00 on Friday.

7. Tara wants to play some of her friend Erica's CDs at the party.

    TARA: _Could I play some of ~~your~~ Erica's CDs at the party?_
    (Could)

    ERICA: _(Yes, you could) Sure_ Which ones should I bring?

8. It's Friday night. A student wants to study in the lounge.

    STUDENT: _Can I study in the lounge?_
    (Can)

    HEATHER: _(No, you can't) I'm sorry_ We're having a party. Want to join us?

4 | EDITING

Read Emil's English test. There are seven mistakes in the use of **can**, **could**, **may**, *and* **do you mind if**. *The first mistake is already corrected. Find and correct six more.*

Class: ___English 102___   Name: ___Emil Kuhn___

Directions: These conversations take place on a train. Find and correct the mistakes.

1. **A:** May we board the train yet?
   can't OR *may not*
   B: No, you ~~mayn't~~ board until 12:30.

2. **A:** Can he comes on the train with me?

   B: Sorry. Only passengers can board.

3. **A:** Do you mind if I'm sitting here?

   B: No, I don't. My friend is sitting here.

4. **A:** Could I looked at your newspaper?

   B: Yes, of course you could.

5. **A:** Do you mind if my son play his
      computer game?

   B: No, not at all. It won't disturb me.

   A: Thanks.

Communication Practice

5 | LISTENING

🎧 *Listen and write the number of each conversation. Then listen again and decide if permission was given or refused. Check the appropriate column.*

	Permission Given	Permission Refused
_____ **a.** roommate / roommate	☐	☐
_____ **b.** child / parent	☐	☐
_____ **c.** travel agent / customer	☐	☐
_1_ **d.** police officer / driver	☑	☐
_____ **e.** boyfriend / girlfriend's mother	☐	☐
_____ **f.** employee / employer	☐	☐
_____ **g.** student / teacher	☐	☐

6 | ASKING PERMISSION

Work in small groups. Read the following situations and decide what to say. Think of as many things to say as possible.

1. You have a small apartment. Two of your friends are coming to visit your town for a week, and they want to stay with you. What can you say to your roommate?

   Examples: Do you mind if Larry and Zoë stay here for a week?
   Could Larry practice his guitar in the evening?
   Can Zoë keep her bike in the hall?

2. You're visiting some good friends. The weather is very cold, but they don't seem to mind. Their windows are open, and the heat is off. You're freezing.

3. You're at a concert with some friends. You like the performer very much. You have your camcorder and your camera with you. Sometimes this performer talks to fans and signs programs after the concert.

4. You have formed a study group with some classmates. You want to use a classroom on Thursday evenings to study. You would like to use one of your school's video cams for speaking practice. Some of your classmates come directly from work. They would like permission to eat their dinner in the classroom. What can you say to your teacher?

7 | ROLE PLAY

Work in pairs. Read the following situations. Take turns being Student A and Student B.

Student A

1. You were absent from class yesterday. Student B, your classmate, always takes good notes.

   Example: A: May I copy your notes from class yesterday?
   B: Sure. Here they are.
   A: Could I call you tonight if I have questions?
   B: Of course.

2. You're at work. You have a terrible headache. Student B is your boss.

3. You're a teenager. You and your friend want to travel to another city to see a concert. You want to borrow your mother's (Student B's) car. Your friend has a license and wants to drive.

4. Student B has invited you to a small party. At the last minute, your two cousins show up. They have nothing to do the night of the party.

Student B

1. Student A is in your class. You are always willing to help your classmates.

2. Student A is your employee. You have a lot of work for Student A to do today.

3. Student A is your son / daughter. You like this friend, and you have no objection to lending him or her the car. However, you want the friend to be careful.

4. Your party is a small party for a few of your close friends. It's also at a restaurant, and you have already arranged for a certain number of people to attend.

8 | WRITING

Write two short notes asking permission. Choose situations from Exercise 7 or use situations of your own. Then exchange notes with two classmates. Write responses to your classmates' notes.

Examples:

Ana,
I missed class yesterday.
Can I copy your notes?
Melissa

Sorry, Melissa, but
I missed class too!
Ana

9 | ON THE INTERNET

 Do a search on **dormitory rules***. Choose a school that interests you and print out or write down some of their rules. Then work with a partner. Role-play a conversation between a student and a dorm counselor.*

1. Ask for information about the rules for the dorm your partner researched. You can ask about:

   - visitors
   - decorating your room
   - study areas
   - quiet hours

2. Answer your partner's questions about the dorm you researched.

   Example: A: Can my sister stay overnight with me?
   B: Yes, she can. But only for two days.

13 Requests: *Can, Could, Will, Would, Would you mind*

Grammar in Context

BEFORE YOU READ

🎧 *What is Marcia's e-mail address? Who did Marcia send e-mails to? Who did she get e-mails from? Read her e-mail messages.*

Mail's Here!

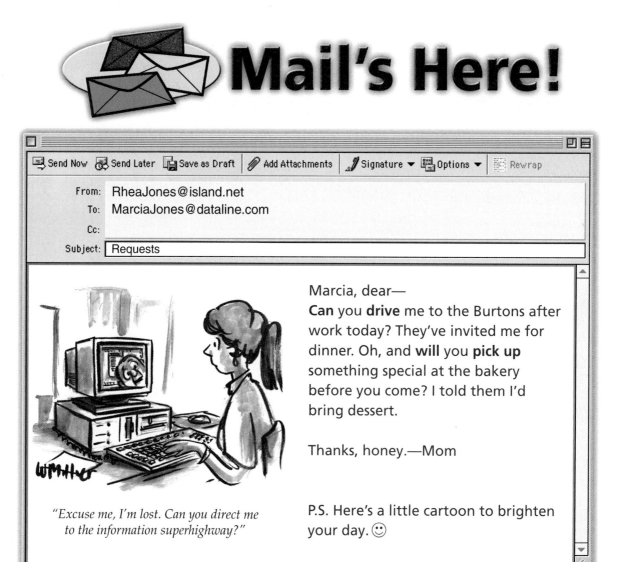

Send Now   Send Later   Save as Draft   Add Attachments   Signature ▾   Options ▾   Rewrap

From: RheaJones@island.net
To: MarciaJones@dataline.com
Cc:
Subject: Requests

Marcia, dear—
Can you **drive** me to the Burtons after work today? They've invited me for dinner. Oh, and **will** you **pick up** something special at the bakery before you come? I told them I'd bring dessert.

Thanks, honey.—Mom

P.S. Here's a little cartoon to brighten your day. ☺

"Excuse me, I'm lost. Can you direct me to the information superhighway?"

Send Now Send Later Save as Draft | Add Attachments | Signature ▼ Options ▼ | Rewrap

From: MarciaJones@dataline.com
To: RheaJones@island.net
Cc:
Subject: Re: Requests

Mom,
I'm sorry, but tonight I **can't**. I have to work late. Do you want me to ask your favorite son-in-law if he can drive you? Let me know.
M.
P.S. Thanks for the cartoon. Very funny!

Send Now Send Later Save as Draft | Add Attachments | Signature ▼ Options ▼ | Rewrap

From: JohnSanchez@dataline.com
To: MarciaJones@dataline.com
Cc:
Subject: Sales Report

Marcia:
I'll be out of town until Thursday. **Would** you please **photocopy** the monthly sales report for me? Thanks a lot!
John

Send Now Send Later Save as Draft | Add Attachments | Signature ▼ Options ▼ | Rewrap

From: MarciaJones@dataline.com
To: AnnChen@dataline.com
Cc:
Subject: Re: Sales Report

Hi, Ann,
I'm sending you a copy of our sales report. **Could** you **make** 25 copies?
And **would you mind delivering** them to me when you're finished? It's a rush! Thanks.
Marcia

AFTER YOU READ

Read the statements. Check **True** *or* **False**.

	True	False
1. Marcia's mother needs a ride to the Burtons.	☐	☐
2. Marcia is going to drive her mother to the Burtons.	☐	☐
3. John needs copies of the sales report.	☐	☐
4. Marcia is going to make the copies herself.	☐	☐

Grammar Presentation

REQUESTS: *CAN, COULD, WILL, WOULD, WOULD YOU MIND*

Questions: *Can / Could / Will / Would*			
Can / Could Will / Would *	Subject	Base Form of Verb	
Can **Could** **Will** **Would**	you	**mail**	this letter for me?
		drive	me to the doctor?
		pick up	some groceries?

Short Answers		
Affirmative		Negative
Sure Certainly Of course	(I **can**). (I **will**).	I'm sorry, but I **can't**.

*Can, *could*, *will*, and *would* are modals. Modals do not have *-s* in the third-person singular.

Questions: *Would you mind*		
Would you mind	Gerund	
Would you mind	**mailing**	this letter for me?
	driving	me to the doctor?
	picking up	some groceries?

Short Answers	
Affirmative	Negative
Not at all. I'd be glad to. No problem.	I'm sorry, but I **can't**.

NOTE: See Grammar Note 4 for a full explanation.

GRAMMAR NOTES	EXAMPLES
1. Use the modals *can*, *could*, *will*, and *would* to make a **request** (ask someone to do something). **USAGE NOTE:** We use *could* and *would* to <u>soften requests</u> and make them more polite.	less formal • **Can** you **turn on** the TV? • **Will** you **bring** dessert? • **Could** you **call** me later? • **Would** you **close** the door? more formal
2. You can also use *please* to make the request <u>more polite</u>. Note the word order.	• **Would** you **close** the door, *please*? OR • **Would** you *please* **close** the door?
3. In **affirmative answers** to requests, we usually use expressions such as *sure*, *certainly*, *of course*, and *no problem*. In **negative answers**, we usually apologize and give an explanation. ▶ **BE CAREFUL!** Do not use *could* or *would* in response to polite requests.	A: **Would** you **shut** the window, please? B: *Sure*. OR *Sure I will*. OR *Certainly*. A: **Could** you **take** this to Ron's office, please? B: *I'm sorry, I can't. I'm expecting a call*. NOT I'm sorry, I ~~couldn't~~. NOT Sure I ~~would~~.
4. We also use *Would you mind* + **gerund** (verb + *-ing*) to make <u>polite requests</u>. ▶ **BE CAREFUL!** When we <u>answer</u> this type of request with *Not at all*, it means that we will do what the person requests.	A: **Would you mind waiting** a minute? Mr. Caras is still in a meeting. B: *Not at all*. *(OK. I'll do it.)*

Reference Notes

For general information on **modals,** see Unit 11, Grammar Note 1, page 126.
Can and *could* are also used to talk about **ability** (see Unit 11) and ask **permission** (see Unit 12).
Can't and *could* are also used to draw **conclusions** (see Unit 37).
Could is also used to express **future possibility** (see Unit 36).
Will is also used to talk about the **future** (see Units 6 and 7).
For a list of **modals and their functions,** see Appendix 19 on page A-8.

Focused Practice

1 | DISCOVER THE GRAMMAR

🎧 *Marcia has a new co-worker. Read their conversations. Underline all the requests.*

1. **MARCIA:** Hi. You must be the new assistant. I'm Marcia. Let me know if you need anything.

   LORNA: Thanks, Marcia. <u>Could you show</u> me the coat closet?

   MARCIA: Certainly. It's right over here.

2. **LORNA:** Marcia, would you help me with the photocopier? I'm having trouble with it.

   MARCIA: Sure. Just put your original in, like this, and press this button.

3. **MARCIA:** I'm leaving for lunch. Would you like to come?

   LORNA: Thanks, but I can't right now. I'm really busy.

   MARCIA: Do you want a sandwich from the coffee shop?

   LORNA: That would be great. Can you get me a tuna sandwich and a soda?

   MARCIA: Sure. Will you answer my phone until I get back?

   LORNA: No problem.

4. **MARCIA:** Lorna, would you mind making a pot of coffee? Some clients are coming in a few minutes, and I have to set up the PowerPoint presentation.

   LORNA: I'm sorry, but I can't do it now. I've got to finish this letter before 2:00.

   MARCIA: That's OK. Thanks anyway.

5. **CLIENT:** I'm Michael Rodrigues. Could you tell Marcia that I'm here for our meeting?

   LORNA: Certainly. I'll call her right now.

6. **LORNA:** Hi, Marcia. Mr. Rodrigues is here for your meeting.

   MARCIA: Thanks. Could you take him to the conference room? I'll be there in a few minutes.

   LORNA: No problem.

   MARCIA: And would you mind offering him a cup of coffee while he waits?

7. **MARCIA:** I'm going home now. Don't forget to turn off the printer before you leave.

   LORNA: I won't.

   MARCIA: By the way, could you give this report to John Sanchez for me?

   LORNA: Sure.

2 | ASKING FOR FAVORS

Grammar Notes 3–4

Mike's roommate, Jeff, is having problems today. Read Jeff's requests. Then circle the letter of the appropriate response to each request.

1. Mike, would you please drive me to class today? My car won't start.
   a. Yes, I would. **b.** I'd be glad to.

2. Would you mind lending me $5? I'm getting paid tomorrow.
   a. Not at all. **b.** Yes.

3. Mike, can you take these books back to the library for me? I'm running late this morning.
   a. Sorry. I'm late for class too. **b.** No, I can't.

4. Could you lock the door on your way out? My hands are full.
   a. Yes, I could. **b.** Sure.

5. Can you turn the radio down? I need to study for my math quiz this morning.
   a. Certainly. **b.** Not at all.

6. Will you pick up some milk on the way home this afternoon?
   a. No, I won't. **b.** I'm sorry, I can't. I'll be at work until 8:00.

3 | WOULD YOU MIND?

Grammar Notes 1–2, 4

Look at the pictures on this and the next page. What is each person thinking? Write the letter of the correct sentence from the box.

a. Repair the photocopier.	**d.** File these reports.	**g.** Buy some cereal.
b. Call back later.	**e.** Shut the door.	**h.** Wait for a few minutes.
c. Get that book.	**f.** Close the window.	**i.** Wash your cups and dishes.

1. ___*d*___ 2. _____ 3. _____

(continued)

4. _____   5. _____   6. _____

7. _____   8. _____   9. _____

What are these people going to say? Complete their requests. Use the words in parentheses and the information from the pictures.

1. _____*Could you file these reports, please?*_____ I've finished reading them.
   (Could)

2. _____ I can't think with all that noise in the hall.
   (Would)

3. _____ on the way home? We don't have any left.
   (Will)

4. _____ It's freezing in here.
   (Can)

5. _____ Mr. Rivera is still in a meeting.
   (Would you mind)

6. _____ It's getting messy in here.
   (Would you mind)

7. _____ I have to leave for a meeting now.
   (Could)

8. _____ I can't reach it.
   (Can)

9. _____ I need to make copies right away.
   (Could)

4 | EDITING

*Read Marcia Jones's response to an e-mail message from her boss. (Her answers are in **red** print.) There are seven mistakes in making and responding to requests. The first mistake is already corrected. Find and correct six more.*

Send Now | Send Later | Save as Draft | Add Attachments | Signature ▼ | Options ▼ | Rewrap

Date: 04-11-05 12:14:39 EST
From: MarciaJones@dataline.com
To: JohnSanchez@dataline.com
CC: AnnChen@dataline.com
Subject: sales meeting—Reply

>>> <JohnSanchez@dataline.com> 04/11/06 10:37am>>>

The meetings are going well but they have been extended a day. Could you ~~call please~~ *please call* Doug Rogers to try to reschedule our sales meeting?

Not at all. I'll do it right away.

We'll need three extra copies of the monthly sales report. Would you ask Ann to take care of that?

Yes, I would. (Ann—could you do this?)

I won't have time to return Emma Lopes' call this week. Would you mind to call her and telling her I'll call her back next week?

No problem. Could you e-mail me her phone number?

I hate to ask, but would you mind to work on Saturday? We'll need the extra time to go over the new information I've gotten.

Sorry, but I couldn't. My in-laws are coming for a visit. But Rob Lin says he can come into the office to help out.

One last thing. I was going to pick up those new business cards, but I won't be back in time. Would you mind doing that for me?

Yes, I would. I'll stop at the printer's during my lunch break.

Communication Practice

5 | LISTENING

🎧 *Marcia Jones has planned a busy weekend. Listen to the conversations. Then listen again and check the things that belong on her schedule.*

☑ **1.** take Ethan to the dentist   ☐ **5.** go to the movies

☐ **2.** take kids to the library   ☐ **6.** walk Mom's dog

☐ **3.** babysit for Kelly's daughter   ☐ **7.** pick up the car at the garage

☐ **4.** go to Kelly's party   ☐ **8.** go to the gym with Jade

6 | I'D BE GLAD TO

Fill out your schedule for the weekend.

SATURDAY		SUNDAY
Morning _____		**Morning**
_____		
_____		
Afternoon _____		**Afternoon**
_____		
_____		
Evening _____		**Evening**
_____		
_____		

Now work in a group. Ask group members to help you with some of the things on your schedule.

Example: **A:** Can you drive me to the mall Saturday morning?
          B: Sorry, I can't. I'm working Saturday morning.   OR   Sure, I'd be glad to.

7 | WRITING

Read the following situations. For each one, write a note making one or more requests.

1. Your roommate is going away for the weekend. Your sister from out of town will be visiting you. Write a note to your roommate.

Example:

Hi Viktor,

My sister is visiting this weekend. Would you mind lending her your bike? I'd like to take her for a ride in the park.

Thanks,
Kunio

2. You work at a restaurant on Mondays, Wednesdays, and Fridays. You have to go to the dentist, but he or she can only see you on Wednesday. Write a note to a co-worker.

3. You're in school. You have to leave class early in order to help your parents. Write a note to a classmate.

4. You're going to have a party at your home. You've invited 20 people. Write a note to your neighbor.

8 | ON THE INTERNET

Send e-mail messages to several classmates. Make a request in each one. Answer messages you receive from your classmates.

Example: Hi Carlos,
I have to miss class tomorrow. Could you make a copy of your notes for me? Also, would you mind . . .

14 Advice: *Should, Ought to, Had better*

Grammar in Context

BEFORE YOU READ

Do you talk to people on the Internet? What are some advantages of Internet communication? What are some problems? Read the article about being polite on the Internet. If you don't understand a cyber word, look up its meaning on the next page.

Netiquette 101
by Emilia Poster

E-mail, bulletin boards, and chat rooms open up a new world of communication—and, sometimes, misunderstanding. To avoid problems, you **should know** these simple rules of netiquette:

When **should** you **post** to a bulletin board or chat room? Newbies **shouldn't jump in** right away—they **ought to lurk** a little first. Look through old messages for answers to common questions. Many sites also have FAQs for basic information. After that, post when you have something new to say. You **should keep** your post short and simple.

Should you **use** capital letters to make a strong statement? NO! A MESSAGE ALL IN CAPITAL LETTERS SEEMS LIKE SHOUTING. You **should follow** the normal rules for capital (big) and lowercase (small) letters.

Did someone make you angry? You**'d better not reply** right away. Count to 10 first. Don't flame another board or chat room member. You **should** never **forget** that people on the Internet are real people with real feelings.

Emoticons help avoid misunderstandings. You **should learn** how to use them to show your feelings.

Internet safety is part of netiquette. When you post to a bulletin board or a chat room, you **should** always **use** a screen name. Never give your real name or other personal information.

Practice these five rules of netiquette, and most of your emoticons will be smilies! ☺

Cyber Words

bulletin board an Internet site where members can post ideas about a special interest

chat room a site for online conversations in "real" time

emoticon a picture of a feeling, for example:

FAQ Frequently Asked Questions

flame send insulting messages to someone

lurk read messages on a bulletin board but not post any messages

netiquette Internet etiquette (rules for polite behavior)

newbie (or newb) someone new to an Internet site

post send messages to a bulletin board or chat room

"Got your e-mail, thanks."

AFTER YOU READ

Read the statements. Check **OK** *or* **Not OK**.

	OK	Not OK
1. Read some messages before you post.	☐	☐
2. Reply immediately when you're angry.	☐	☐
3. Use all capital letters in your posts.	☐	☐
4. Use emoticons to show feelings.	☐	☐
5. Use your real name in chat rooms.	☐	☐
6. Learn the rules of netiquette.	☐	☐
7. Always flame people when you don't like their messages.	☐	☐
8. Write long, complicated messages.	☐	☐
9. Think about people's feelings when you post a message.	☐	☐

Grammar Presentation

ADVICE: *SHOULD, OUGHT TO, HAD BETTER*

Statements		
Subject	*Should / Ought to / Had Better**	**Base Form of Verb**
I You He She We You They	**should** (**not**) **ought to** **had better** (**not**)	**reply**.

Contractions		
should not	=	**shouldn't**
had better	=	**'d better**

*Should and *ought to* are modals. *Had better* is similar to a modal. These forms do not have *-s* in the third-person singular.

Yes / No Questions		
Should	**Subject**	**Base Form of Verb**
Should	I he she we they	**reply**?

Short Answers					
Affirmative			Negative		
Yes,	you he she you they	**should**.	**No**,	you he she you they	**shouldn't**.

Wh- Questions				
Wh- Word	*Should*	**Subject**	**Base Form of Verb**	
How When Where	**should**	I he she we they	**send**	it?

GRAMMAR NOTES	**EXAMPLES**
1. Use the modals *should* and *ought to* to say that something is **advisable** (a good idea).	• Derek **should answer** that e-mail.
	• You **ought to read** the FAQ.
USAGE NOTES: We do not usually use the <u>negative</u> of *ought to* in American English. We use *shouldn't* instead.	• We **shouldn't post** long messages. NOT COMMON We ~~ought not to~~ post long messages.
We often <u>soften advice</u> with *maybe*, *perhaps*, or *I think*.	• Ryan, *maybe* you **shouldn't spend** so much time on the Internet.

Pronunciation Note
Ought to is often pronounced "oughta" in informal speech.

2. Use *had better* for **strong advice**—when you believe that something bad will happen if the person does not follow the advice.	• Kids, you**'d better get** off-line now or you won't have time for your homework.
USAGE NOTE: The full form *had better* is very formal. We usually use the **contraction**.	• You**'d better choose** a screen name. NOT COMMON You ~~had better~~ choose a screen name.
The <u>negative</u> of *had better* is *had better not*.	• You**'d better not use** your real name. NOT You ~~had not better~~ use your real name.
▶ **BE CAREFUL!** *Had better* always refers to the **present** or the **future**, never to the past (even though it uses the word *had*).	• You**'d better not call** them *now*. They're probably sleeping.
	• You**'d better post** that *tomorrow* or it'll be late.

3. Use *should* for **questions**. We do not usually use *ought to* or *had better* for questions.	• **Should** I **join** this chat room?
	• When **should** I **sign on**?

Reference Notes
For general information on **modals,** see Unit 11, Grammar Note 1 on page 126.
Sometimes we use *must* or *have to* to give **very strong advice.** This kind of advice is similar to talking about **necessity** or **obligation** (see Unit 34).
For a list of **modals and their functions,** see Appendix 19 on page A-8.

Focused Practice

1 DISCOVER THE GRAMMAR

Read these posts to an online bulletin board for high school students. Underline the words that give or ask for advice.

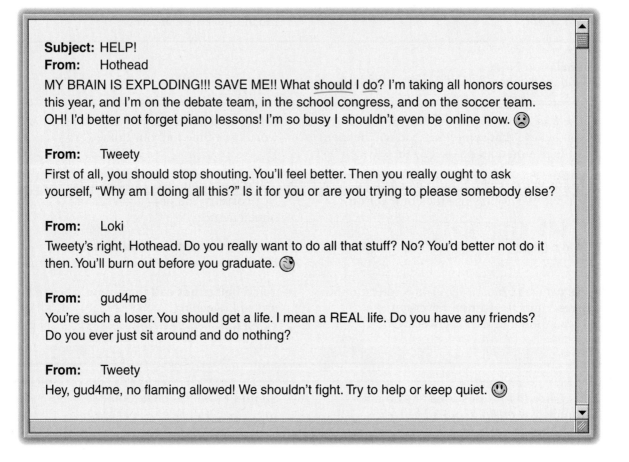

Subject: HELP!
From: Hothead

MY BRAIN IS EXPLODING!!! SAVE ME!! What <u>should</u> I <u>do</u>? I'm taking all honors courses this year, and I'm on the debate team, in the school congress, and on the soccer team. OH! I'd better not forget piano lessons! I'm so busy I shouldn't even be online now. 😞

From: Tweety

First of all, you should stop shouting. You'll feel better. Then you really ought to ask yourself, "Why am I doing all this?" Is it for you or are you trying to please somebody else?

From: Loki

Tweety's right, Hothead. Do you really want to do all that stuff? No? You'd better not do it then. You'll burn out before you graduate. 😊

From: gud4me

You're such a loser. You should get a life. I mean a REAL life. Do you have any friends? Do you ever just sit around and do nothing?

From: Tweety

Hey, gud4me, no flaming allowed! We shouldn't fight. Try to help or keep quiet. 😊

2 FRIENDLY ADVICE
Grammar Notes 1–2

Read these posts to a chat room about learning English. Complete them with the correct form (affirmative or negative) of the words in parentheses. Use contractions when possible.

curly: I think I _____*should watch*_____ more movies to improve my English. Any ideas?
          1. (should / watch)

usedit: I loved *Sixth Sense*. But you _____ it if you don't like scary films.
          2. (had better / rent)

agurl: That's right. You _____ the remote in your hand. That way you
          3. (had better / keep)
          can fast-forward through the scary parts.

592XY: I think you _____ *Groundhog Day*. The same thing happens
          4. (ought to / see)
          again and again. It's great listening practice—and it's funny!

pati: Do you have a DVD player? If not, maybe you _____ one.
                                                                    5.(should / get)
DVDs have English subtitles.

usedit: But you _____ the subtitles right away. First you
                              6.(should / use)
_____ a few times. That's what rewind buttons are for!
7.(should / listen)

592XY: Good advice. And you really _____ a plot summary before you
                                                   8.(ought to / read)
watch. You can find one online. It's so much easier when you know the story.

agurl: Curly, you're a math major, right? You _____ *A Beautiful Mind.*
                                                             9.(ought to / watch)
It's about a math genius.

curly: Thanks, guys. Those are great ideas. But you _____ me any
                                                                    10.(had better / give)
more advice, or I'll never work on my other courses!

---

3 | COMPUTER TIPS   *Grammar Note 3*

Complete these posts to an online bulletin board. Choose the correct words from the box to complete the questions. Give short answers.

ask them to stop	buy one online	check the spelling
forward the e-mail	~~post right away~~	try to repair it

1. Q: I want to join a new online discussion group. *Should I post right away* ?

A: *No, you shouldn't* . It's always a good idea to "lurk" before you post.

2. Q: My friends e-mail me a lot of jokes. A few of them are funny, but I really don't like receiving them. _____?

A: _____. These jokes can waste a lot of time!

3. Q: My computer is seven years old and has problems. _____?

A: _____. That's very old for a computer! Buy a new one!

4. Q: I just received a warning about a computer virus. The e-mail says to tell everyone I know about it. _____?

A: _____. These warnings are almost always false.

5. Q: I hate to go shopping, but I really need a jacket. _____?

A: _____. It's safe. Just buy from a company you know.

6. Q: I type fast and make spelling mistakes. Is that bad? _____?

A: _____. Use a spell checker! Mistakes are bad netiquette!

4 | SAFETY RULES! *Grammar Notes 1–2*

*Rewrite these Internet safety tips. Use **should**, **ought to**, or **had better**. Choose between affirmative and negative.*

> **The Internet is a wonderful place to visit and hang out. Here are some tips to make your trip there a safe one!**

1. I often use my real name online. Is that a problem?

Yes! *You should always use a screen name.*
(Always use a screen name.)

Protect your identity!

2. Someone in my chat group just asked for my address.

_____
(Don't give out any personal information.)

People can use it to steal your identity and your money.

3. My brother wants my password to check out a group before joining.

_____
(Don't give it to anyone.)

Not even your brother! He might share it, and then people can steal your information.

4. I sent a file to someone, and she told me it had a virus.

_____
(Get virus protection and use it.)

A virus can hurt your computer and destroy important files (and other people's too).

5. I update my virus protection every month. Is that really necessary?

Yes! _____
(Keep your virus protection up-to-date.)

Remember: *Old* virus protection is *no* virus protection!

6. I got an e-mail about a home-based business. I could make $15,000 a month.

_____
(Don't believe any "get rich quick" offers.)

They sound good, but people almost always lose money.

7. I got an interesting e-mail. I don't know who sent it, but it's got a file attached.

_____
(Don't open any e-mail attachments from strangers.)

They could contain dangerous viruses.

8. The Internet sounds too dangerous for me!

Not really. _____ ,
(Be careful!)

but enjoy yourself—it's an exciting world out there!

5 | EDITING

*Read these posts to a bulletin board for international students in the United States. There are twelve mistakes in the use of **should**, **ought to**, and **had better**. The first mistake is already corrected. Find and correct eleven more.*

Justme: My friend asked me to dinner and she told me I should ~~to~~ bring some food! What kind of an invitation is that? What I should bring to this strange dinner party?

Sasha: LOL!* Your friend is having a potluck—a dinner party where everybody brings something. It's really a lot of fun. You ought bring a dish from your country. People will enjoy that.

Toby: HELP! My first day of class, and I lost my wallet! What ought I do first? My student ID, credit card, and cash are all gone.

R2D2: First of all, you'd not better panic because you need to be calm so you can speak clearly. You should to call your credit card company right away. Did you lose your wallet at school? Then you ought to going to the Lost and Found Department at your school.

Smiley: What should an international student does to make friends? At my college people always smile and say, "Hi, how are you?" but they don't wait for an answer!

4gud: New students should joining some clubs and international student organizations. They also ought to find a student in each class to study with and ask about homework assignments.

Newguy: Hi. I'm new to this board. I'm from Vietnam, and I'm going to school in Canada next year. How should I will get ready?

Smiley: Welcome Newguy! I'm at school in Montreal, and my best advice is—you're better bring a lot of warm clothes. You won't believe how cold it gets here.

Sasha: You ought check the school's website. They might have a Vietnam Students' Association. If they do, you should e-mail the Association with your questions. Good luck!

*LOL = Laughing out Loud

Communication Practice

6 | LISTENING

○ *A radio show host is giving advice to callers about buying a new computer. Listen to the show. Then listen again and check the sentences that agree with his advice.*

☐ **1.** Repair a seven-year-old computer.

☑ **2.** Read online computer reviews.

☐ **3.** Throw away your old computer.

☐ **4.** Always buy the cheapest computer.

☐ **5.** Order a computer from a big online company.

☐ **6.** Shop at a local computer store.

☐ **7.** Consider a service contract.

☐ **8.** Get the most memory you can afford.

7 | NEW COUNTRY, NEW CUSTOMS

Work with a partner. Imagine that your partner has been offered a job in a country that you know very well. Give some advice about customs there. Then switch roles. Use the topics below and some of your own.

- calling your boss by his or her first name
- shaking hands when you first meet someone
- calling a co-worker by a nickname
- asking for a second helping of food when you are a guest
- crossing the street before the light turns green

Add your own topics.

- _____
- _____

Examples: You'd better not call your boss by her first name.
You should shake hands when you first meet someone.

8 | PROBLEM SOLVING

Work in small groups. Take turns telling each other about problems you are having. They can be real problems or invented problems, or you can choose from the problems below. Your classmates will give you advice.

- having trouble making friends

- not earning enough money

- not having enough free time

Example: A: I'm having trouble making friends.
B: Maybe you should come to the student lounge.
C: I think you ought to spend more time with the rest of us.

9 | THIS PLACE NEEDS WORK!

Work in pairs. Look at a classroom at the EFL Computer Training Institute. Give advice for ways to improve the institute. Then compare your ideas with the ideas of another pair.

Example: A: They should empty the trash.
B: Yes, and they ought to . . .

10 | WRITING

Look at the picture in Exercise 9. Imagine you are a student at the EFL Computer Training Institute. Write a letter of complaint to Mr. Thompson, the owner of the school. Give advice on improvements the institute should make.

Example: Dear Mr. Thompson:

I am a student at the EFL Computer Training Institute. My classes are very good, but the Institute had better make some improvements or many students are going to leave. First, I think you should . . .

11 | ON THE INTERNET

Do a search on **advice on learning English***. Then discuss your search results with your classmates.*

Example: A: You should always speak English with your classmates.
B: You shouldn't worry about speaking fast. It's not important.
C: I think . . .

Do you agree with the advice?

Suggestions: *Let's, Could, Why don't, Why not, How about*

Grammar in Context

BEFORE YOU READ

🎧 *What do you know about youth hostels? Would you like to stay in one of the hostels in the photos below? Read the information from a youth hostel website.*

Let's Travel!

A LOT OF STUDENTS WANT TO TRAVEL—but they don't have much money or don't want to travel alone. Sound familiar? If so, **why don't** you **travel** and **stay** at youth hostels? They are cheap, and you'll meet friendly people from all over the world.

There are more than 4,000 hostels in over 60 different countries. They vary from simple buildings to magnificent old castles. Interested in a more active vacation? **How about checking into** a lodge near a volcano in Costa Rica? Hike through the rain forest during the day. In the evening, you **could watch** red-hot lava coming out of the volcano.

Carbisdale Castle, Scotland

Arenal Observatory Lodge, Costa Rica

Do you prefer cities? **Why not stay** at the Jockey Club Mt. Davis Youth Hostel in Hong Kong? It overlooks the harbor and isn't far from the excitement of downtown.

Tired of being on land? **How about a room** on the *af Chapman* in Stockholm, Sweden? Built in 1888, this sailing ship has been rocking tired tourists to sleep for more than 50 years.

Wherever you go, you'll meet talkative travelers, share stories with them, and gain a greater understanding of the world and its people. So what are you waiting for?

(select a country) ▼ and **let's go!**

AFTER YOU READ

Check the correct answers.

The website suggests _____.

☐ **1.** spending your vacation in the dorm

☐ **2.** staying at expensive hotels

☐ **3.** checking into a lodge

☐ **4.** avoiding the Jockey Club Mt. Davis Youth Hostel

☐ **5.** sleeping on the *af Chapman*

☐ **6.** talking to other travelers

Grammar Presentation

SUGGESTIONS: *LET'S, COULD, WHY DON'T, WHY NOT, HOW ABOUT*

Let's		
Let's (not)	**Base Form of Verb**	
Let's (not)	**take**	the ferry.
	stay	in a castle.

Could			
Subject	**Could***	**Base Form of Verb**	
I You He She We They	**could**	**take**	the ferry.
		stay	in a castle.

*Could is a modal. Modals have only one form.
They do not have *-s* in the third-person singular.

Why don't				
Why	**Don't**	**Subject**	**Base Form of Verb**	
Why	**don't**	I we you they	**take**	the ferry?
	doesn't	he she	**stay**	in a castle?

Why not		
Why not	**Base Form of Verb**	
Why not	**take**	the ferry?
	stay	in a castle?

How about		
How about	**Gerund / Noun**	
How about	**staying**	in a castle?
	a castle?	

GRAMMAR NOTES

EXAMPLES

1. Use *let's*, *could*, *why don't*, *why not*, and *how about* to make **suggestions**.

A: **Let's take** a trip this summer.

B: We **could go** to Costa Rica.

A: **Why don't** we **ask** Luke to go too?

B: OK. **Why doesn't** Tom **call** him tonight?

A: **Why not call** him right now?

B: **How about staying** at youth hostels?

A: **How about a lodge** in the rain forest?

USAGE NOTE: We often use *maybe* in suggestions with *could*.

• *Maybe* we **could stay** near the volcano.

2. *Let's* always includes the speaker. It means "Here's a suggestion for you and me."

• **Let's go** to Miami. We need a vacation.
(I suggest that we go to Miami.)

• **Let's not stay** at a hostel.
(I suggest that we don't stay at a hostel.)

3. Note the **different forms** to use with these expressions.

BASE FORM OF THE VERB

• **Let's** *take* the ferry.

• We **could** *take* the ferry.

• **Why don't** we *take* the ferry?

• **Why not** *take* the ferry?

GERUND OR NOUN

• **How about** *taking* the ferry?

• **How about** *the ferry*?

4. Notice the **punctuation** at the end of each kind of suggestion.

STATEMENTS

• **Let's** go to a concert**.**

• **Maybe** we **could** go to a concert**.**

QUESTIONS

• **Why don't** we go to a concert**?**

• **Why not** go to a concert**?**

• **How about** going to a concert**?**

(continued)

---

5. To **agree with a suggestion**, we usually answer with an <u>informal expression</u>.

A: Let's take a walk.
B: *Good idea*.
Great.
I'd like that.
OK.
Sure.

To **disagree**, we often give an explanation and make another suggestion.

A: Why don't we go to the park?
B: *We go there a lot*. *How about the river*?

Reference Note
Making suggestions is sometimes similar to **giving advice** (see Unit 14).

Focused Practice

1 | DISCOVER THE GRAMMAR

🎧 *Emily and Megan are visiting Hong Kong. Read their conversation. Underline all the suggestions.*

EMILY: <u>Why don't we go to the races</u>? I hear they're really exciting.

MEGAN: I'd like to, but I need to go shopping.

EMILY: Then let's go to the Temple Street Market tonight. We might even see some Chinese opera in the street while we're there.

MEGAN: That sounds like fun. But if we do that, why not go to the races this afternoon?

EMILY: OK, but let's get something to eat first in one of those floating restaurants.

MEGAN: I don't think we'll have time. Maybe we could do that tomorrow. Right now, how about getting *dim sum* at the Kau Kee Restaurant next door? Then we could take the Star Ferry to Hong Kong Island and the racecourse.

EMILY: Sounds good. Here's an idea for tomorrow. Why not take one of those small boats— *kaido*—to Lantau Island? When we come back, we could have dinner at the Jumbo Palace.

MEGAN: Let's do that. It's a little expensive, but it sounds like fun.

Now look at this page from a Hong Kong guidebook and check the places Emily and Megan will visit and the transportation they will take.

- **Hong Kong Space Museum.** One of the world's most advanced. See the Sky Show and a movie on the Omnimax movie screen.
- ✓ **Temple Street Night Market.** Find great bargains, visit a fortune-teller, and, with luck, hear Chinese opera performed in the street.

- **Harbour City.** Shop for clothing, electronics, and antiques in this huge, modern mall. Beautiful harbour views from the open rooftop.
- **Happy Valley Racecourse.** Watch Hong Kong's favorite sport. Feel the excitement as millions of Hong Kong dollars ride on every horse race.

TRANSPORTATION

- **Railway lines** make local stops in both Kowloon and on Hong Kong Island. Use the Kwung Tong Line in Kowloon and the Island Line on Hong Kong Island.
- **The Star Ferry** is the queen of Hong Kong water transportation, and it's a bargain, too. There are several routes connecting Kowloon and Hong Kong Island.
- *Kaido* are small wooden ferries that carry 20–40 passengers.
- **Citybus** passengers ride the double-decker buses in air-conditioned comfort all over Hong Kong, Kowloon, and nearby islands. Tourists like the view from the top deck.

PLACES TO EAT

- **Jumbo Palace ($$$)** A traditional-style floating restaurant specializing in seafood.
- **Yunk Kee Restaurant ($)** Award-winning Cantonese food—famous for its roast duck.
- **Kau Kee Restaurant ($)** A favorite place for *dim sum*—a great way to try a variety of dishes.
- **Bo Kong Vegetarian Restaurant ($$)** Simple but tasty dishes. This attractive restaurant is popular with local celebrities.
- **Peak Lookout ($$$)** The food is not exciting, but you won't notice because the view of the harbour and the islands is so spectacular.

2 | MAKING PLANS

Complete the conversations with the appropriate expression in parentheses.

1. **A:** I feel like having seafood for dinner, but we went to Jumbo Palace last night.

    B: _____ *Why not* _____ go again? The food's great, and so is the view.

(Why not / Let's not)

2. **A:** I'm really tired. _____ resting before we go out?

(Let's / How about)

    B: That's a good idea. I'm tired too.

3. **A:** I want to explore downtown Hong Kong.

    B: _____ take a double-decker Citybus? We'll see a lot more that way.

(Let's not / Why don't we)

4. **A:** A group of foreign students just checked into the hostel.

    B: _____ ask them to join us for dinner.

(How about / Maybe we could)

5. **A:** I don't want to go home tomorrow. I'm having a really good time here.

    B: So am I. _____ leave tomorrow.

(Let's / Let's not)

3 | LET'S . . .

*Complete the suggestions with phrases from the box. Add pronouns and change the verbs
as necessary. Punctuate correctly.*

buy another one	~~buy tickets~~	come with us
go to the beach	take a trip together	try that new seafood place

1. **A:** There's an Oasis concert at the Hong Kong Convention Centre next weekend.

    B: We're near there now. Why don't *we buy tickets?* _____

2. **A:** It's going to be hot tomorrow.

    B: I know. How about_____

3. **A:** Sweaters are on sale. Maybe we could buy one for Brian's birthday.

    B: We got him a sweater last year. Let's not_____

4. **A:** I don't know what to do on spring vacation. I'm sick of staying in the dorm.

    B: Me too. Maybe _____

5. **A:** Emily doesn't have any plans either.

    B: Why doesn't_____

6. **A:** I'm hungry.

    B: Let's _____

4 | EDITING

Read these comments from a suggestions book at a hostel. There are nine mistakes in the use of expressions of suggestion. The first mistake is already corrected. Find and correct eight more. Remember to check the punctuation.

SUGGESTIONS

The rooms here are very nice, but why don't you ~~having~~ *have* better lamps so we can read at night?
Petra De Graff, Netherlands

How about have a list of inexpensive restaurants in the area?
Jessica Edwards, Canada

The breakfast is delicious, but why not has music in the breakfast room? Everyone likes music.
Liv Lindberg, Sweden

The countryside around here is very beautiful. Maybe you could having some bikes for us to use so we could explore a little?
Yan Ying Tan, Taiwan

I like staying in old, historic hostels, but I miss some of the modern conveniences. How about having Internet access. It would be nice to send and get e-mail! And why not accepting credit cards?
Carlos Ezcurra, Argentina

You provide sheets, so why you don't provide towels too? They're just as important as sheets!
Ian Harlow, Scotland

Here's a suggestion for all of us hostel guests. Let's don't be so messy! It will be more pleasant for everyone if we clean up our own stuff.
Anonymous

Communication Practice

5 | LISTENING

🎧 *Emily and Megan have just arrived on Lantau Island in Hong Kong. Look at the map. Then listen to the conversation. Listen again. On the map, check the things they decide to do and the places they decide to see.*

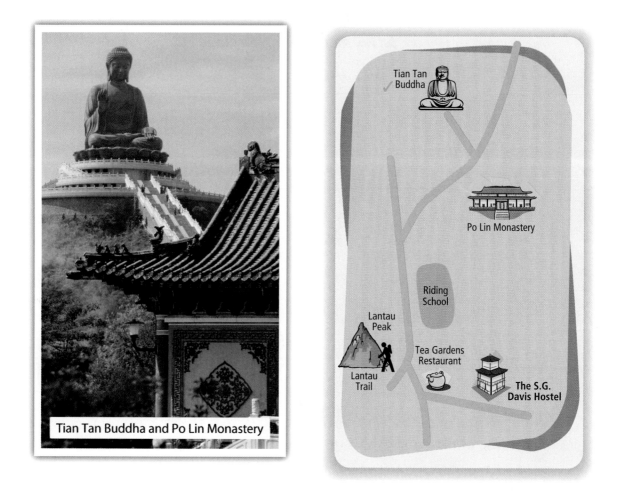

Tian Tan Buddha and Po Lin Monastery

6 | HOW ABOUT . . .?

Work with a partner. Imagine you are both visiting Hong Kong. Look at the guidebook on page 169 and talk about what you would like to do. Make suggestions about activities.

Example: **A:** I want to buy some souvenirs.
B: Let's go to the Temple Street Night Market.

7 | THINGS TO DO

Work with a group to plan a trip to an interesting place in your area. Discuss the following:

- where to go

- when to go

- how to get there

- what to do there

- who will call or write for more information

Example: A: How about visiting San Diego?
B: Maybe we could go next weekend.
C: How about going to the zoo?
A: Why not take the bus?
B: Why don't the two of you call for information?

8 | WRITING

Write a letter to someone who is going to visit you. Make suggestions about the things you can do together.

Example: Dear Kim,
I am so excited about your visit! Let's make some plans right now. You arrive on Friday, the 10th. Why don't we spend the next day at the museum? There's a great exhibit on . . .

9 | ON THE INTERNET

Ⓒ *Work with a partner. First choose a country and city you are both interested in visiting. Then research the hostels there. (You could check out* **Hostelling International**). *Discuss the hostel possibilities and agree on one to stay at.*

Example: A: Let's go to England.
B: I've been there. How about Scotland? It's a beautiful country, and we could still practice our English . . .
A: Maybe we could stay at Carbisdale Castle. It looks great in the photo.
B: That's true. But why don't we stay in Edinburgh? There are several hostels in the old section of the city . . .

III From **Grammar** to **Writing**
Using Appropriate Modals

When you write a note, you do more than give information. You perform social functions such as asking for permission and making requests. Modals help you perform these functions politely.

Example: I want you to call me in the morning. $\longrightarrow$
Could you **please** call me in the morning?

1 | *Read this note from Ed to his co-worker, Chen. Work with a partner and decide which sentences should have modals. Underline the sentences.*

    From the Desk of Ed Hansen . . .

Chen,—Here is our project summary. <u>Read it.</u> I really think it's much too long.

What do you think? Tell me whether to shorten it. We will meet tomorrow to

discuss it. My advice is that we finish the draft by Friday. By the way, Nadia

is in town. I want to invite her to our meeting. —Ed

---

2 | *Complete a second draft of the note. Use modals to express the functions in parentheses.*

    From the Desk of Ed Hansen . . .

Chen,—Here is our project summary. _____Would you mind_____ reading it? I really think
                                    (make a request)

it's much too long. What do you think? _____ I shorten it?
                                              (ask advice)

_____ meet tomorrow to discuss it. We _____ finish
   (make a suggestion)   **(give advice)**

the final draft by Friday. By the way, Nadia is in town. _____ I
                                                            (ask permission)

invite her to our meeting? —Ed

---

3 Complete Chen's note to Ed. Use modals to express the following ideas:

- Shorten the summary. *(advice)*
- I want to meet tomorrow morning instead. *(suggestion)*
- Reserve the conference room for the meeting. *(request)*
- Of course Nadia will come to the meeting. *(permission)*
- We're going to have lunch together after the meeting. *(suggestion)*

 From the Desk of Chen Wu . . .

Ed—Sorry, I was very busy this morning, so I wasn't able to finish reading the summary until now. *I think you should shorten it.*

See you tomorrow morning. —Chen

4 Before you write . . .

1. Work with a partner. Choose one of the situations below. Role-play the situation. Use modals to express the ideas.

   SITUATION 1: **A salesperson and his or her boss**
   You work in a sales office. Recently a customer complained to your boss because he had to wait for service. You want to meet with your boss to explain what happened. You'd like to bring a co-worker who saw the incident. You think the company needs another receptionist for busy times.

   SITUATION 2: **A student and his or her English teacher**
   You would like your English teacher to write a letter of recommendation for you. You want him or her to mention that you have good computer skills and are an A student in the class. You're not sure how many hours to work a week, so you ask your teacher. You want to miss class so that you can go to your job interview.

2. Work with another pair. Watch their role play. Make a list of functions they expressed (for example, advice, suggestion, ability) and the modals they used to express those functions. Discuss your list with them—did they express what they wanted to?

3. Perform your role play and discuss it with the other pair.

5 Write a note as one of the characters in the role play. Use modals and information from the feedback you received on your role play.

Review Test

I *Circle the letter of the appropriate response to each question.*

1. Could you speak English when you were a child?
   a. I'd be glad to.
   b. Yes, I could.

2. Can you swim?
   a. Yes, I can. I'd be glad to.
   b. Yes, I can. I really enjoy it.

3. Would you turn off the lights before you leave?
   a. Of course.
   b. Yes, I would.

4. May I ask a question?
   a. Yes, you may. What is it?
   b. You may. I'm not sure.

5. Would you mind lending me some money? I left my wallet at home.
   a. Yes, I would. Here's $10.
   b. Not at all. Here's $10.

6. Why don't we go to the beach today?
   a. Good idea.
   b. Because the car broke down.

7. Could you explain this word to me?
   a. Sorry, but I don't understand it either.
   b. No, I couldn't. I never heard it before!

8. Maybe I'll wear a suit. What do you think?
   a. Maybe you shouldn't.
   b. Maybe you won't.

9. Were you able to get tickets for the concert last week?
   a. No, I wasn't.
   b. Why not?

II *Read each sentence. Write its function. Use the words in the box.*

| ability | advice | permission | request | suggestion |

1. Passengers may not use cell phones on the airplane. _____*permission*_____

2. Could you please turn the light out before you leave? _____

3. Why not take the train? _____

4. Of course you can use my pen. _____

5. When Eva was little, she couldn't reach the elevator button. _____

6. Do you mind if my sister comes with us? _____

7. Let's take a taxi. _____

8. If you don't know who sent that e-mail, you'd better not open it. _____

9. Would you mind calling back in about half an hour? _____

10. Will you please explain that to me again? _____

11. I can't lift that box by myself. _____

12. Maybe we could go to a later movie. _____

13. You shouldn't use your real name in an Internet chat room. _____

14. Ty didn't study hard, but he was able to pass the final exam. _____

III *Circle the correct words to complete the conversations.*

1. A: This dorm room is depressing me.

B: May we / (Why not) redecorate? We have some free time.
   a.

A: OK. Where should we / were we able to start?
   b.

B: Maybe we could / couldn't put up new curtains.
   c.

A: Great. Let's / Why not go to the store right now?
   d.

B: We can't / 'd better measure the windows first.
   e.

A: These curtains are pretty. Why not / How about putting them up right away?
   f.

B: We may / should wash the windows first. They're really dirty.
   g.

A: OK. The windows are clean. Let's / May we put up the curtains now.
   h.

B: The room looks great. Why don't we / We should buy some new posters next.
   i.

(continued)

2. A: Dancing Wheels is performing next weekend. <u>Let's / Would you mind</u> get tickets.
a.

B: Good idea. <u>Could / Should</u> you pick them up? I'm really busy this week.
      b.

A: No problem. I'll <u>can / be able to</u> get them after class today. <u>Do you mind if / Why not</u>
          c.   d.
I get a ticket for Carlos too?

B: <u>Yes, I do. / Not at all.</u> I haven't seen him in ages. Maybe we <u>could / will</u> all go out to
    e.   f.
dinner before the theater. I hear that new Indian restaurant is very good.

A: OK, but we <u>could / 'd better</u> make a reservation. It's also very popular.
           g.

3. A: I'm buying a new computer this year. Any suggestions?

B: <u>How about / Why don't</u> you ask Anatol? He knows a lot about computers.
    a.

A: Good idea. <u>Could / Should</u> you give me his e-mail address?
      b.

B: I don't have it, but you <u>'d better / could</u> ask Karin. She'll have it.
          c.

A: <u>Do you mind if / Would you mind</u> asking her for me? You know her better.
    d.

B: Sure.

IV | *Each sentence has four underlined words or phrases. The four underlined parts of the sentences are marked A, B, C, or D. Circle the letter of the <u>one</u> underlined word or phrase that is NOT CORRECT.*

1. <u>When</u> I was 10, I <u>could</u> hit a ball far, but I <u>wasn't</u> able <u>run</u> fast.   **A**   **B**   **C**   Ⓓ
  A   B   C   D

2. Why <u>don't</u> we <u>have</u> dinner and then <u>go</u> see *Possible Dreams.*   **A**   **B**   **C**   **D**
        A   B   C   D

3. You <u>drove</u> all day today, so <u>maybe</u> you'd <u>not better</u> <u>drive</u> tonight.   **A**   **B**   **C**   **D**
     A   B   C   D

4. <u>Will</u> you mind <u>bringing</u> your camera to the party <u>tomorrow</u> <u>?</u>   **A**   **B**   **C**   **D**
  A   B   C D

5. Dad, <u>may</u> I <u>borrow</u> the car tomorrow or <u>does</u> Mom <u>has</u> to use it?   **A**   **B**   **C**   **D**
        A   B   C   D

6. I <u>can't help</u> you with this, so <u>maybe</u> you should <u>to talk</u> to Mr. Ho.   **A**   **B**   **C**   **D**
   A B   C   D

7. <u>Should</u> I <u>give</u> my host flowers, or <u>should</u> I <u>bringing</u> candy?   **A**   **B**   **C**   **D**
    A   B   C   D

8. <u>May be</u> you <u>ought</u> <u>to</u> just <u>bring</u> flowers.
   A   B C   D

A B C D

9. Silva <u>wasn't</u> a strong child, but she <u>could</u> win first prize in
        A   B

gymnastics <u>when</u> she <u>was</u> ten.
         C   D

A B C D

10. I think I <u>was</u> able <u>to</u> <u>finish</u> my <u>homework</u> early tomorrow.
          A   B C   D

A B C D

11. <u>It's</u> really late, so <u>let's</u> <u>us</u> <u>go</u> out to dinner tonight, OK?
    A   B C D

A B C D

V   *Find and correct the mistake in each conversation.*

1. **A:** Can Elena ~~dances~~? *dance*

   B: Yes, she's great. She's able to do all kinds of difficult steps.

2. **A:** When you were a child, were you able to skate?

   B: Yes. In fact, I once could win a competition in my school.

3. **A:** Could please you help me?

   B: Sure. What seems to be the problem?

4. **A:** Would you mind giving me a ride home?

   B: Yes, I would. When would you like to leave?

5. **A:** You really ought update your virus protection.

   B: OK. I'll do it today.

6. **A:** We would better hurry, or we'll be late.

   B: Don't worry. We can still get there on time.

7. **A:** Could I borrow the car tonight?

   B: Sorry, but you couldn't. I need it myself.

8. **A:** Do you mind if my friend coming to the party with me?

   B: Not at all. There's always room for one more!

▶ *To check your answers, go to the Answer Key on page RT-2.*

PART
IV
Present Perfect

16 Present Perfect: *Since* and *For*

Grammar in Context

BEFORE YOU READ

🎧 *Where can you find an article like this? Look at the information below the photo. How long has Bob Burnquist been a professional? Read the article about this champion skateboarder.*

KING OF SKATE

by Mariana Andrade

When he was only 11 years old, Bob Burnquist's life changed. A skate park opened just three blocks from his house in São Paulo, Brazil. Bob got his very first skateboard and started skating. He **hasn't stopped since then**.

At first he did it just for fun, but soon he turned pro. His first big international contest was in Canada, in 1995. **Since then** he **has taken** home many more first-place prizes and gold medals. He **has** also **earned** enough money to support himself while doing what he loves most. In 2002 he was voted "King of Skate" in a California contest.

Bob **has lived** in California **since 1995**, but he frequently returns to Brazil. He**'s had** dual citizenship (Brazil and the United States) **for many years**. Does he consider himself "American"? "I am American, South American. . . . A citizen of the world."

The skateboard isn't the only board he uses. Bob also enjoys snowboarding and surfing. **Since he moved to California**, he **has been** close to snow-topped mountains and the beach. His backyard and, of course, the streets provide opportunity for skating. As he once said, "If you snowboard, surf, and skate, you pretty much cover the whole Earth."

Sports Cards

© Stan Liu

Bob Burnquist

Date of Birth: October 10, 1976
Place of Birth: Rio de Janeiro, Brazil
Residence: California, USA
Citizenship: Brazilian, USA
Started Skateboarding: 1987
Turned Professional: 1991
Other Interests: Reading, travel, photography, snowboarding, mountain biking, surfing
Motto: "Be good, be positive, respect individuality and nature."

Sports Cards

AFTER YOU READ

*Read the statements. Check **True** or **False**.*

	True	False
1. Bob Burnquist still skates.	☑	☐
2. His only first-place prize was in 1995.	☐	☑
3. He lives in Brazil.	☐	☑
4. He lives close to the beach.	☐	☑

Grammar Presentation

PRESENT PERFECT: *SINCE* AND *FOR*

Statements				
Subject	*Have* (*not*)	**Past Participle**		*Since / For*
I You* We They	**have** (**not**)	**been**†	here	**since** 1995. **for** a long time.
He She It	**has** (**not**)	**lived**		

* *You* is both singular and plural.
† *Been* is an irregular past participle. See Grammar Notes on page 185 and
Appendix 1 on page A-1 for a list of irregular verbs.

Yes / No Questions				
Have	**Subject**	**Past Participle**		*Since / For*
Have	I you we they	**been**	here	**since** 1995? **for** a long time?
Has	he she it	**lived**		

Short Answers					
Affirmative			**Negative**		
Yes,	you I / we you they	**have.**	**No**,	you I / we you they	**haven't.**
	he she it	**has.**		he she it	**hasn't.**

(continued)

Wh- Questions					Short Answers
Wh- Word	*Have*	**Subject**	**Past Participle**		
How long	**have**	I you we they	**been**	here?	**Since** 1995. **For** many years.
	has	he she it	**lived**		

Contractions		
Affirmative		Negative
I have = **I've**	he has = **he's**	have not = **haven't**
you have = **you've**	she has = **she's**	has not = **hasn't**
we have = **we've**	it has = **it's**	
they have = **they've**		

GRAMMAR NOTES

EXAMPLES

1. Use the **present perfect** with *since* or *for* to talk about something that began in the past and continues into the present (and may continue into the future).

- Bob **has been** a skater *since* 1987. *(He became a skater in 1987, and he is still a skater.)*
- He **has been** a skater *for* many years. *(He became a skater many years ago, and he is still a skater.)*

2. Use *since* + **point in time** *(since yesterday, since 5:00, since Monday, since 1995)* to show <u>when</u> something started.

Since can also introduce a time clause.

- He **has won** many contests *since 1995*.
- He **has become** famous *since then*.

- He **has loved** sports *since he was a child*.

3. Use *for* + **length of time** *(for 10 minutes, for two weeks, for years, for a long time)* to show <u>how long</u> something has lasted.

- Bob **has owned** a restaurant *for years*.

4. Form the present perfect with:
have + past participle

Past participles can be regular or irregular.

- He **has lived** there for years.
- They **have been** skating partners since 1998.

a. The **regular** form of the past participle is **base form of verb + -d** or **-ed**.

This form is the same as the regular simple past form of the verb.

▶ **BE CAREFUL!** There are often **spelling changes** when you add **-ed** to the verb.

- He has **loved** sports since he was a kid.
- He has **wanted** to skate for a long time.

- He hasn't **stopped** since then.

b. There are many **irregular** past participles. A few common ones are listed below. Notice that irregular verbs with similar base forms often have similar past participles.

- He has **bought** two new skateboards since March.
- They haven't **won** a contest for several years.

Base Form of the Verb	Past Participle	Base Form of the Verb	Past Participle
be	**been**	pay	**paid**
see	**seen**	say	**said**
meet	**met**	do	**done**
sleep	**slept**	go	**gone**
sell	**sold**	drive	**driven**
tell	**told**	give	**given**
buy	**bought**	know	**known**
think	**thought**	grow	**grown**
begin	**begun**	eat	**eaten**
sing	**sung**	fall	**fallen**
have	**had**	speak	**spoken**
make	**made**	break	**broken**
put	**put**	get	**gotten**
read	**read**	write	**written**

Reference Note
For a more complete list of **irregular past participles**, see Appendix 1 on page A-1.

Focused Practice

1 | DISCOVER THE GRAMMAR

Read the information about Caterina and Roque. Then circle the letter of the sentence
(a or b) that best describes the situation.

1. Caterina has been a skater since 1998.
   a. She is still a skater.
   b. She is not a skater anymore.

2. She has had long hair since she was a little girl.
   a. She has short hair now.
   b. She has long hair now.

3. She has lived in the same apartment for ten years.
   a. She lived in a different apartment eleven years ago.
   b. She moved a few years ago.

4. Caterina and Roque have been married for five years.
   a. They are not married now.
   b. They got married five years ago.

5. They haven't been on a vacation since 2001.
   a. They are on a vacation now.
   b. They were on a vacation in 2001.

6. Caterina hasn't won a contest for two years.
   a. She won a championship two years ago.
   b. She didn't win a championship two years ago.

2 | FOR LOVE OF THE SPORT   *Grammar Notes 1–3*

*Complete these sentences about Brazilian sportswriter Mariana Andrade. Use **since** or **for**.*

1. Mariana Andrade has lived in São Paulo ___since___ 1995.

2. She has been a sportswriter ___for___ four years.

3. ___Since___ June she has written several articles about skateboarding.

4. This sport has been very popular in Brazil ___for___ many years.

5. Mariana has met Burnquist twice ___since___ she started her job.

6. She loves to skate, but she hasn't skated ___for___ a long time.

7. She has been married to Alvaro, another skater, ___since___ 2003.

8. They've had their own house ___for___ two years, and they've been parents ___since___ July.

3 | SKATING SUCCESS

Complete this article about Roque Guterres with the correct form of the verbs in parentheses. Use Appendix 1 on page A-1 for help with irregular verbs.

Roque Guterres _____*has loved*_____ skating since he was a little boy. He began
                           1. (love)

skating when he was 10, and he ____*has not stopped*____ since that time. Roque
                                    2. (not stop)

____*has been*____ a professional skater now for several years. He and Caterina
   3. (be)

____*have lived*____ in Rio since they got married. They ____*have had*____
   4. (live)   **5. (have)**

the same one-bedroom apartment for five years. They ____*have not taken*____ a vacation
                                                        6. (not take)

for many years, but they ____*have gone*____ to several skating contests since Roque
                              7. (go)

turned pro. Roque ____*has skated*____ in four international contests since last year.
                        8. (skate)

He ____*has won*____ two second-place prizes since then. Since he was a child, he
        9. (win)

____*has wanted*____ to be a pro. His dream ____*has come*____ true
   10. (want)   **11. (come)**

since then.

4 | SKATEBOARDING FACTS

*Complete these sentences with the present perfect form of the verbs in parentheses and
with* **since** *or* **for***. Use Appendix 1 on page A-1 for help with irregular verbs.*

 Skateboarding _____*has been*_____ popular __*for*__ more than 50 years.
                              1. (be)   **2.**

 Skateboards ____*have been*____ around __*since*__ the 1930s. The first ones
                            3. (be)   **4.**

   were simple wooden boxes on metal wheels. They ____*have changed*____ a lot
                                                       5. (change)

   __*since*__ then!
      6.

 The first skateboarding contest took place in California in 1963. __*Since*__ then,
                                                                                7.

   thousands of contests ____*have taken*____ place all over the world.
                               8. (take)

 In 1976, the first outdoor skate park opened in Florida. __*Since*__ then, hundreds of
                                                                      9.

   parks ____*have opened*____ in countries around the world.
              10. (open)

 Skateboarding can be dangerous. __*Since*__ last year, more than 15,600 people in the
                                              11.

   United States alone ____*has gone*____ to hospital emergency rooms because
                             12. (go)

   of injuries.

(continued)

When he was seven years old, Jon Comer lost his right foot as a result of a car accident. But that didn't stop him. _Since_ then, he _has become_ one of the
13.   14.(become)
best-known professional skateboarders in the world.

Tony Hawk _has not competed_ professionally _for_ many years, but he
15.(not compete)   16.
is still the most famous and successful skateboarder in the world.

5 | A RÉSUMÉ

Ingrid Schwab is applying for a job as a college sports instructor. Look at her résumé and the interviewer's notes. Complete the interview. Use the words in parentheses to write questions. Then answer the questions. Use contractions when possible.
*Note: **The year is 2006.***

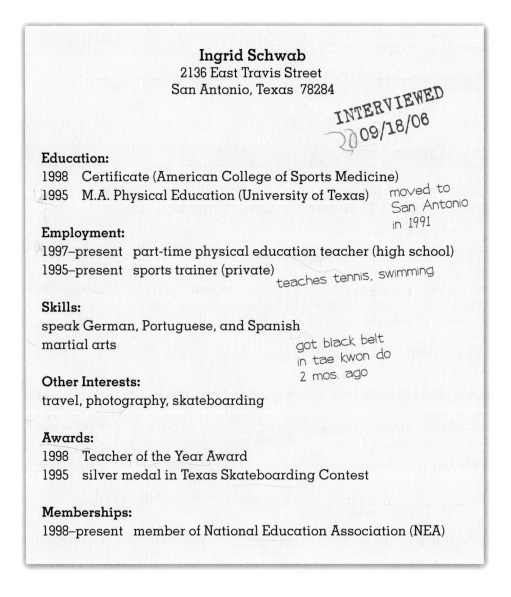

Ingrid Schwab
2136 East Travis Street
San Antonio, Texas 78284

INTERVIEWED
09/18/06

Education:
1998   Certificate (American College of Sports Medicine)
1995   M.A. Physical Education (University of Texas)   *moved to San Antonio in 1991*

Employment:
1997–present   part-time physical education teacher (high school)
1995–present   sports trainer (private)   *teaches tennis, swimming*

Skills:
speak German, Portuguese, and Spanish
martial arts   *got black belt in tae kwon do 2 mos. ago*

Other Interests:
travel, photography, skateboarding

Awards:
1998   Teacher of the Year Award
1995   silver medal in Texas Skateboarding Contest

Memberships:
1998–present   member of National Education Association (NEA)

1. (How long / live in San Antonio)

INTERVIEWER: _How long have you lived in San Antonio?_

INGRID: _I've lived in San Antonio for 15 years._

OR

I've lived in San Antonio since 1991.

2. (How long / have your M.A. degree)

INTERVIEWER: _How long have your_

INGRID: _until 1995._

3. (have any more training since you got your M.A.)

INTERVIEWER: _Have you had_

INGRID: _American C of S. M_

4. (How long / be a physical education teacher)

INTERVIEWER: _How long have you been a physical education teacher?_

INGRID: _2 years._

5. (How long / work as a sports trainer)

INTERVIEWER: _How long have you worked as a sports trainer?_

INGRID: _14 years_

6. (How long / have a black belt in tae kwon do)

INTERVIEWER: _How long have you had a black belt in tae kwondo?_

INGRID: _2 month_

7. (win any awards since then)

INTERVIEWER: I see you won a medal in skateboarding. _Have you won_

INGRID: _1995_ . I won the Teacher of the Year Award in 1998.

8. (How long / be a member of the NEA)

INTERVIEWER: _How long have you been a_

INGRID: _11 years_

6 | EDITING

*Read these posts to an online skateboard message board. There are ten mistakes in the use of the present perfect with **since** and **for**. The first mistake is already corrected. Find and correct nine more.*

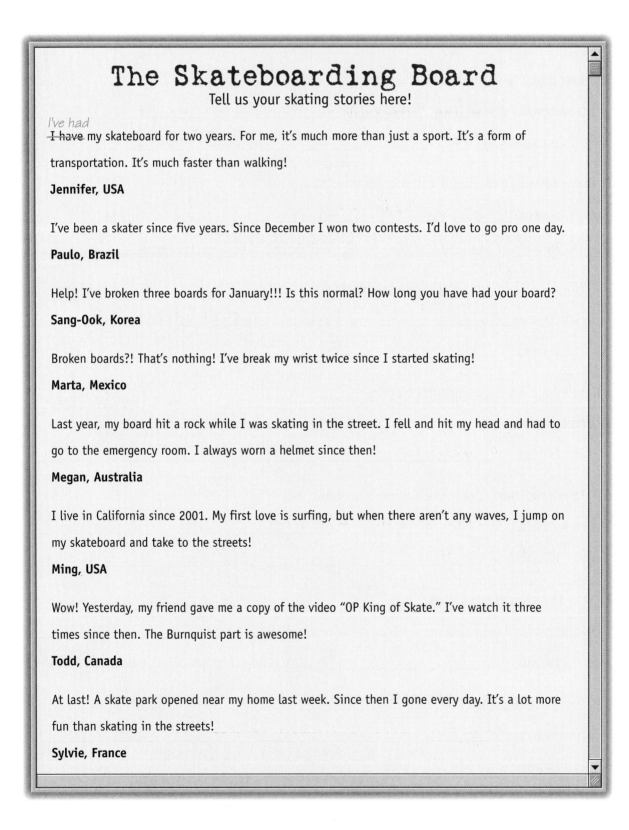

The Skateboarding Board
Tell us your skating stories here!

~~I have~~ *I've had* my skateboard for two years. For me, it's much more than just a sport. It's a form of transportation. It's much faster than walking!

Jennifer, USA

I've been a skater since five years. Since December I won two contests. I'd love to go pro one day.

Paulo, Brazil

Help! I've broken three boards for January!!! Is this normal? How long you have had your board?

Sang-Ook, Korea

Broken boards?! That's nothing! I've break my wrist twice since I started skating!

Marta, Mexico

Last year, my board hit a rock while I was skating in the street. I fell and hit my head and had to go to the emergency room. I always worn a helmet since then!

Megan, Australia

I live in California since 2001. My first love is surfing, but when there aren't any waves, I jump on my skateboard and take to the streets!

Ming, USA

Wow! Yesterday, my friend gave me a copy of the video "OP King of Skate." I've watch it three times since then. The Burnquist part is awesome!

Todd, Canada

At last! A skate park opened near my home last week. Since then I gone every day. It's a lot more fun than skating in the streets!

Sylvie, France

Communication Practice

7 | LISTENING

🎧 *Antonio Serrano is looking for a job as a radio sports announcer. Listen to this interview. Then listen again and complete the interviewer's notes. Use* **since** *and* **for**.

> **WSPR** Radio
> _____
>
> Antonio Serrano   interviewed 9/8
>
> He's been a sports announcer _____*for 20 years*_____.
>   **1.**
>
> He's had two jobs _____.
>   **2.**
>
> He's lived in Los Angeles _____.
>   **3.**
>
> He hasn't worked _____.
>   **4.**
>
> He's been a student at UCLA _____.
>   **5.**

8 | ROLE PLAY: A JOB INTERVIEW

Write a résumé. Use Ingrid's résumé on page 188 as a model. You can use real or imaginary information. Then role-play a job interview with a partner. Take turns being the interviewer and the candidate. Use the script below to help you complete the interview.

Example: A: How long have you been a lab technician?
            B: I've been a lab technician for five years.

INTERVIEWER: How long have you been a(n) _____?

CANDIDATE: I've _____.

INTERVIEWER: And how many jobs have you had since _____?

CANDIDATE: I've _____.

INTERVIEWER: I see from your résumé that you live in _____.
             How long have you lived there?

CANDIDATE: _____.

INTERVIEWER: Your English is quite good. How long have you studied it?

CANDIDATE: _____.

INTERVIEWER: Well, thank you very much. We'll be in touch with you.

9 | THE BEST PERSON FOR THE JOB

*A business college needs a new math teacher. Look at these two résumés. In small groups, decide who to hire and why. Use **since** and **for**.*

Example: **A:** Wu Hao has had the same job since he got his Ph.D.
B: Erika Jones has a lot of experience. She's been a teacher since 1981.

Wu Hao

Education:
1995 Ph.D in Mathematics (UCLA)

Teaching Experience:
1995–present Bryant University

Courses Taught:
Algebra
Trigonometry
Calculus
Business Mathematics

Publications:
"Introducing Computers into the College Math Class" (*The Journal of Mathematics*, 1997)

Awards:
Teacher of the Year, 1997
Distinguished Professor, 2004

Erika Jones

Education:
1981 Ph.D in Mathematics (UCLA)

Teaching Experience:
2001–present	NYC Technical College
1996–2000	UCLA
1987–1995	University of Wisconsin, Madison
1984–1986	Brown University
1981–1983	UCLA

Courses Taught:
Mathematical Analysis 1
Mathematical Analysis 2

Publications:
"Imaginary Numbers" (*MJS*, 1986)
"Number Theory" (*Mathematics*, 1986)
"How Real Are Real Numbers?" (*Math Education*, 1989)

10 | WRITING

*Write a paragraph about someone's accomplishments. It can be someone famous or someone you know. Use the present perfect with **since** or **for**.*

Example: Ingrid has been a high school physical education teacher and a private sports trainer for many years. She has received two awards since 1998, one for teaching and the other for skateboarding. She has been a member of the National Education Association since 1998. Ingrid speaks four languages. She has been a student of martial arts for a long time, and she has had her black belt in tae kwon do for two months.

11 | ON THE INTERNET

Find information online about a current famous professional athlete. How long has that person been professional? How many events has he or she won since 2005? What else has he or she accomplished?

Present Perfect:
Already and *Yet*

BEFORE YOU READ

How do you feel about parties? Which do you prefer: giving a party or going to one? Why? Read the magazine article.

It's Party Time!

It's almost the end of the year, and you**'ve already been** to several parties, but you **haven't given** one **yet**. You're a little nervous, but you decide it's time to take the plunge.

First things first: **Have** you **chosen** the day **yet**? What about the time?

OK. You**'ve already chosen** the day and the time and **sent** the invitations. But you **haven't decided** on the menu **yet**, and now your party is just a week away! Don't panic!

We spoke to Patty Cake, a professional party planner. She says, "It *is* very important to be organized, but remember: You don't need a whole new set of skills. Think about your everyday life. You**'ve already done** many of the things you need to do for a party. You know how to shop for food, put it on plates, and introduce friends to one another. Now, you just need to bring all these skills together."

Still need help? Party planners, like Patty Cake, can offer specific advice. "We**'ve already helped** hundreds of people plan successful parties—big and small. If you **haven't tried** a party-planning service **yet**, you should give it a chance," says Cake. And you don't have to spend a lot of money. Free advice is available on the Internet. There, you will also find handy lists where you can check off things you**'ve already done** (and see the things you **haven't done yet**!). So, take a deep breath, relax, and enjoy the party!

AFTER YOU READ

Reread the first three paragraphs of the article. Check the correct answers.

The person _____.

☐ **1.** went to several parties

☐ **2.** gave a party

☐ **3.** chose a date for the party

☐ **4.** chose the time

☐ **5.** sent invitations

☐ **6.** decided on a menu

Grammar Presentation

PRESENT PERFECT: *ALREADY* AND *YET*

Affirmative Statements: *Already*				
Subject	*Have*	*Already*	**Past Participle**	
They	**have**	*already*	**mailed**	the invitations.
She	**has**		**gotten**	her invitation.

Negative Statements: *Yet*				
Subject	*Have not*	**Past Participle**		*Yet*
They	**haven't**	**mailed**	the invitations	*yet*.
She	**hasn't**	**gotten**	her invitation	

Yes / No Questions: *Yet*				
Have	**Subject**	**Past Participle**		*Yet*
Have	they	**mailed**	the invitations	*yet*?
Has	she	**gotten**	her invitation	

Short Answers				
Affirmative		**Negative**		
Yes,	they **have.**	**No,**	they **haven't.**	
	she **has.**		she **hasn't.**	

GRAMMAR NOTES	EXAMPLES
1. Use the **present perfect** with *already* in <u>affirmative</u> <u>statements</u> to talk about something that has happened before now.	• I've *already* **mailed** the invitations. • Jenna **has** *already* **met** Carlos.
▶ **BE CAREFUL!** We do not usually use past time expressions with the present perfect and *already*.	NOT Jenna has already met Carlos ~~last month~~.

2. *Already* usually goes between *have* and the past participle. *Already* can also go at the end of the clause.	• I've *already* **baked** the cake. OR • I've **baked** the cake *already*.

3. Use the **present perfect** with *yet* in <u>negative</u> <u>statements</u> to talk about something that has not happened before now. It is possible that we expected something to have happened earlier, and it is still possible that it will happen in the future.	• I **haven't cleaned** *yet*. A: Jenna **hasn't called** *yet*. B: Oh, I'm sure we'll hear from her later.

4. *Yet* usually goes at the end of the clause. *Yet* can also go between *have not* and the past participle.	• They **haven't arrived** *yet*. OR • They **haven't** *yet* **arrived**.

5. Use *yet* in <u>questions</u> to ask if something has happened before now. **USAGE NOTE:** We sometimes use *already* in <u>questions</u> to express surprise that something happened sooner than expected.	• **Have** you **bought** the soda *yet*? • **Has** Carlos **arrived** *already*? The party doesn't start until 8:00!

6. For **negative answers** to *yes / no* questions, you can use **haven't** or **not yet**.	A: Has the party started yet? B: No, it **hasn't**. OR No, **not yet**. OR **Not yet**.

Reference Note
For a list of **irregular past participles**, see Appendix 1 on page A-1.

Is he back <u>yet</u> ? → もう帰りましたか?

already → 早くも (thus early) と驚きを示す

Focused Practice

1 | DISCOVER THE GRAMMAR

*Read the first sentence. Then decide if the second sentence is **True (T)** or **False (F)**.*

1. I've already given many parties.

___F___ This will be my first party.

2. I haven't baked the cake yet.

___T___ I plan to bake a cake.

3. Have the guests arrived yet?

F ✓ I'm surprised that the guests are here.

4. Has Jenna left already?

___T___ I'm surprised that Jenna left.

5. Have you had a cup of tea yet?

___T___ I don't know if you had a cup of tea.

6. Carlos has already met my sister.

___F___ I need to introduce Carlos to my sister.

2 | PARTY TALK

Grammar Notes 1–6

*Complete these conversations. Use the present perfect form of the verbs in parentheses with **already** or **yet** and short answers. Use contractions when possible. Go to Appendix 1 on page A-1 for help with irregular verbs.*

1. **A:** This is a great party. _____Have_____ you _____tried_____ the cake _____yet_____?
(try)

   B: _____No_____, I _____haven't_____. But I'm going to have a piece now.

2. **A:** Jenna, I'd like you to meet my friend Carlos.

   B: We _have_ _already_ _met_. Marta introduced us.
(meet)

3. **A:** Would you like another cup of coffee?

   B: No, thanks. I _have_ _already_ _had_ three cups!
(have)

4. **A:** I don't see Jenna. _Has_ she _left_ _yet_? It's still early!
(leave)

   B: _No_, she _hasn't_. She's in the kitchen.

5. **A:** _Have_ you _seen_ Coppola's new movie _yet_?
(see)

   B: _Yes_, I _have_. It's great. What about you?

   A: I _have_ _seen_ it _yet_, but I want to.
(see)

6. **A:** This was a great party. I'm giving my own party next week.

   I _have_ _already_ _planned_ the whole thing, but I'm
(plan)

   still a little nervous about it.

   B: Don't worry. If you do all the planning, the rest will take care of itself!

3 | **FIRST THINGS FIRST**

*Read Fabrizio's party-planning checklist. Write statements about the things that he **has already done** and the things that he **hasn't done yet**. Use contractions when possible. Go to Appendix 1 on page A-1 for help with irregular verbs.*

Things to Do

- ☑ pick a date
- ☐ choose a time
- ☑ find a location
- ☑ write a guest list
- ☑ buy invitations
- ☐ send invitations
- ☐ ask friends to help
- ☐ plan the menu
- ☑ pick out music
- ☐ shop for food
- ☐ clean the house
- ☑ borrow some chairs

1. He's already picked a date.
2. He hasn't chosen a time yet.
3. He's already found.
4. He's already written.
5. He's already bought.
6. He hasn't sent invitations yet.
7. He hasn't ask friends to help yet.
8. He hasn't planned.
9. He's already picked out.
10. He hasn't shopped for food yet.
11. He hasn't cleaned the house yet.
12. He's already borrowed.

4 | EDITING

*Read this online bulletin board. There are nine mistakes in the use of the present perfect with **already** and **yet**. The first mistake is already corrected. Find and correct eight more.*

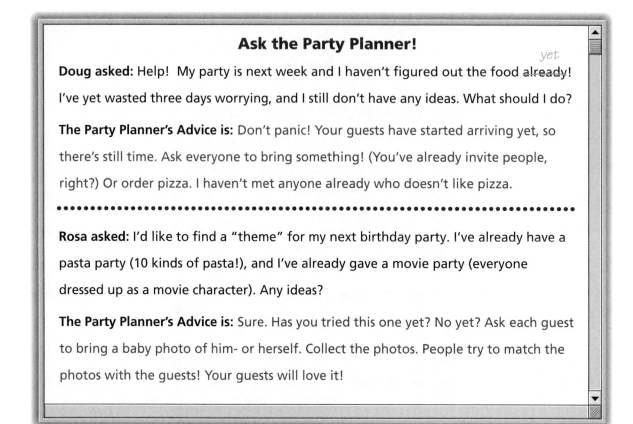

Ask the Party Planner!

                                                                    yet
Doug asked: Help! My party is next week and I haven't figured out the food ~~already~~!
I've yet wasted three days worrying, and I still don't have any ideas. What should I do?

The Party Planner's Advice is: Don't panic! Your guests have started arriving yet, so
there's still time. Ask everyone to bring something! (You've already invite people,
right?) Or order pizza. I haven't met anyone already who doesn't like pizza.

•••

Rosa asked: I'd like to find a "theme" for my next birthday party. I've already have a
pasta party (10 kinds of pasta!), and I've already gave a movie party (everyone
dressed up as a movie character). Any ideas?

The Party Planner's Advice is: Sure. Has you tried this one yet? No yet? Ask each guest
to bring a baby photo of him- or herself. Collect the photos. People try to match the
photos with the guests! Your guests will love it!

Communication Practice

5 | LISTENING

🎧 *Some friends are planning a party. Listen to their conversation. Listen again and check the things they've already done.*

✓ 1. *find a place*
2. *invite people*
3. *borrow extra chairs*
4. *figure out food*
5. *buy soda*
6. *select music*

6 │ INFORMATION GAP: CHORES

Work in pairs (A and B). Student A, follow the instructions on this page. Student B, turn to page 201 and follow the instructions there.

1. Look at the picture of the Meiers' dining room and at Gisela's To Do list. Cross out the chores that Gisela has already done.

2. Answer your partner's questions about Gisela's chores.

   Example: B: Has Gisela vacuumed the carpet yet?
   A: No, she hasn't.   OR   No, not yet.

3. Look at Helmut's To Do list. Ask your partner questions to find out which chores Helmut has already done. Cross out those chores.

   Example: A: Has Helmut bought film yet?
   B: Yes, he has.   OR   Yes, he's already bought film.

To Do–Helmut
buy film
bake the cake
put the turkey in the oven
mop the floor
wash the dishes
cut up the vegetables

To Do—Gisela
vacuum the carpet
buy flowers
wash the windows
set the table
hang the balloons
wrap the gift

Now compare lists with your partner. Are they the same?

7 | WHAT ABOUT YOU?

Write a list of things that you planned or wanted to do by this time (for example, find a new job, paint the apartment). Include things that you have already done and things that you haven't done yet. Exchange lists with a classmate and ask and answer questions about the items on the lists.

Example: A: Have you found a new job yet?
B: No, not yet. I'm still looking.   OR   Yes, I have.

8 | WRITING

Imagine you and a friend are giving a party tonight. Leave a note for your friend to explain what you've already done and what you haven't done yet.

Example: I've already bought the soda, but I haven't gotten the potato chips yet . . .

9 | ON THE INTERNET

*Think of an activity you are planning—a job search, travel, a car purchase, moving, a party. Look for an online To Do list. For example, type in **to do list + job search**. What have you already done? What haven't you done yet? Discuss your list with a partner.*

Example: I'm looking for a job. I've already written a résumé, but I haven't gotten any references yet.

INFORMATION GAP FOR STUDENT B

1. Look at the picture of the Meiers' kitchen and at Helmut's To Do list. Cross out the chores that Helmut has already done.

2. Look at Gisela's To Do list. Ask your partner questions to find out which chores Gisela has already done. Cross out those chores.

   Example: **B:** Has Gisela vacuumed the carpet yet?
   A: No, she hasn't.   OR   No, not yet.

3. Answer your partner's questions about Helmut's chores.

   Example: **A:** Has Helmut bought film yet?
   B: Yes, he has.   OR   Yes, he's already bought film.

To Do—Helmut
~~buy film~~
bake the cake
put the turkey in the oven
mop the floor
wash the dishes
cut up the vegetables

To Do—Gisela
vacuum the carpet
buy flowers
wash the windows
set the table
hang the balloons
wrap the gift

Now compare lists with your partner. Are they the same?

18 | Present Perfect: Indefinite Past

Grammar in Context

BEFORE YOU READ

🎧 *What do you think the article is about? Would you like to do the things in the photos? Why or why not? Read the article.*

Been There? Done That? Maybe it's time for something new ... (or maybe not!)

by Rosa García

Today's world is getting smaller. People are traveling the globe in record numbers. They**'ve been** to Rome. They**'ve seen** the ancient pyramids of Egypt. They**'ve gone** skiing in the Swiss Alps. Now, they're looking for new places to see and new things to do. They want adventure. *Travel Today* **has just come out** with its annual survey. As part of the survey, the magazine asks its readers the following question: "What would you like to do that you**'ve never done** before?"

happen or occur once every year.

Here are some of their answers:

I**'ve made** several trips to Egypt, but I**'ve never ridden** a camel. I'd like to do that some day.

Hot-air ballooning! My boyfriend **has tried** this several times, but I**'ve never done** it.

I**'ve ice skated** and I**'ve climbed** mountains, but I**'ve never been** ice climbing. That's something I'd definitely like to try!

Moving along.
Camel safari in the desert

Up, up, and away!
Hot-air ballooning over Turkey

Work or play?
Ice climbing in the USA

These are just a few activities that travelers can choose from today. All you need is time, money (a lot of it!), and a sense of adventure. But you don't have to go to a faraway place in an unusual type of transportation to have a great vacation! **Have** you **ever spent** the day walking in the woods or **watched** the sun set over the ocean? These can be wonderful adventures too! And a lot more affordable!

Have you ~ yet? → いつもやる時 (朝食等)
Have you ever ~? → 通常ではない (旅とか)

AFTER YOU READ

Which activities have the readers of Travel Today *tried? Check them.*

☐ **1.** skiing in the Alps   ☐ **4.** ice skating

☐ **2.** riding a camel   ☐ **5.** mountain climbing

☐ **3.** hot-air ballooning   ☐ **6.** ice climbing

Grammar Presentation

PRESENT PERFECT: INDEFINITE PAST

Statements			
Subject	*Have (not)*	**Past Participle**	
They	**have (not)**	**visited**	Egypt.
She	**has (not)**	**been**	there.

See page 183 in Unit 16 for a complete presentation of
present perfect forms.

Statements with Adverbs					
Subject	*Have (not)*	**Adverb**	**Past Participle**		**Adverb**
They	**have**	*never* *just* *recently*	**visited**	Egypt.	
She	**has**		**been**	there.	
They	**have (not)**		**visited**	Egypt	*twice.* *lately.* *recently.*
She	**has (not)**		**been**	there	

Yes / No Questions				
Have	**Subject**	*(Ever)*	**Past Participle**	
Have	they	*(ever)*	**visited**	Egypt?
Has	she		**been**	there?

Short Answers				
Affirmative			**Negative**	
Yes,	they **have.**	**No,**	they **haven't.**
	she **has.**		she **hasn't.**

Wh- Questions				
Wh- Word	*Have*	**Subject**	**Past Participle**	
How often	**have**	they	**visited**	Egypt?
	has	she	**been**	there?

GRAMMAR NOTES	EXAMPLES

1. Use the **present perfect** to talk about things that happened at an **indefinite time** in the past.

You can use the present perfect when you <u>don't know</u> when something happened or when the specific time is <u>not important</u>.

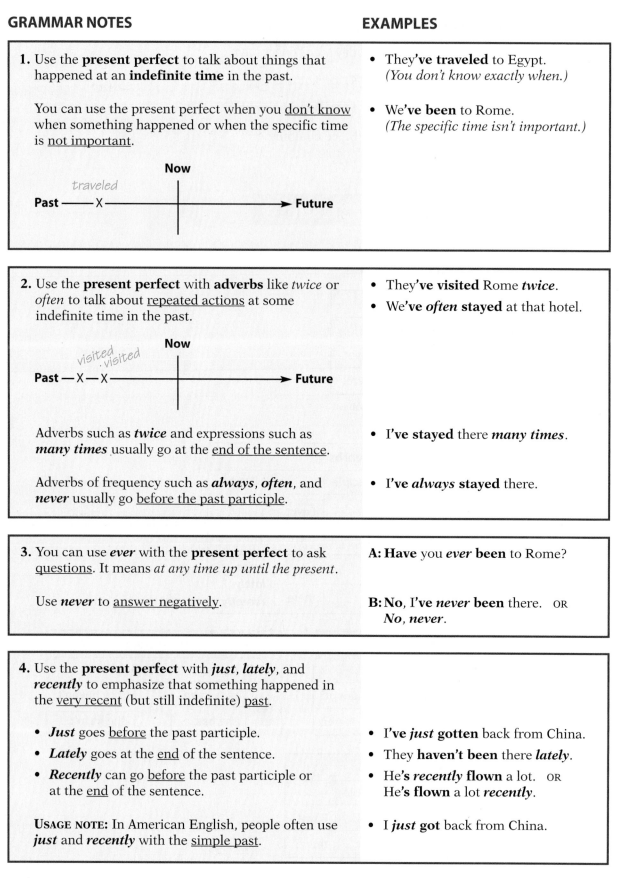

- They**'ve traveled** to Egypt.
  (You don't know exactly when.)

- We**'ve been** to Rome.
  (The specific time isn't important.)

---

2. Use the **present perfect** with **adverbs** like *twice* or *often* to talk about <u>repeated actions</u> at some indefinite time in the past.

- They**'ve visited** Rome *twice*.
- We**'ve** *often* **stayed** at that hotel.

Adverbs such as *twice* and expressions such as *many times* usually go at the <u>end of the sentence</u>.

- I**'ve stayed** there *many times*.

Adverbs of frequency such as *always*, *often*, and *never* usually go <u>before the past participle</u>.

- I**'ve** *always* **stayed** there.

---

3. You can use *ever* with the **present perfect** to ask <u>questions</u>. It means *at any time up until the present*.

Use *never* to <u>answer negatively</u>.

A: Have you *ever* **been** to Rome?

B: No, I**'ve** *never* **been** there.   OR
No, *never*.

---

4. Use the **present perfect** with *just*, *lately*, and *recently* to emphasize that something happened in the <u>very recent</u> (but still indefinite) <u>past</u>.

- *Just* goes <u>before</u> the past participle.
- *Lately* goes at the <u>end</u> of the sentence.
- *Recently* can go <u>before</u> the past participle or at the <u>end</u> of the sentence.

USAGE NOTE: In American English, people often use *just* and *recently* with the <u>simple past</u>.

- I**'ve** *just* **gotten** back from China.
- They **haven't been** there *lately*.
- He**'s** *recently* **flown** a lot.   OR
  He**'s flown** a lot *recently*.

- I *just* **got** back from China.

Reference Note
For a list of **irregular past participles**, see Appendix 1 on page A-1.

Focused Practice

1 | DISCOVER THE GRAMMAR

*Read the first sentence. Then decide if the second sentence is **True (T)** or **False (F)**.*

1. Adventure vacations have become very popular.

_T_   They are popular now.

2. I have never been to the Himalayas.

_F_   I went to the Himalayas a long time ago.

3. I've just returned from China.

_T_   I was in China a short time ago.

4. Greg asks you, "Have you ever been to Costa Rica?"

_F_   Greg wants to know when you were in Costa Rica.

5. Marta asks you, "Have you read any good travel books lately?"

_T_   Marta wants to know about a travel book you read last year.

6. We have visited Egypt several times.

_T_   This is not our first visit to Egypt.

2 | INTERVIEW

Grammar Notes 1–4

🎧 *Complete this interview between* Travel Today **(TT)** *and travel writer Rosa García* **(RG)**.
Use the present perfect form of the verbs in parentheses. Use contractions when possible.

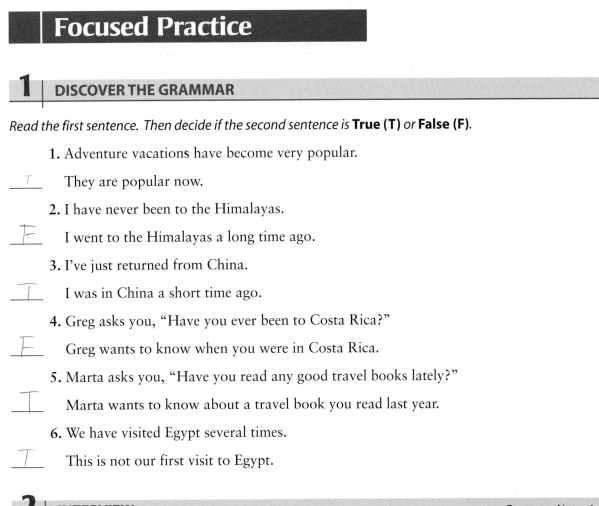

TT: As a travel writer, you _____'ve visited_____ many places. Any favorites?
    1. (visit)

RG: Thailand. It's a beautiful, amazing country. I __have been__ there five times, and I can't
    2. (be)

wait to go back.

TT: What __have you been__ [*has been*] your most unusual travel experience?
    3. (be)

RG: My *most* unusual? I __have had__ so many! I __have swum__ [*swum*] near sharks
    4. (have)   **5. (swim)**

(in a cage, of course!), I __have eaten__ dinner next to an active volcano,
    6. (eat)

I __have slept__ in an ice hotel in Finland . . .
    7. (sleep)

TT: The world __have become__ [*has*] a lot smaller. There are fewer and fewer "undiscovered"
    8. (become)

places. __Have__ you ever __found__ a really great place and decided not to tell
    9. (find)

your readers about it?

(continued)

RG: No. I _have thought_ about doing that a few times, but I _have_ never
10.(think)

kept a place secret. I _have_ always _written_ about it.
11.(keep)   12.(write)

TT: Where _have_ you just _come_ back from?
13.(come)

RG: I _have_ just _returned_ from a hot-air ballooning trip in Australia.
14.(return)

It was really fantastic.

TT: Where are you going next?

RG: On an African safari! I _have_ never _gone_ on one, and I'm really excited.
15.(go)

TT: Good luck! I look forward to your African safari article.

---

3 | SURVEY   *Grammar Note 1*

*Look at the survey. Then write sentences about things Andy **has done** and things he **hasn't done**. Use contractions when possible.*

Travel Time Survey

Name: _Andy Cheng_

Have you ever done the following activities?
Check the ones you have done.

1. rent a car ☐
2. rent a motorcycle ☑
3. ride a camel ☐
4. jump out of an airplane with a parachute ☑
5. go up in a hot-air balloon ☑
6. spend time on a desert island ☐
7. eat some really unusual food ☑
8. take photos of wild animals up close ☐
9. cross the Andes on horseback ☐
10. sail a boat on the Nile River ☑
11. swim with dolphins in the ocean ☑
12. be on a safari ☐
13. fly around the world ☐
14. go on an organized trip ☐

1. *He hasn't rented a car.* OR *He's never rented a car.*

2. *He's rented a motorcycle.*

3. He has ridden a camel.

4. He hasn't jumped out of an airplane with a parachute.

5. He hasn't gone up in a hot-air ballon.

6. He has spent time on a desert island.

7. He hasn't eaten some really unnsual food.

8. He has taken photos of wild animals up close.

9. He has crossed the Andes on horseback.

10. He hasn't sailed a boat on the Nile River.

11. He hasn't swrm with dolphins in the ocean.

12. He has been on a safari.

13. He has flown around the world.

14. He has gone on an organized trip.

4 | FIRST TIME UP

Grammar Notes 1–4

🎧 *Complete this conversation with the words in parentheses and the present perfect form of the verbs. Include short answers. Use contractions when possible.*

EVAN: Hot-air ballooning! What's it like? _I've never done this before_ !
  1. **(I / never / do / this / before)**

ANDY: You'll love it. I've gone up a few times,
  2. **(I / go up)**

  but I haven't done it lately .
  3. **(I / not do / it / lately)**

EVAN: ~~Have you~~ travelled Have you traveled a lot ?
  4. **(you / travel / a lot)**

ANDY: Yes, I have . I'm a travel writer, so it's part of my job.
  5.

EVAN: That's great! Have you ever been on a safari?
  6. **(you / ever / be)**

ANDY: No, I haven't , but I have always wanted to go .
  7.   8. **(I / always / want / to go)**

EVAN: Me too. I've been to Africa several times .
  9. **(I / be / to Africa / several times)**

  In fact, I've just gotton back from a trip there.
  10. **(I / just / get)**

  But I've never been on a safari.
  11. **(I / never / be)**

ANDY: Look. They've just finished getting the balloon ready.
  12. **(They / just / finish)**

  It's time to go up!

5 | SOUVENIRS

Look at some of Rosa's things. Write sentences using the present perfect form of the verbs in the box.

| be | ride | see | stay | travel | write |

1. ___She's been to Egypt twice.___

2. ___She's ridden on the a Camel___

3. ___She's travelled to many countries. with Suitcase___

4. ___She's stayed at Ho TEL Roma___

5. ___She's written several books a book___

6. ___She's seen CATS___

6 | EDITING

Read these comments found on a hot-air ballooning website. There are twelve mistakes in the use of the present perfect and adverbs. The first mistake is already corrected. Find and correct eleven more.

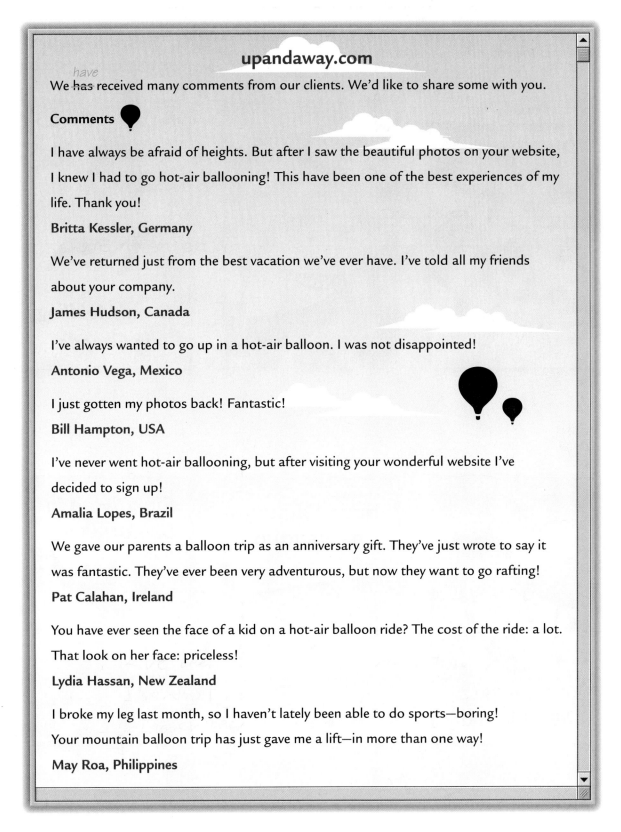

upandaway.com

have
We ~~has~~ received many comments from our clients. We'd like to share some with you.

Comments

I have always be afraid of heights. But after I saw the beautiful photos on your website, I knew I had to go hot-air ballooning! This have been one of the best experiences of my life. Thank you!

Britta Kessler, Germany

We've returned just from the best vacation we've ever have. I've told all my friends about your company.

James Hudson, Canada

I've always wanted to go up in a hot-air balloon. I was not disappointed!

Antonio Vega, Mexico

I just gotten my photos back! Fantastic!

Bill Hampton, USA

I've never went hot-air ballooning, but after visiting your wonderful website I've decided to sign up!

Amalia Lopes, Brazil

We gave our parents a balloon trip as an anniversary gift. They've just wrote to say it was fantastic. They've ever been very adventurous, but now they want to go rafting!

Pat Calahan, Ireland

You have ever seen the face of a kid on a hot-air balloon ride? The cost of the ride: a lot. That look on her face: priceless!

Lydia Hassan, New Zealand

I broke my leg last month, so I haven't lately been able to do sports—boring! Your mountain balloon trip has just gave me a lift—in more than one way!

May Roa, Philippines

Communication Practice

7 | LISTENING

Olivia is talking to a travel agent about different vacation possibilities. Look at the choices below. Listen to the conversation. Then listen again and check the activities she's done before. Then circle the number of the best vacation choice for her.

1. ☑

2. ☐

3. ☐

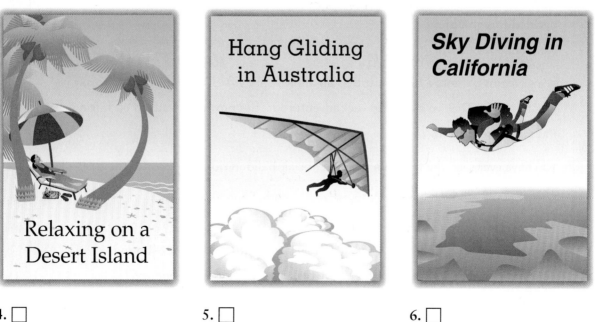

4. ☐

5. ☐

6. ☐

8 | HAVE YOU EVER?

Ask your classmates questions. Find out how many people have ever done any of the following things. Add four more activities. When someone answers yes, ask more questions. Get the stories behind the answers. Share your answers and stories with the class.

- ride a horse
- take a long trip by car
- climb a mountain
- swim in a river
- sail a boat
- go camping
- _____
- _____
- _____
- _____

Example: A: Have you ever ridden a horse?
B: Yes, I have. I was visiting a friend . . .

9 | WRITING

Read this quote. Then write a paragraph that answers the questions below.

"My favorite thing is to go where I've never been."
Diane Arbus (1923–1971, photographer, USA)

What does Arbus mean? Do you feel the same way? Where have you been? Where have you never been that you would like to go?

Example: I've read the quote by Diane Arbus. I think it means . . .

10 | ON THE INTERNET

Do a search on **adventure vacation**. *Describe some of the activities you find. Have you ever done any of them? Would you like to try one? Why or why not?*

Example: I've never been on an African safari, but I'd like to go on one. I love animals . . .

19 Present Perfect and Simple Past

Grammar in Context

BEFORE YOU READ

🎧 *What do you think a "commuter marriage" is? What is happening in the cartoon? How do you think the people feel? Read the excerpt from an article in* Modern Day *magazine.*

LIFESTYLES

Commuter Marriages

Many modern marriages are finding interesting solutions to difficult problems. Take Joe and Maria Tresante, for example. Joe and Maria **married** in June 2000. They **lived** in Detroit for three years. Then in 2003 Joe, a college professor, **got** a great job offer in Los Angeles. At the same time, Maria's company **moved** to Boston. They are still married, but they **have lived** apart ever since. They **have decided** to travel back and forth between Boston and Los Angeles until one of them finds a different job. Sociologists call this kind of marriage a "commuter marriage." "It **hasn't been** easy," says Maria. "Last month I **saw** Joe three times, but this month I**'ve** only **seen** him once."

It also **hasn't been** inexpensive. In addition to the cost of frequent air flights, their phone bills **have gone up**. Last month, they **started** to communicate more by e-mail with the hope of lowering their expenses.

Is all this trouble and expense worth it? "Yes," says the couple. "It **was** a difficult decision, but so far it **has worked out** for us. It's better for us both to have jobs that we like." The Tresantes **have had to** work hard to make their marriage succeed, but the effort **has paid off**. The couple notes, "We**'ve been** geographically separated, but we**'ve grown** closer emotionally."

Boston

L.A.

AFTER YOU READ

Read the statements. Check **True** *or* **False**.

	True	False
1. Joe and Maria used to live in Detroit.	☐	☐
2. They are now living together in Los Angeles.	☐	☐
3. They are happy with their marriage.	☐	☐
4. It costs a lot to live apart.	☐	☐
5. Joe and Maria communicate by e-mail.	☐	☐

Grammar Presentation

PRESENT PERFECT AND SIMPLE PAST

Present Perfect
She **has been** here since 2003.
They**'ve lived** here for 20 years.
We**'ve spoken** once today.
He **hasn't flown** this month.
Has she **called** him today?

Simple Past
She **was** in Detroit in 2000.
They **lived** there for 10 years.
We **spoke** twice yesterday.
She **didn't fly** last month.
Did she **call** him yesterday?

GRAMMAR NOTES

1. Use the **present perfect** to talk about things that started in the past, <u>continue up to the present</u>, and may continue into the future.

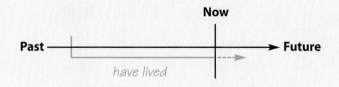

Use the **simple past** to talk about things that happened in the past and have <u>no connection to the present</u>.

EXAMPLES

- They **have lived** apart for the past three years.
  (They started living apart three years ago and are still living apart.)

- They **lived** together in Detroit for three years.
  (They lived in Detroit until 2003. They no longer live in Detroit.)

(continued)

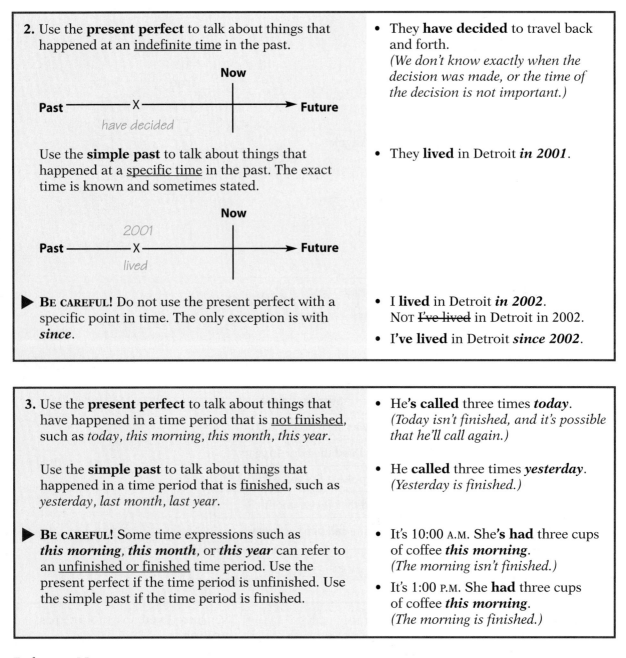

2. Use the **present perfect** to talk about things that happened at an <u>indefinite time</u> in the past.

Now

Past ————X————→ Future

have decided

Use the **simple past** to talk about things that happened at a <u>specific time</u> in the past. The exact time is known and sometimes stated.

Now

2001

Past ————X————→ Future

lived

▶ **BE CAREFUL!** Do not use the present perfect with a specific point in time. The only exception is with *since*.

- They **have decided** to travel back and forth.
  (We don't know exactly when the decision was made, or the time of the decision is not important.)

- They **lived** in Detroit *in 2001*.

- I **lived** in Detroit *in 2002*.
  NOT <s>I've lived</s> in Detroit in 2002.
- **I've lived** in Detroit *since 2002*.

---

3. Use the **present perfect** to talk about things that have happened in a time period that is <u>not finished</u>, such as *today, this morning, this month, this year*.

Use the **simple past** to talk about things that happened in a time period that is <u>finished</u>, such as *yesterday, last month, last year*.

▶ **BE CAREFUL!** Some time expressions such as *this morning*, *this month*, or *this year* can refer to an <u>unfinished or finished</u> time period. Use the present perfect if the time period is unfinished. Use the simple past if the time period is finished.

- He**'s called** three times *today*.
  (Today isn't finished, and it's possible that he'll call again.)

- He **called** three times *yesterday*.
  (Yesterday is finished.)

- It's 10:00 A.M. She**'s had** three cups of coffee *this morning*.
  (The morning isn't finished.)
- It's 1:00 P.M. She **had** three cups of coffee *this morning*.
  (The morning is finished.)

Reference Notes
For the **simple past**, see Unit 3.
For the **present perfect** with *since* and *for*, see Unit 16.
For the **present perfect** for **indefinite past**, see Unit 18.
For a list of **irregular verbs**, see Appendix 1 on page A-1.

Focused Practice

1 | DISCOVER THE GRAMMAR

*Read the information about Joe and Maria. Then circle the letter of the sentence (**a** or **b**) that best describes the situation.*

1. It's 2005. Joe's family moved to Houston in 1995. They still live there.
   a. Joe's family lived in Houston for 10 years.
   (b.) Joe's family has lived in Houston for 10 years.

2. Last year Joe and Maria enjoyed their vacation in Canada.
   (a.) They had a good time.
   b. They've had a good time.

3. Joe is telling his friend about his present job. His friend asks,
   a. "How long were you there?"
   (b.) "How long have you been there?"

4. Joe is telling Maria that the weather in Los Angeles has been too hot for the past five days.
   (a.) The weather is uncomfortable now.
   b. The weather is comfortable now.

5. Joe studied the piano for 10 years, but he doesn't play anymore.
   a. Joe has played the piano for 10 years.
   (b.) Joe played the piano for 10 years.

6. Maria wants to move to Los Angeles from Boston, but she must find a job first. <u>She is interviewing for a job in Los Angeles.</u> She says,
   (a.) "I lived in Boston for two years." → She doesn't get job yet.
   b. "I've lived in Boston for two years."

7. This month Maria and Joe have met once in Boston and once in Los Angeles. <u>They will meet</u> once more in New York.
   Still not a. They've seen each other twice this month.
   (b.) They saw each other twice this month.

8. Maria's mother visited Maria in Boston. When she got home, <u>she wrote,</u>
   a. "It was a great visit." → single past
   (b.) "It has been a great visit."

9. Maria and Joe haven't e-mailed each other this week.
   a. Joe's computer was broken.
   (b.) Joe's computer has been broken.

2 | IT HASN'T BEEN EASY

Grammar Notes 1–3

Complete this entry in Maria's journal. Circle the correct verb forms.

Thursday, September 28

It's 8:00 P.M. It **'s been** / was a hard day, and it's not over yet! I still have to work on that
<u>1.</u>   → *begun is one time.*

report. I **'ve begun** / began it last night, but so far I **'ve written** / wrote only two pages. And it's due
<u>2.</u>   *so X=3*   <u>3.</u>

tomorrow! Work **has been** / was so difficult lately. I **'ve worked** / worked late every night this
<u>4.</u>   <u>5.</u>

week. I feel exhausted and I **haven't gotten** / didn't get much sleep last night. And, of course, I
<u>6.</u>

miss Joe. Even though I **'ve seen** / **saw** him last week, it seems like a long time ago. This commuter
<u>7.</u>

relationship is beginning to get me down. We **'ve lived** / lived apart for too long. Oh, there's the
<u>8.</u>

phone. I hope it's Joe.

3 | PHONE CONVERSATION

Grammar Notes 1–3

🎧 *Complete the phone conversation between Maria and Joe. Use the present perfect or
the simple past form of the verbs in parentheses.*

JOE: Hi, hon! How _____ was _____ your day? I bet you're glad it's over.
                        1. (be)

MARIA: I'm OK—a little tired. I only _____ slept _____ a few hours last night. I'm
                                    2. (sleep)

writing this big report, and I __ haven't stopped __ worrying about it all week.
                                3. (not stop)

JOE: You __ have been __ tired for weeks. You need to relax a little. Listen—
            4. (be)

why don't I come see you this weekend? We __ have seen __ each other
                                            5. (see)

only twice this month.   *this ~ → still unfinish*

MARIA: Sounds great, but remember the last time you __ came __?
                                                    6. (come)

I __ didn't do __ any work, and I still __ haven't caught up __.
   7. (not do)   **8. (not catch up)**

JOE: I understand. Now, why don't you have a cup of coffee and relax?

MARIA: Coffee! You're kidding! I __ have already had __ five cups today. And yesterday
                                9. (already have)

I __ drank __ at least six. I can't drink another drop.
     10. (drink)

JOE: You __ have had __ a rough week. Try to get some sleep.
         11. (have)

MARIA: I can't go to sleep yet. I __ haven't finished __ my report, and it's due tomorrow.
                                12. (not finish)   *you can say " didn't finish"*

JOE: Well, I hope it goes fast. Good night, hon. I'll call you tomorrow.

MARIA: Bye honey. Speak to you tomorrow.

4 | CHANGES

Joe and Maria met in the 1990s. Since then Joe has changed. Use the words below and write down how Joe has changed.

In the 1990s	Since then
1. have / long hair	wear his hair / very short
2. be / clean shaven	grow / a beard
3. be / heavy	lose / weight
4. be / a student	become / a professor
5. live / in a dormitory	buy / a house
6. be / single	get / married

1. *In the 1990s Joe had long hair.*

   Since then, he has worn his hair very short.

2. In the 1990s Joe was clean shaven.
   Since then, he has grown a beard.

3. ~ Joe was heavy.
   ~, he has lost weight.

4. ~ Joe was a student.
   ~ he has become a professor.

5. ~ Joe lived in a dormitory.
   ~, he has bought a house.

6. ~ Joe Joe was single.
   ~, he has gotten married.

5 | AN INTERVIEW

Read the magazine article on page 212 again. Imagine that you wrote the article. You asked Joe and Maria questions to get your information. What were they? Use the words in parentheses and write the questions.

1. (How long / be married)

   How long have you been married?

2. (How long / live in Detroit)

(continued)

3. (When / get a job offer)

_____

4. (When / your company move)

_____

5. (How long / live apart)

_____

6. (How often / see each other last month)

_____

7. (How often / see each other this month)

_____

8. (When / start to communicate by e-mail)

_____

6 | EDITING

Read this entry from Maria's journal. There are eight mistakes in the use of the present perfect and the simple past. The first mistake is already corrected. Find and correct seven more.

> I've just finished reading a fascinating article about Felicia Mabuza-Suttle.
>
> _I've read_
> Actually, ~~I read~~ several articles about her this year. She's a very famous
> international businesswoman and talk-show host in South Africa. Guess what! We
> have something in common! She and her husband had a "commuter marriage" for
> more than 15 years, and they are still happily married! She lives in Johannesburg,
> South Africa; he lives in Atlanta, Georgia. That's a whole ocean apart! They have
> met in the 1970s. In the first 10 years of their marriage they have lived in more
> than 10 cities. Then, in the early 1990s she has returned to South Africa to help
> her country. It wasn't an easy life, but they both feel it's been very worthwhile.
>
> Their situation makes our problems seem not that bad. Joe and I are only
> 3,000 miles apart, and we have managed to see each other a lot since we left
> Detroit. But, to be honest, I have been happier when we have lived together in
> Detroit. I hope we can live together again someday soon.

Communication Practice

7 | LISTENING

🎧 *A school newspaper is interviewing two college professors. Listen to the interview. Then listen again and check the items that are now true.*

The professors _____.

☑ **1.** are married

☐ **2.** live in different cities

☐ **3.** are at the same university

☐ **4.** live in Boston

☐ **5.** are in Austin

☐ **6.** have a house

8 | SOME NUMBERS

Look at the chart. Work in pairs and discuss the information. Use the words in the box.

↑ increase	↓ decrease
get higher	get lower
go up	go down

Marriage Statistics for the United States				
	1980	**1990**	**1995**	**2000**
Number of marriages	2,406,700	2,448,000	2,336,000	2,329,000
Number of divorces	1,182,000	1,175,000	1,169,000	1,155,000
Percentage of men (20–24) never married	68.8%	79.7%	80.7%	83.7%
Percentage of women (20–24) never married	50.2%	64.1%	66.7%	72.8%
Average age of first marriage: men women	24.7 22.0	26.1 23.9	26.9 24.5	26.8 25.1

Example: **A:** The number of marriages has decreased since 1980.
B: That's right. In 1980 there were 2,406,700 marriages. And in 2000 there were 2,329,000.

9 | A COUNTRY YOU KNOW WELL

Work in small groups. Tell your classmates about some changes in a country you know well.

Example: In 2004, a new president took office. Since then, the economy has improved.

10 | LOOKING BACK

Work in pairs. Look at Maria's records from last year and this year. It's now the end of August. Compare what Maria did last year with what she's done this year.

LAST YEAR					
January	**February**	**March**	**April**	**May**	**June**
• business trip to N.Y. • L.A. – 2X	• L.A. – 2X • 1 seminar	• business trip to N.Y. • L.A. – 1X	• L.A. – 3X • 1 lecture	• 10 vacation days • Jay's wedding	• 2 seminars • L.A. – 2X
July	**August**	**September**	**October**	**November**	**December**
• L.A. – 1X • Sue's wedding	• L.A. – 1X	• L.A. – 2X • 1 lecture	• business trip to Little Rock	• 1 seminar	• 10 vacation days

THIS YEAR					
January	**February**	**March**	**April**	**May**	**June**
• L.A. – 1X	• business trip to N.Y. • 1 lecture	• L.A. – 1X • Nan's wedding	• L.A. – 1X	• business trip to Miami • L.A. – 1X	• 5 vacation days • 1 seminar
July	**August**	**September**	**October**	**November**	**December**
• Barry's wedding	• L.A. – 1X • 1 lecture				

Example: A: Last year she went on three business trips.
B: So far this year she's only gone on two.

11 | WRITING

How has your family changed in the last five years? Write a paragraph about some of the changes. Use the present perfect and the simple past.

Example: Five years ago, all my brothers and sisters lived at home. Since then, we have all moved away . . .

12 | ON THE INTERNET

Do a search on **Felicia Mabuza-Suttle***. What has she accomplished? What degrees has she gotten? What awards has she received? When did she receive them? Write about her. Use the present perfect and the simple past.*

Example: Felicia Mabuza-Suttle has been a talk-show host in South Africa for many years . . .

Grammar in Context

BEFORE YOU READ

🎧 *Look at the key facts about African elephants. Why do you think the elephant population has changed so much? Look at the map of Africa. What parts of Africa have elephants? Professor Jane Owen has been studying elephants for several decades. Read the excerpt from her latest article in* Science Today.

AFRICAN ELEPHANTS

Jane Owen, Ph.D.

AFRICA

HABITAT

Elephants and their ancestors **have been living** on this planet for 5 million years. Scientists **have found** their bones in many places, including Europe and the Americas. Present-day African elephants **have** also **survived** in different kinds of environments, including very dry areas in Niger, grasslands in East Africa, and forests in West Africa.

KEY FACTS

Largest Size

Height: 13 feet	**Trunk:** 40 pounds
Length: 25 feet	**Tusks:** 11 feet
Weight: 8 tons	**Tail:** 4 feet

Life Span
60–65 years

Estimated Population

1979: 1,300,000	**1997:** 650,000
1989: 600,000	**2003:** 435,000

ELEPHANTS AND HUMANS

Because of their great size and strength, elephants **have** always **fascinated** humans. Our fascination **has caused** African elephants to become almost extinct. Poachers (illegal hunters) **have killed** hundreds of thousands of elephants for the ivory of their tusks. After 1989 it became illegal to sell ivory. The elephant population grew after that, but recently it **has been dropping** again. According to recent reports, many governments **have lost** control of poachers. At present, there may be only 400,000 African elephants left.

AFTER YOU READ

Read the statements. Check **True** *or* **False**.

	True	False
1. There were elephants on Earth 5 million years ago.	☐	☐
2. All elephants live in grasslands.	☐	☐
3. Poachers killed hundreds of thousands of elephants before 1989.	☐	☐
4. The number of elephants is increasing.	☐	☐

Grammar Presentation

PRESENT PERFECT PROGRESSIVE AND PRESENT PERFECT

PRESENT PERFECT PROGRESSIVE

Statements				
Subject	*Have* (**not**)	*Been*	Base Form of Verb + *-ing*	(*Since / For*)
I You* We They	**have** (**not**)	**been**	**writing**	(**since** 2004). (**for** years).
He She It	**has** (**not**)			

* *You* is both singular and plural.

Yes / No Questions				
Have	Subject	*Been*	Base Form of Verb + *-ing*	(*Since / For*)
Have	you	**been**	**writing**	(**since** 2004)? (**for** years)?
Has	he			

Short Answers						
Affirmative			Negative			
Yes,	I / we	**have.**	**No,**	I / we	**haven't.**
	he	**has.**		he	**hasn't.**

Wh- Questions				
Wh- Word	*Have*	Subject	*Been*	Base Form of Verb + *-ing*
How long	**have**	you	**been**	**writing**?
	has	he		

(continued)

PRESENT PERFECT PROGRESSIVE AND PRESENT PERFECT

Present Perfect Progressive
They **have been living** here for 5 million years.
I**'ve been reading** this book since Monday.
Dr. Owen **has been writing** articles since 1990.
She**'s been working** in Niger for a year.

Present Perfect
They **have lived** here for 5 million years.
I**'ve read** two books about elephants.
Dr. Owen **has written** many articles.
She**'s worked** in many countries.

GRAMMAR NOTES

EXAMPLES

1. The **present perfect progressive** often shows that something is <u>unfinished</u>. It started in the past and is still continuing. The emphasis is on the <u>continuation</u> of the action.

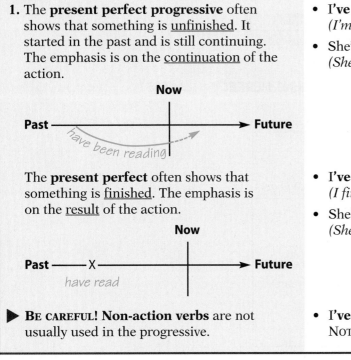

The **present perfect** often shows that something is <u>finished</u>. The emphasis is on the <u>result</u> of the action.

▶ **BE CAREFUL! Non-action verbs** are not usually used in the progressive.

- I**'ve been reading** a book about elephants. *(I'm still reading it.)*
- She**'s been writing** an article. *(She's still writing it.)*

- I**'ve read** a book about elephants. *(I finished the book.)*
- She**'s written** an article. *(She finished the article.)*

- I**'ve had** a headache all day. NOT I~~'ve been having~~ a headache all day.

2. We often use the **present perfect progressive** to talk about <u>how long</u> something has been happening.

We often use the **present perfect** to talk about:

- <u>how much</u> someone has done

- <u>how many things</u> someone has done

- <u>how many times</u> someone has done something

- I**'ve been reading** books about elephants *for two months*.

- I**'ve read** *a lot* about it.

- She**'s written** *three* articles.

- I**'ve read** that book *twice*.

3. Sometimes you can use either the **present perfect progressive** or the **present perfect**. The meaning is basically the same. This is especially true with verbs such as *live*, *study*, *teach*, and *work* with *for* or *since*.

- She**'s been studying** African elephants *for* three years.

  OR

- She**'s studied** African elephants *for* three years.
  (In both cases, she is still studying them.)

USAGE NOTES

We often use the **present perfect progressive** to show that something is <u>temporary</u>.

We use the **present perfect** to show that something is <u>permanent</u>.

- They**'ve been living** here *since* 1995, but they are moving next month.

- They**'ve lived** here *since* they were children. They've always lived here.

Reference Notes
For a list of **non-action verbs**, see Appendix 2 on page A-2.
For use of the **present perfect** with *since* and *for*, see Unit 16 on page 184.

Focused Practice

1 | DISCOVER THE GRAMMAR

Read the first sentence. Then decide if the second sentence is **True (T)** *or* **False (F)**.

1. Professor Owen has been reading a book about African wildlife.

_F_   She finished the book.

2. She's read a book about African wildlife.

_T_   She finished the book.

3. She's written a magazine article about the rain forest.

_T_   She finished the article.

4. She's been waiting for some supplies.

_F_   She received the supplies.

5. They've lived in Uganda since 1992.

_T/F_   They are still in Uganda.

6. They've been living in Uganda since 1992.

_T_   They are still in Uganda.

7. We've been discussing environmental problems with the leaders of many countries.

_F_   The discussions are probably over.

8. We've discussed these problems with many leaders.

_T_   The discussions are probably over.

[Handwritten notes:] They lived in Uganda for 5 years. They have live in Uganda for 5 years. They have been living in Uganda for 5 years.

one time → have ~

2 | PROFESSOR OWEN'S WORK

Grammar Notes 1–3

Complete these statements. Circle the correct form of the verbs. In some cases, both forms are correct.

1. Professor Owen is working on two articles for the next issue of *National Wildlife* magazine. She has written / (has been writing) these articles since Monday.

2. *National Wildlife* magazine has published / has been publishing its annual report on the environment. It is an excellent report.

3. More than 500 African elephants have already died / have been dying this year.

4. Professor Owen has given / has been giving many talks about elephants in past lecture series.

5. She has spoken / has been speaking at our school many times.

6. Congress has created / has been creating a new study group to discuss the problem of endangered animals. The group has already met twice.

7. The new group has a lot of work to do. Lately, the members have studied / have been studying the problem of the spotted owl.

8. Professor Owen was late for a meeting with the members of Congress. When she arrived the chairperson said, "At last, you're here. We have waited / have been waiting for you."

9. Professor Owen has lived / has been living in Kenya for the last two years, but she will return to the United States in January.

10. She has worked / has been working with environmentalists in Kenya and Tanzania.

3 | WHAT'S BEEN HAPPENING?

Grammar Note 1

Compare these two pictures of Professor Jane Owen.

noun action can't use progressive.

Complete the sentences describing what is going on in the pictures. Use the present perfect progressive form of the verbs in parentheses. Choose between affirmative and negative forms.

1. She __'s been working__ in her office.
   (work)
2. She __has been following__ an elephant in the field.
   (follow)
3. She __has been writing__ an article.
   (write)
4. She __hasn't been reading__ the newspaper.
   (read)
5. She __has been drinking__ coffee.
   (drink)
6. She __hasn't been drinking__ tea.
   (drink)
7. She __hasn't been eating__ her sandwich.
   (eat)
8. She __hasn't been watching__ TV.
   (watch)
9. She __has been working__ hard.
   (work)
10. It __has been raining__ all day.
    (rain)

4 | GRANDDAD

Grammar Notes 1–3

Complete this entry from Professor Owen's field journal. Use the present perfect progressive or the present perfect form of the verbs in parentheses.

We __'ve been hearing__ about Granddad since we arrived here in Amboseli Park.
     1. (hear)

He is one of the last "tuskers." Two days ago, we finally saw him. His tusks are more than seven

feet long. I __have__ never __seen__ anything like them.
                          2. (see)

Granddad __has lived__ [has been living] here for more than 60 years. He
          3. (live)

__has experienced__ everything, and he __has been surviving__ [has survived] countless threats from
   4. (experience)   5. (survive)

human beings. Young men __has been testing__ [have tested] their courage against him, and poachers
                          6. (test)

__have been hunting__ [have hunted] him for his ivory. His experience and courage
   7. (hunt)

__has been saving__ [have saved] him so far.
   8. (save)

For the last two days, Granddad __has moved__ [has been moving] slowly through the tall grass.
                                   9. (move)

He __has ate__ and __rested__ [resting] [has been eating]. Luckily, it __has rained__
      10. (eat)   11. (rest)   12. (rain)

a lot this year, and even the biggest elephants __have found__ enough food and water.
                                                13. (find)

Watching this elephant __has been being__ an incredible experience. I hope he is still
                        14. (be)

here when we come back next year!

5 | HOW LONG AND HOW MUCH?

Grammar Note 2

Professor Owen is doing fieldwork in Africa. Imagine you are about to interview her. Use the words below to ask her questions. Use her notes to complete her answers. Choose between the present perfect progressive and the present perfect.

FIELD NOTES
3/23/05

GRANDDAD
  Order: *Proboscidea*
  Family: *Elephantidae*
  Genus and Species: *Loxodonta africana*

• eats about 500 pounds of vegetation/day
• drinks about 40 gallons of water at a time
• walks 5 miles/hour (50 miles/day)

1. (How long / you / observe / Granddad)

   YOU: *How long have you been observing Granddad?* _____

   OWEN: *I've been observing him for* _____ two days.

2. (How much vegetation / he / eat)

   YOU: _____

   OWEN: _____

3. (How often / he / stop for water)

   YOU: _____

   OWEN: _____ four times.

4. (How much water / he / drink)

   YOU: _____

   OWEN: _____

5. (How long / he / walk today)

   YOU: _____

   OWEN: _____ nine hours.

6. (How far / he / travel today)

   YOU: _____

   OWEN: _____

6 | EDITING

Read this student's journal entry. There are eight mistakes in the use of the present perfect progressive and the present perfect. The first mistake is already corrected. Find and correct seven more.

IE T

> studying
> This year in class we've been ~~studied~~ endangered species.
> studied
> We've already ~~been~~ studying the panda and the tiger. Now
> have
> we're learning about the African elephant. Elephants ~~has~~ been
> roaming the Earth for millions of years! I have to write a
> been researching
> research paper on the topic. I've ~~researched~~ it on the Web
> been finishing
> since Monday. It's now Friday, and I haven't ~~finished~~ yet.
> read
> There's so much information! I've already ~~been reading~~ more
> ordering
> than ten articles, and I've even been ~~ordered~~ a book about
> endangered species. I really find this topic interesting, and I've
> learned
> been ~~learning~~ a lot! The paper has to be ten pages long. So far,
> m written
> I've ~~been writing~~ about five pages. I've been thinking about a
> title for my paper, but I haven't been deciding on one yet.
> ?

Communication Practice

7 | LISTENING

🎧 *Listen to the conversations. Then listen again and circle the letter of the pictures that illustrate the situations.*

1.

a.

b.

(continued)

2. a. b.

3. a. b.

4. a. b.

5. a. b.

8 | THINGS CHANGE

*Have a class discussion. Talk about things that have changed or have been changing in
your city or town. Use the present perfect progressive and the present perfect.*

Example: **A:** Traffic has been getting worse. I've been spending a lot more time driving to class.
B: Me too. I think more and more people have been driving to work.

9 | ON THE INTERNET

 These two animals have been on the World Wildlife Fund's list of the ten most endangered species. Do a search on one of them.

Arabian oryx

Monarch butterfly

Find out about its . . .

- geographic location (habitat)
- size
- habits

Learn . . .

- why it has become endangered
- what governments or other groups have been doing to save it

Now get together in small groups and discuss your findings.

10 | WRITING

Write a paragraph about one of the animals discussed in this unit. Use the topics from Exercise 9 to guide your writing.

Example: The Arabian oryx is about three feet tall. Its horns are . . .
It has become endangered because . . .

From **Grammar** to **Writing**
The Topic Sentence and Paragraph Unity

A paragraph is a group of sentences about one main idea. Writers often state the main idea in one sentence, called the topic sentence. The topic sentence is often near the beginning of the paragraph.

1 | *Read this personal statement for a job application. First cross out any sentences that do not belong in the paragraph. (Later you will choose a topic sentence.)*

Please describe your work experience.

<u>   </u>
(topic sentence)

While I was in high school, I worked as a server at Darby's during the summer and on weekends. ~~Summers here are very hot and humid.~~ I worked with many different kinds of customers, and I learned to be polite even with difficult people. They serve excellent food at Darby's. I received a promotion after one year. Since high school, I have been working for Steak Hut as the night manager. I have developed management skills because I supervise six employees. One of them is a good friend of mine. I have also learned to order supplies and to plan menus. Sometimes I am very tired after a night's work.

Now choose one of the sentences below as the topic sentence, and write it as the first sentence of the paragraph.

- I feel that a high school education is necessary for anyone looking for a job.

- My restaurant experience has prepared me for a position with your company.

- Eating at both Darby's and Steak Hut in Greenville is very enjoyable.

- I prefer planning menus to any other task in the restaurant business.

2 | *You can use a tree diagram to develop and organize your ideas. Complete the tree diagram for the paragraph in Exercise 1.*

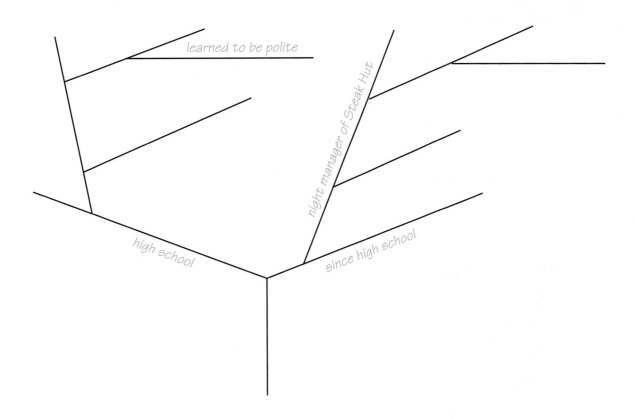

3 | *Before you write . . .*

1. On a separate piece of paper, make a tree diagram for your accomplishments. Do not include a topic sentence.

2. Work with a small group. Look at each other's diagrams and develop a topic sentence for each one.

3. Ask and answer questions to develop more information about your accomplishments.

4 | *Write a personal statement about your accomplishments. Use your tree diagram as an outline.*

IV Review Test

I *Complete the following conversations. Use the present perfect form of the verbs in parentheses.*

1. **A:** I've just decided to give a big New Year's party.

   B: _____*Have*_____ you ever _____*given*_____ a big party before?
   (give)

   A: Nope. This will be my first.

2. **A:** How long _____ you _____ a party planner?
   (be)

   B: A long time. I started helping my friends plan their parties in college.

3. **A:** Marla _____ just _____ back from vacation.
   (get)

   B: Really? Where did she go this time?

4. **A:** It's time to pay the bills.

   B: They're not as bad as they look. I _____ already _____
   (pay)
   the phone bill.

5. **A:** _____ you ever _____ a letter of complaint?
   (write)

   B: Yes, I have. I got great results.

6. **A:** Can I throw this magazine out?

   B: Not yet. Jennifer _____ it yet.
   (not read)

7. **A:** How many skating contests _____ you _____?
   (win)

   B: A lot. I've stopped counting.

8. **A:** What have you told the kids about our holiday plans?

   B: I _____ them anything yet. Let's wait until our plans are definite.
   (not tell)

9. **A:** _____ the letter carrier _____ yet?
   (come)

   B: Yes, he has. About an hour ago. You got two letters.

10. **A:** Would you like some coffee?

    B: No, thanks. I _____ three cups already.
    (have)

11. **A:** _____ you _____ a topic for your research paper?
    (choose)

    B: Yes. I'm going to write about Asian elephants.

II *Complete the conversations with* **since** *or* **for**.

1. **A:** What happened? I've been waiting for you _____*since*_____ 7:00.

    B: My train broke down. I sat in the tunnel for an hour.

2. **A:** How long have you lived in San Francisco?

    B: _____ I was born. How about you?

    A: I've only been here _____ a few months.

3. **A:** When did you and Alan meet?

    B: I've known Alan _____ ages. We went to elementary school together.

4. **A:** Has Greg worked at Café Fidelio for a long time?

    B: Not too long. He's only been there _____ 2004.

5. **A:** Why didn't you answer the door? I've been standing here ringing the doorbell _____ five minutes.

    B: I didn't hear you. I was taking a shower.

6. **A:** How long have you had trouble sleeping, Mr. Yang?

    B: _____ March. It started when I moved.

7. **A:** Celia has been studying English _____ she was 10.

    B: That's why she speaks so well.

8. **A:** Did you know that Gary plans to change jobs?

    B: He's been saying that _____ the past two years. He never does anything about it.

III *Each sentence has four underlined words or phrases. The four underlined parts of the sentences are marked A, B, C, or D. Circle the letter of the <u>one</u> underlined word or phrase that is NOT CORRECT.*

1. I <u>'ve wanted</u> to visit Bali <u>since</u> years, but I <u>haven't been</u> there <u>yet</u>.   **A** **(B)** **C** **D**
         A   **B**   **C**   **D**

2. We <u>went</u> there last year <u>after</u> we <u>have</u> <u>visited</u> Japan.   **A** **B** **C** **D**
         A   **B**   **C** **D**

3. <u>Have</u> you <u>been</u> <u>living</u> in California <u>since</u> a long time?   **A** **B** **C** **D**
     A   **B**   **C**   **D**

4. I <u>lived</u> here <u>since</u> I <u>got</u> married <u>in</u> 1998.   **A** **B** **C** **D**
      A   **B**   **C**   **D**

(continued)

5. We 've been wait for Chen for an hour, but he hasn't arrived yet.   **A B C D**
    A   B   C   D

6. Todd is excited right now because he's lately won an award.   **A B C D**
    A   B   C D

7. It's only 9:00, and she already had four cups of tea this morning.   **A B C D**
    A   B   C   D

8. I 'm watching television for the last three hours and now I feel   **A B C D**
       A   B   C   D
worried about that test tomorrow.

9. Paz been working for Intellect since he moved to Silicon Valley.   **A B C D**
     A   B   C   D

10. Has he moved here a long time ago, or has he just arrived?   **A B C D**
     A   B   C   D

IV *Circle the letter of the correct answer to complete each sentence.*

1. _____ you ever appeared on a game show, Mr. Smith?   **A B Ⓒ D**

    (**A**) Did   (**C**) Have

    (**B**) Has   (**D**) Was

2. No, but I've _____ wanted to.   **A B C D**

    (**A**) ever   (**C**) don't

    (**B**) yet   (**D**) always

3. Why _____ you decide to try out for *Risk*?   **A B C D**

    (**A**) did   (**C**) have

    (**B**) were   (**D**) are

4. My wife _____ your show for years now.   **A B C D**

    (**A**) watches   (**C**) was watching

    (**B**) is watching   (**D**) has been watching

5. She has always _____ I should apply as a contestant.   **A B C D**

    (**A**) saying   (**C**) said

    (**B**) says   (**D**) say

6. You're a librarian. How long _____ that kind of work?   **A B C D**

    (**A**) did you do   (**C**) do you do

    (**B**) have you done   (**D**) were you doing

7. I've been a reference librarian since _____. **A B C D**

    (**A**) a long time   (**C**) 1998

    (**B**) three years   (**D**) I've graduated

8. Have you been interested in game shows since you _____ a librarian?   **A B C D**

    (**A**) became   (**C**) become

    (**B**) have become   (**D**) have been becoming

9. I've only _____ them for about a year.   **A B C D**

    (**A**) watching   (**C**) been watching

    (**B**) watch   (**D**) watches

10. Have you been studying the rules for the show _____ we called?   **A B C D**

    (**A**) for   (**C**) since

    (**B**) when   (**D**) as soon as

11. I _____ them for weeks, but I still don't understand them.   **A B C D**

    (**A**) read   (**C**) was reading

    (**B**) reading   (**D**) 've been reading

V   *Complete each conversation with the correct form of the verb in parentheses. Choose between affirmative and negative forms.*

1. (see)

    A: _____*Have*_____ you _____*seen*_____ *Day After Tomorrow* yet?
                                a.

    B: Yes, I have. I _____ it last night.
                     b.

2. (drink)

    A: Who _____ all the soda? We needed it for the party.
              a.

    B: Not me. I _____ any soda at all since last week. I _____
                     b.   **c.**
    water all week. It's much healthier.

3. (write)

    A: Susan Jackson _____ a lot of travel books lately.
                        a.

    B: _____ she _____ *Rafting in Costa Rica*?
                                    b.

    A: Yes, she did. She _____ that one about five years ago.
                           c.

(continued)

4. (cook)

   A: You _____ for hours. When are we eating dinner?

a.

   B: I just finished. I _____ something special for you. It's called

b.
   "ants on a tree."

   A: Gross!

   B: I _____ it for you many times before. It's just meatballs with rice.

c.

5. (have)

   A: I _____ a lot of trouble with my new car lately.

a.

   B: Really? You _____ it very long!

b.

   A: I know. I _____ it for only a year. I _____ my old car

c.   d.
   for 10 years before I sold it. I _____ any trouble with it at all!

e.

6. (look)

   A: Linda _____ really discouraged yesterday afternoon.

a.

   B: I know. She _____ for an apartment and hasn't found anything yet.

b.

   A: There's an apartment available on the fourth floor in our building.

   _____ she _____ at it?

                               c.

   B: She _____ at it last week, but she didn't rent it because it's too small.

d.

VI *Find and correct the mistake in each sentence.*

have
1. I ~~am~~ applied for the position of junior accountant in my department.

2. I have been working as a bookkeeper in this company since four yours.

3. I have did a good job.

4. I have already been getting a promotion.

5. I has gained a lot of experience in retail sales.

6. In addition, I have took several accounting courses.

7. Since February my boss liked my work a lot.

8. She has gave me more and more responsibility.

9. I have already show my accounting skills.

10. This has been being a very good experience for me.

▶ *To check your answers, go to the Answer Key on page RT-3.*

APPENDICES

1 | Irregular Verbs

Base Form	Simple Past	Past Participle
arise	arose	arisen
awake	awoke	awoken
be	was/were	been
beat	beat	beaten/beat
become	became	become
begin	began	begun
bend	bent	bent
bet	bet	bet
bite	bit	bitten
bleed	bled	bled
blow	blew	blown
break	broke	broken
bring	brought	brought
build	built	built
burn	burned/burnt	burned/burnt
burst	burst	burst
buy	bought	bought
catch	caught	caught
choose	chose	chosen
cling	clung	clung
come	came	come
cost	cost	cost
creep	crept	crept
cut	cut	cut
deal	dealt	dealt
dig	dug	dug
dive	dived/dove	dived
do	did	done
draw	drew	drawn
dream	dreamed/dreamt	dreamed/dreamt
drink	drank	drunk
drive	drove	driven
eat	ate	eaten
fall	fell	fallen
feed	fed	fed
feel	felt	felt
fight	fought	fought
find	found	found
fit	fit/fitted	fit
flee	fled	fled
fling	flung	flung
fly	flew	flown
forbid	forbade/forbid	forbidden
forget	forgot	forgotten
forgive	forgave	forgiven
freeze	froze	frozen
get	got	gotten/got

Base Form	Simple Past	Past Participle
give	gave	given
go	went	gone
grind	ground	ground
grow	grew	grown
hang	hung	hung
have	had	had
hear	heard	heard
hide	hid	hidden
hit	hit	hit
hold	held	held
hurt	hurt	hurt
keep	kept	kept
kneel	knelt/kneeled	knelt/kneeled
knit	knit/knitted	knit/knitted
know	knew	known
lay	laid	laid
lead	led	led
leap	leaped/leapt	leaped/leapt
leave	left	left
lend	lent	lent
let	let	let
lie *(lie down)*	lay	lain
light	lit/lighted	lit/lighted
lose	lost	lost
make	made	made
mean	meant	meant
meet	met	met
pay	paid	paid
prove	proved	proved/proven
put	put	put
quit	quit	quit
read /rid/	read /rɛd/	read /rɛd/
ride	rode	ridden
ring	rang	rung
rise	rose	risen
run	ran	run
say	said	said
see	saw	seen
seek	sought	sought
sell	sold	sold
send	sent	sent
set	set	set
sew	sewed	sewn/sewed
shake	shook	shaken
shave	shaved	shaved/shaven
shine *(intransitive)*	shone/shined	shone/shined
shoot	shot	shot

(continued)

Base Form	Simple Past	Past Participle
show	showed	shown
shrink	shrank/shrunk	shrunk/shrunken
shut	shut	shut
sing	sang	sung
sink	sank/sunk	sunk
sit	sat	sat
sleep	slept	slept
slide	slid	slid
speak	spoke	spoken
speed	sped/speeded	sped/speeded
spend	spent	spent
spill	spilled/spilt	spilled/spilt
spin	spun	spun
spit	spit/spat	spat
split	split	split
spread	spread	spread
spring	sprang	sprung
stand	stood	stood
steal	stole	stolen
stick	stuck	stuck
sting	stung	stung
stink	stank/stunk	stunk

Base Form	Simple Past	Past Participle
strike	struck	struck/stricken
swear	swore	sworn
sweep	swept	swept
swim	swam	swum
swing	swung	swung
take	took	taken
teach	taught	taught
tear	tore	torn
tell	told	told
think	thought	thought
throw	threw	thrown
understand	understood	understood
upset	upset	upset
wake	woke	woken
wear	wore	worn
weave	wove/weaved	woven/weaved
weep	wept	wept
win	won	won
wind	wound	wound
withdraw	withdrew	withdrawn
wring	wrung	wrung
write	wrote	written

2 | Non-action Verbs

Appearance	Emotions	Mental States		Possession and Relationship	Senses and Perceptions	Wants and Preferences
appear	admire	agree	know	belong	feel	desire
be	adore	assume	mean	contain	hear	hope
look (seem)	appreciate	believe	mind	have	notice	need
represent	care	consider	presume	own	observe	prefer
resemble	detest	disagree	realize	possess	perceive	want
seem	dislike	disbelieve	recognize		see	wish
signify	doubt	estimate	remember		smell	
	envy	expect	see (understand)		sound	
Value	fear	feel (believe)	suppose		taste	
cost	hate	find (believe)	suspect			
equal	like	guess	think (believe)			
weigh	love	hesitate	understand			
	miss	hope	wonder			
	regret	imagine				
	respect					
	trust					

3 | Verbs and Expressions Used Reflexively

allow yourself	behave yourself	forgive yourself	pride yourself on
amuse yourself	believe in yourself	help yourself	push yourself
ask yourself	blame yourself	hurt yourself	remind yourself
avail yourself of	cut yourself	imagine yourself	see yourself
be hard on yourself	deprive yourself of	introduce yourself	take care of yourself
be yourself	dry yourself	kill yourself	talk to yourself
be pleased with yourself	enjoy yourself	look at yourself	teach yourself
be proud of yourself	feel sorry for yourself	prepare yourself	tell yourself

(s.o. = someone s.t. = something)

PHRASAL VERB	MEANING
ask s.o. **over**	invite to one's home
blow s.t. **out**	stop burning by blowing air on it
blow s.t. **up**	make explode
bring s.o. or s.t. **back**	return
bring s.o. **up**	raise (a child)
bring s.t. **up**	bring attention to
burn s.t. **down**	burn completely
call s.o. **back**	return a phone call
call s.t. **off**	cancel
call s.o. **up**	contact by phone
carry s.t. **out**	complete (a plan)
clean s.o. or s.t. **up**	clean completely
clear s.t. **up**	explain
close s.t. **down**	close by force
cover s.o. or s.t. **up**	cover completely
cross s.t. **out**	draw a line through
do s.t. **over**	do again
drink s.t. **up**	drink completely
drop s.o. or s.t. **off**	take someplace in a car and leave there
empty s.t. **out**	empty completely
figure s.o. **out**	understand (the behavior)
figure s.t. **out**	solve, understand after thinking about it
fill s.t. **in**	complete with information
fill s.t. **out**	complete (a form)
find s.t. **out**	learn information
give s.t. **back**	return
give s.t. **up**	quit, abandon
hand s.t. **in**	give work (to a boss/teacher), submit
hand s.t. **out**	distribute
hand s.t. **over**	give
help s.o. **out**	assist
keep s.o. or s.t. **away**	cause to stay at a distance
keep s.t. **on**	not remove (a piece of clothing/jewelry)
keep s.o. or s.t. **out**	not allow to enter
lay s.o. **off**	end employment
leave s.t. **on**	1. not turn off (a light/radio) 2. not remove (a piece of clothing/jewelry)
leave s.t. **out**	not include, omit
let s.o. **down**	disappoint
let s.o. or s.t. **in**	allow to enter
let s.o. **off**	allow to leave (from a bus/car)
light s.t. **up**	illuminate
look s.o. or s.t. **over**	examine
look s.t. **up**	try to find (in a book/on the Internet)

PHRASAL VERB	MEANING
make s.t. **up**	create
pass s.t. **on**	give to
pass s.t. **out**	distribute
pass s.o. or s.t. **over**	decide not to use
pass s.o. or s.t. **up**	decide not to use, reject
pay s.o. or s.t. **back**	repay
pick s.o. or s.t. **out**	choose
pick s.o. or s.t. **up**	1. lift 2. go get someone or something
pick s.t. **up**	1. get (an idea/a new book) 2. answer the phone
point s.o. or s.t. **out**	indicate
put s.t. **away**	put in an appropriate place
put s.t. **back**	return to its original place
put s.o. or s.t. **down**	stop holding
put s.t. **off**	delay
put s.t. **on**	cover the body (with clothes/lotion)
put s.t. **together**	assemble
put s.t. **up**	erect
set s.t. **up**	1. prepare for use 2. establish (a business)
shut s.t. **off**	stop (a machine/light)
straighten s.t. **up**	make neat
switch s.t. **on**	start (a machine/light)
take s.o. or s.t. **back**	return
take s.t. **off**	remove
talk s.o. **into**	persuade
talk s.t. **over**	discuss
tear s.t. **down**	destroy
tear s.t. **off**	remove by tearing
tear s.t. **up**	tear into small pieces
think s.t. **over**	consider
think s.t. **up**	invent
throw s.t. **away/out**	put in the trash, discard
try s.t. **on**	put clothing on to see if it fits
try s.t. **out**	use to see if it works
turn s.o. or s.t. **down**	reject
turn s.t. **down**	lower the volume (a TV/radio)
turn s.t. **in**	give work (to a boss/teacher), submit
turn s.o. or s.t. **into**	change from one form to another
turn s.o. **off**	[slang] destroy interest in
turn s.t. **off**	stop (a machine/light), extinguish
turn s.t. **on**	start (a machine/light)
turn s.t. **up**	make louder (a TV/radio)
use s.t. **up**	use completely, consume
wake s.o. **up**	awaken
work s.t. **out**	solve, find a solution to a problem
write s.t. **down**	write on a piece of paper
write s.t. **up**	write in a finished form

5 | Intransitive Phrasal Verbs

Phrasal Verb	Meaning
blow up	explode
break down	stop working (a machine)
burn down	burn completely
call back	return a phone call
clear up	become clear
close down	stop operating
come about	happen
come along	come with, accompany
come back	return
come in	enter
come off	become unattached
come out	appear
come up	arise
dress up	wear special clothes
drop in	visit by surprise
drop out	quit
eat out	eat in a restaurant
empty out	empty completely
find out	learn information

Phrasal Verb	Meaning
follow through	complete
fool around	act playful
get ahead	make progress, succeed
get along	have a good relationship
get back	return
get by	survive
get through	finish
get together	meet
get up	get out of bed
give up	quit
go on	continue
grow up	become an adult
hang up	end a phone call
keep away	stay at a distance
keep on	continue
keep out	not enter
keep up	go as fast
lie down	recline
light up	illuminate

Phrasal Verb	Meaning
look out	be careful
make up	end a disagreement, reconcile
play around	have fun
run out	not have enough
set out	begin a project
show up	appear
sign up	register
sit down	take a seat
slip up	make a mistake
stand up	rise
start over	start again
stay up	remain awake
straighten up	make neat
take off	depart (a plane)
turn up	appear
wake up	stop sleeping
watch out	be careful
work out	1. be resolved 2. exercise

6 | Irregular Plural Nouns

Singular	Plural
half	halves
knife	knives
leaf	leaves
life	lives
loaf	loaves
shelf	shelves
wife	wives

Singular	Plural
man	men
woman	women
child	children
foot	feet
tooth	teeth
goose	geese
mouse	mice

Singular	Plural
deer	deer
fish	fish
sheep	sheep
person	people

7 | Non-count Nouns

REMEMBER: Non-count nouns are singular.

Activities	Food		Ideas and Feelings	Liquids and Gases	School Subjects	Very Small Things
baseball	bread	ice cream	anger	air	art	dust
biking	butter	lettuce	beauty	gasoline	English	pepper
football	cake	meat	fear	milk	math	rice
golf	cheese	pasta	freedom	oil	music	salt
hiking	chicken	pizza	friendship	oxygen	photography	sand
running	chocolate	salad	happiness	water	science	sugar
sailing	coffee	soup	hate			
soccer	cream	spaghetti	hope	Materials		Weather
swimming	fat	tea	loneliness	cotton		fog
tennis	fish	yogurt	love	glass		ice
				gold		rain
				leather		snow
				paper		wind
				wood		
				wool		

NAMES OF CATEGORIES

equipment	(BUT: computers, phones, TVs . . .)
food	(BUT: bananas, eggs, vegetables . . .)
furniture	(BUT: beds, chairs, lamps, tables . . .)
homework	(BUT: assignments, pages, problems . . .)
jewelry	(BUT: bracelets, earrings, necklaces . . .)
mail	(BUT: letters, packages, postcards . . .)
money	(BUT: dinars, dollars, euros, pounds . . .)
work	(BUT: jobs, projects, tasks . . .)

OTHER

(Some non-count nouns don't fit into any list. You must memorize these non-count nouns.)

advice
garbage/trash
information
traffic
news

8 | Proper Nouns

REMEMBER: Write proper nouns with a capital letter.

PEOPLE
• first names	Anne, Eduardo, Mehmet, Olga, Shao-fen
• family names	Chen, García, Haddad, Smith
• titles	Doctor, Grandma, Professor
• title + names	Mr. García, Professor Smith, Uncle Steve

PLACES
• continents	Africa, Asia, Australia, Europe, South America
• countries	Argentina, China, France, Nigeria, Turkey, the United States
• provinces/states	Brittany, Ontario, Szechwan, Texas
• cities	Beijing, Istanbul, Rio de Janeiro, Toronto
• streets	Adalbertstrasse, the Champs-Elysées, Fifth Avenue
• structures	Harrods, the Louvre, the Petronas Towers, the Golden Gate Bridge
• schools	Midwood High School, Oxford University
• parks	Central Park, the Tivoli Gardens
• mountains	the Andes, the Himalayas, the Pyrenees, the Rocky Mountains
• oceans	the Arctic, the Atlantic, the Indian Ocean, the Pacific
• rivers	the Amazon, the Ganges, the Seine
• lakes	Baikal, Erie, Tanganyika, Titicaca
• deserts	the Gobi, the Kalahari, the Sahara

LANGUAGES
Arabic, Chinese, Portuguese, Russian, Spanish

NATIONALITIES
Brazilian, Japanese, Mexican, Saudi, Turkish

RELIGIONS
Buddhism, Christianity, Hinduism, Islam, Judaism

COURSES
Introduction to Computer Sciences, Math 201

PRODUCT BRANDS
Adidas, Dell, Kleenex, Mercedes, Samsung

TIME
• months	January, March, December
• days	Monday, Wednesday, Saturday
• holidays	Bastille Day, Buddha Day, Christmas, Hanukah, New Year's Day, Ramadan

9 | Adjectives That Form the Comparative and Superlative in Two Ways

ADJECTIVE	COMPARATIVE	SUPERLATIVE
cruel	crueler/more cruel	cruelest/most cruel
deadly	deadlier/more deadly	deadliest/most deadly
friendly	friendlier/more friendly	friendliest/most friendly
handsome	handsomer/more handsome	handsomest/most handsome
happy	happier/more happy	happiest/most happy
likely	likelier/more likely	likeliest/most likely
lively	livelier/more lively	liveliest/most lively
lonely	lonelier/more lonely	loneliest/most lonely
lovely	lovelier/more lovely	loveliest/most lovely
narrow	narrower/more narrow	narrowest/most narrow
pleasant	pleasanter/more pleasant	pleasantest/most pleasant
polite	politer/more polite	politest/most polite
quiet	quieter/more quiet	quietest/most quiet
shallow	shallower/more shallow	shallowest/most shallow
sincere	sincerer/more sincere	sincerest/most sincere
stupid	stupider/more stupid	stupidest/most stupid
true	truer/more true	truest/most true

ADJECTIVE	ADVERB	COMPARATIVE	SUPERLATIVE
bad	badly	worse	the worst
far	far	farther/further	the farthest/furthest
good	well	better	the best
little	little	less	the least
many/a lot of	—	more	the most
much*/a lot of	much*/a lot	more	the most

*Much is usually only used in questions and negative statements.

-ed	-ing	-ed	-ing	-ed	-ing
alarmed	alarming	disturbed	disturbing	moved	moving
amazed	amazing	embarrassed	embarrassing	paralyzed	paralyzing
amused	amusing	entertained	entertaining	pleased	pleasing
annoyed	annoying	excited	exciting	relaxed	relaxing
astonished	astonishing	exhausted	exhausting	satisfied	satisfying
bored	boring	fascinated	fascinating	shocked	shocking
charmed	charming	frightened	frightening	surprised	surprising
confused	confusing	horrified	horrifying	terrified	terrifying
depressed	depressing	inspired	inspiring	tired	tiring
disappointed	disappointing	interested	interesting	touched	touching
disgusted	disgusting	irritated	irritating	troubled	troubling

REMEMBER: We do not usually use more than three adjectives before a noun.

1. Order of Adjectives from Different Categories

Adjectives from different categories usually go in the following order. Do not use a comma between these adjectives.

Opinion	Size*	Age	Shape	Color	Origin	Material	Nouns used as Adjectives	
beautiful	enormous	antique	flat	blue	Asian	cotton	college	
comfortable	huge	modern	oval	gray	European	gold	flower	
cozy	little	new	rectangular	green	Greek	plastic	kitchen	+ NOUN
easy	tall	old	round	purple	Pacific	stone	mountain	
expensive	tiny	young	square	red	Southern	wooden	vacation	

*EXCEPTION: Big and small usually go first in a series of adjectives: *a small comfortable apartment*

EXAMPLES: I bought an **antique Greek flower** vase.   NOT a ~~Greek antique~~ flower vase
She took some **easy college** courses.   NOT some ~~college easy~~ courses
We sat at an **enormous round wooden** table.   NOT a ~~wooden enormous~~ round table

2. Order of Adjectives from the Same Category

Adjectives from the same category do not follow a specific order. Use a comma between these adjectives.

EXAMPLES: We rented a **beautiful, comfortable, cozy** apartment. OR
We rented a **cozy, comfortable, beautiful** apartment. OR
We rented a **comfortable, cozy, beautiful** apartment.

13 | Verbs Followed by the Gerund (Base Form of Verb + *-ing*)

acknowledge	celebrate	dislike	finish	mind *(object to)*	quit	risk
admit	consider	endure	forgive	miss	recall	suggest
advise	delay	end up	give up *(stop)*	postpone	recommend	support
appreciate	deny	enjoy	imagine	practice	regret	tolerate
avoid	detest	escape	justify	prevent	report	understand
can't help	discontinue	explain	keep *(continue)*	prohibit	resent	
can't stand	discuss	feel like	mention	put off	resist	

14 | Verbs Followed by the Infinitive (*To* + Base Form of Verb)

agree	can't wait	fail	learn	pay	refuse	wait
appear	choose	help	manage	plan	request	want
arrange	consent	hesitate	mean *(intend)*	prepare	rush	wish
ask	decide	hope	need	pretend	seem	would like
attempt	deserve	hurry	neglect	promise	volunteer	
can't afford	expect	intend	offer			

15 | Verbs Followed by the Gerund or the Infinitive

begin	continue	hate	love	remember*	stop*
can't stand	forget*	like	prefer	start	try

*These verbs can be followed by either the gerund or the infinitive, but there is a big difference in meaning *(see Unit 32)*.

16 | Verbs Followed by Object + Infinitive

advise	convince	get	need*	persuade	require	want*
allow	encourage	help*	order	promise*	teach	warn
ask*	expect*	hire	pay*	remind	tell	wish
cause	forbid	invite	permit	request	urge	would like*
choose*	force					

*These verbs can also be followed by an infinitive without an object (example: *ask to leave* or *ask someone to leave*).

17 | Adjective + Preposition Combinations

accustomed to	bad at	different from	interested in	safe from	surprised
afraid of	bored with/by	excited about	nervous about	satisfied with	at/about/by
amazed at/by	capable of	famous for	opposed to	shocked at/by	terrible at
angry at	careful of	fond of	pleased about	sick of	tired of
ashamed of	concerned about	glad about	ready for	slow at/in	used to
aware of	content with	good at	responsible for	sorry for/about	worried about
awful at	curious about	happy about	sad about		

admit to	believe in	deal with	look forward to	rely on	thank someone for
advise against	choose between	dream about/of	object to	resort to	think about
apologize for	complain about	feel like	pay for	succeed in	wonder about
approve of	count on	insist on	plan on	talk about	

19 | **Modals and Their Functions**

FUNCTION	MODAL OR EXPRESSION	TIME	EXAMPLES
Ability	can can't	Present	• Sam **can swim**. • He **can't skate**.
	could couldn't	Past	• We **could swim** last year. • We **couldn't skate**.
	be able to* not be able to*	All verb forms	• Lea **is able to run** fast. • She **wasn't able to run** fast last year.
Permission	can	Present or Future	• **Can** I **sit** here? • **Can** I **call** tomorrow? • Yes, you **can**.
	can't		• No, you **can't**. Sorry.
	could		• **Could** he **leave** now?
	may		• **May** I **borrow** your pen? • Yes, you **may**.
	may not		• No, you **may not**. Sorry.
Requests	can	Present or Future	• **Can** you **close** the door, please? • Sure, I **can**.
	can't		• Sorry, I **can't**.
	could		• **Could** you please **answer** the phone?
	will		• **Will** you **wash** the dishes, please?
	would		• **Would** you please **mail** this letter?
Advice	should	Present or Future	• You **should study** more.
	shouldn't		• You **shouldn't miss** class.
	ought to**		• We **ought to leave**.
	had better**		• We**'d better go**.
	had better not**		• We**'d better not stay**.
Necessity	have to*	All verb forms	• He **has to go** now. • I **had to go** yesterday. • I **will have to go** soon.
	not have to*		• He **doesn't have to go** yet.
	have got to*	Present or Future	• He**'s got to leave**!
	must		• You **must use** a pen for the test.
Prohibition	must not	Present or Future	• You **must not drive** without a license.
	can't		• You **can't drive** without a license.

*The meaning of this expression is similar to the meaning of a modal. Unlike a modal, it has -s for third-person singular.
**The meaning of this expression is similar to the meaning of a modal. Like a modal, it has no -s for third-person singular.

Function	Modal or Expression	Time	Examples
Possibility	must must not have to* have got to*	Present	• This **must be** her house. Her name is on the door. • She **must not be** home. I don't see her car. • She **has to know** him. They went to school together. • He's **got to be** guilty. We saw him do it.
	may may not might might not could	Present or Future	• She **may be** home now. • It **may not rain** tomorrow. • Lee **might be sick** today. • He **might not come** to class. • They **could be** at the library. • It **could rain** tomorrow.
Impossibility	can't couldn't	Present or Future	• That **can't be** Ana. She left for France yesterday. • It **can't snow** tomorrow. It's going to be too warm. • He **couldn't be** guilty. He wasn't in town when the crime occurred. • The teacher **couldn't give** the test tomorrow. Tomorrow's Saturday.

*The meaning of this expression is similar to the meaning of a modal. Unlike a modal, it has -s for third-person singular.

20 | Spelling Rules for the Simple Present: Third-Person Singular (he, she, it)

1. Add **-s** for most verbs.

work	work**s**
buy	buy**s**
ride	ride**s**
return	return**s**

2. Add **-es** for verbs that end in **-ch**, **-s**, **-sh**, **-x**, or **-z**.

watch	watch**es**
pass	pass**es**
rush	rush**es**
relax	relax**es**
buzz	buzz**es**

3. Change the **y** to **i** and add **-es** when the base form ends in **consonant** + **y**.

study	stud**ies**
hurry	hurr**ies**
dry	dr**ies**

Do not change the **y** when the base form ends in **vowel** + **y**. Add **-s**.

play	play**s**
enjoy	enjoy**s**

4. A few verbs have **irregular forms**.

be	**is**
do	**does**
go	**goes**
have	**has**

21 | Spelling Rules for Base Form of Verb + -ing (Progressive and Gerund)

1. Add *-ing* to the base form of the verb.

read	read**ing**
stand	stand**ing**

2. If the verb ends in a **silent -e**, drop the final *-e* and add *-ing*.

leave	leav**ing**
take	tak**ing**

3. In **one-syllable** verbs, if the last three letters are a consonant-vowel-consonant combination (CVC), double the last consonant and add *-ing*.

   C V C
   ↓ ↓ ↓
   s i t   sit**ting**

   C V C
   ↓ ↓ ↓
   p l a n   plan**ning**

   Do not double the last consonant in verbs that end in *-w*, *-x*, or *-y*.

sew	sew**ing**
fix	fix**ing**
play	play**ing**

4. In verbs of **two or more syllables** that end in a consonant-vowel-consonant combination, double the last consonant only if the last syllable is stressed.

admít	admit**ting**	*(The last syllable is stressed.)*
whísper	whisper**ing**	*(The last syllable is not stressed, so don't double the -r.)*

5. If the verb ends in *-ie*, change the *ie* to *y* before adding *-ing*.

die	d**ying**

STRESS
´ shows main stress.

22 | Spelling Rules for Base Form of Verb + -ed (Simple Past and Past Participle of Regular Verbs)

1. If the verb ends in a **consonant**, add *-ed*.

return	return**ed**
help	help**ed**

2. If the verb ends in *-e*, add *-d*.

live	live**d**
create	create**d**
die	die**d**

3. In **one-syllable** verbs, if the last three letters are a consonant-vowel-consonant combination (CVC), double the last consonant and add *-ed*.

   C V C
   ↓ ↓ ↓
   h o p   hop**ped**

   C V C
   ↓ ↓ ↓
   g r a b   grab**bed**

   Do not double the last consonant in verbs that end in *-w*, *-x*, or *-y*.

bow	bow**ed**
mix	mix**ed**
play	play**ed**

4. In verbs of **two or more syllables** that end in a consonant-vowel-consonant combination, double the last consonant only if the last syllable is stressed.

prefér	prefer**red**	*(The last syllable is stressed.)*
vísit	visit**ed**	*(The last syllable is not stressed, so don't double the -t.)*

5. If the verb ends in **consonant + y**, change the *y* to *i* and add *-ed*.

worry	worr**ied**
carry	carr**ied**

6. If the verb ends in **vowel + y**, add *-ed*. (Do not change the *y* to *i*.)

play	play**ed**
annoy	annoy**ed**

   EXCEPTIONS:

lay	la**id**
pay	pa**id**
say	sa**id**

23 | Spelling Rules for the Comparative *(-er)* and Superlative *(-est)* of Adjectives

1. With **one-syllable** adjectives, add *-er* to form the comparative. Add *-est* to form the superlative.

cheap	cheap**er**	cheap**est**
bright	bright**er**	bright**est**

2. If the adjective ends in *-e*, add *-r* or *-st*.

nice	nice**r**	nice**st**

3. If the adjective ends in **consonant + y**, change *y* to *i* before you add *-er* or *-est*.

pretty	prett**ier**	prett**iest**

   EXCEPTION:

shy	shy**er**	shy**est**

4. If a one-syllable adjective ends in a consonant-vowel-consonant combination (CVC), double the last consonant before adding *-er* or *-est*.

   C V C
   ↓ ↓ ↓
   b i g   big**ger**   big**gest**

   Do not double the consonant in adjectives ending in *-w* or *-y*.

slow	slow**er**	slow**est**
gray	gray**er**	gray**est**

24 | Spelling Rules for Adverbs Ending in *-ly*

1. Add *-ly* to the corresponding adjective.

nice	nice**ly**
quiet	quiet**ly**
beautiful	beautiful**ly**

2. If the adjective ends in **consonant + y**, change the *y* to *i* before adding *-ly*.

easy	eas**ily**

3. If the adjective ends in *-le*, drop the *e* and add *-y*.

possible	possibl**y**

   Do not drop the *e* for other adjectives ending in *-e*.

extreme	extreme**ly**

   EXCEPTION:

true	tru**ly**

4. If the adjective ends in *-ic*, add *-ally*.

basic	basic**ally**
fantastic	fantastic**ally**

25 | Spelling Rules for Regular Plural Nouns

1. Add *-s* to most nouns.

book	book**s**
table	table**s**
cup	cup**s**

2. Add *-es* to nouns that end in *-ch*, *-s*, *-sh*, or *-x*.

watch	watch**es**
bus	bus**es**
dish	dish**es**
box	box**es**

3. Add *-s* to nouns that end in **vowel + y**.

day	day**s**
key	key**s**

4. Change the *y* to *i* and add *-es* to nouns that end in **consonant + y**.

baby	bab**ies**
city	cit**ies**
strawberry	strawberr**ies**

5. Add *-s* to nouns that end in **vowel + o**.

radio	radio**s**
video	video**s**
zoo	zoo**s**

6. Add *-es* to nouns that end in **consonant + o**.

potato	potato**es**
tomato	tomato**es**

   EXCEPTIONS: kilo—kilos, photo—photos, piano—pianos

1. SIMPLE PRESENT, PRESENT PROGRESSIVE, AND IMPERATIVE

Contractions with *Be*

I am	=	I'm
you are	=	you're
he is	=	he's
she is	=	she's
it is	=	it's
we are	=	we're
you are	=	you're
they are	=	they're

SIMPLE PRESENT	PRESENT PROGRESSIVE
I'm a student.	I'm studying here.
He's my teacher.	He's teaching verbs.
We're from Canada.	We're living here.

I am not	=	I'm not		
you are not	=	you're not	OR	you aren't
he is not	=	he's not	OR	he isn't
she is not	=	she's not	OR	she isn't
it is not	=	it's not	OR	it isn't
we are not	=	we're not	OR	we aren't
you are not	=	you're not	OR	you aren't
they are not	=	they're not	OR	they aren't

SIMPLE PRESENT	PRESENT PROGRESSIVE
She's not sick.	She's not reading.
He isn't late.	He isn't coming.
We aren't twins.	We aren't leaving.
They're not here.	They're not playing.

Contractions with *Do*

do not	=	don't
does not	=	doesn't

SIMPLE PRESENT	IMPERATIVE
They don't live here.	Don't run!
It doesn't snow much.	

2. SIMPLE PAST AND PAST PROGRESSIVE

Contractions with *Be*

was not	=	wasn't
were not	=	weren't

SIMPLE PAST	PAST PROGRESSIVE
He wasn't a poet.	He wasn't singing.
They weren't twins.	They weren't sleeping.
We didn't see her.	

Contractions with *Do*

did not	=	didn't

3. FUTURE

Contractions with *Will*

I will	=	I'll
you will	=	you'll
he will	=	he'll
she will	=	she'll
it will	=	it'll
we will	=	we'll
you will	=	you'll
they will	=	they'll

will not	=	won't

FUTURE WITH *WILL*
I'll take the train.
It'll be faster that way.
We'll go together.
He won't come with us.
They won't miss the train.

Contractions with *Be going to*

I am going to	=	I'm going to
you are going to	=	you're going to
he is going to	=	he's going to
she is going to	=	she's going to
it is going to	=	it's going to
we are going to	=	we're going to
you are going to	=	you're going to
they are going to	=	they're going to

FUTURE WITH *BE GOING TO*
I'm going to buy tickets tomorrow.
She's going to call you.
It's going to rain soon.
We're going to drive to Boston.
They're going to crash!

4. PRESENT PERFECT AND PRESENT PERFECT PROGRESSIVE

Contractions with *Have*

I have	=	I**'ve**
you have	=	you**'ve**
he has	=	he**'s**
she has	=	she**'s**
it has	=	it**'s**
we have	=	we**'ve**
you have	=	you**'ve**
they have	=	they**'ve**
have not	=	**haven't**
has not	=	**hasn't**

> You**'ve** already **read** that page.
> We**'ve been writing** for an hour.
> She**'s been** to Africa three times.
> It**'s been raining** since yesterday.
> We **haven't seen** any elephants yet.
> They **haven't been living** here long.

5. MODALS AND SIMILAR EXPRESSIONS

cannot or can not	=	**can't**
could not	=	**couldn't**
should not	=	**shouldn't**
had better	=	**'d better**
would prefer	=	**'d prefer**
would rather	=	**'d rather**

> She **can't dance**.
> We **shouldn't go**.
> They**'d better decide**.
> I**'d prefer** coffee.
> I**'d rather take** the bus.

27 | Capitalization and Punctuation Rules

	USE FOR . . .	EXAMPLES
capital letter	• the pronoun *I* • proper nouns • the first word of a sentence	• Tomorrow **I** will be here at 2:00. • His name is **Karl**. He lives in **Germany**. • **When** does the train leave? **At** 2:00.
apostrophe (')	• possessive nouns • contractions	• Is that **Marta's** coat? • **That's** not hers. **It's** mine.
comma (,)	• after items in a list • before sentence connectors *and*, *but*, *or*, and *so* • after the first part of a sentence that begins with *because* • after the first part of a sentence that begins with a preposition • after the first part of a sentence that begins with a time clause or an *if* clause	• He bought **apples**, **pears**, **oranges**, and **bananas**. • They watched TV, **and** she played video games. • *Because* it's raining, we're not walking to the office. • *Across from* the **post office**, there's a good restaurant. • *After* he arrived, we ate dinner. • *If* it rains, we won't go.
exclamation mark (!)	• at the end of a sentence to show surprise or a strong feeling	• You're here! That's great! • Stop! A car is coming!
period (.)	• at the end of a statement	• Today is Wednesday.
question mark (?)	• at the end of a question	• What day is today**?**

These are the pronunciation symbols used in this text. Listen to the pronunciation of the key words.

VOWELS				CONSONANTS			
Symbol	**Key Word**	**Symbol**	**Key Word**	**Symbol**	**Key Word**	**Symbol**	**Key Word**
i	beat, feed	ə	banana, among	p	pack, happy	ʃ	ship, machine, station, special, discussion
ɪ	bit, did	ɚ	shirt, murder	b	back, rubber		
eɪ	date, paid	aɪ	bite, cry, buy, eye	t	tie	ʒ	measure, vision
ɛ	bet, bed	aʊ	about, how	d	die	h	hot, who
æ	bat, bad	ɔɪ	voice, boy	k	came, key, quick	m	men
ɑ	box, odd, father	ɪr	beer	g	game, guest	n	sun, know, pneumonia
ɔ	bought, dog	ɛr	bare	tʃ	church, nature, watch	ŋ	sung, ringing
oʊ	boat, road	ɑr	bar	dʒ	judge, general, major	w	wet, white
ʊ	book, good	ɔr	door	f	fan, photograph	l	light, long
u	boot, food, student	ʊr	tour	v	van	r	right, wrong
ʌ	but, mud, mother			θ	thing, breath	y	yes, use, music
				ð	then, breathe	t̬	butter, bottle
				s	sip, city, psychology		
				z	zip, please, goes		

> **STRESS**
> ′ shows main stress.

---

29 | Pronunciation Rules for the Simple Present: Third-Person Singular (he, she, it)

1. The third-person singular in the simple present always ends in the letter -s. There are, however, three different pronunciations for the final sound of the third-person singular.

/s/	/z/	/ɪz/
talks	loves	dances

2. The final sound is pronounced /s/ after the voiceless sounds /p/, /t/, /k/, and /f/.

top	tops
get	gets
take	takes
laugh	laughs

3. The final sound is pronounced /z/ after the voiced sounds /b/, /d/, /g/, /v/, /m/, /n/, /ŋ/, /l/, /r/, and /ð/.

describe	describes
spend	spends
hug	hugs
live	lives
seem	seems
remain	remains
sing	sings
tell	tells
lower	lowers
bathe	bathes

4. The final sound is pronounced /z/ after all **vowel sounds**.

agree	agrees
try	tries
stay	stays
know	knows

5. The final sound is pronounced /ɪz/ after the sounds /s/, /z/, /ʃ/, /ʒ/, /tʃ/, and /dʒ/. /ɪz/ adds a syllable to the verb.

miss	misses
freeze	freezes
rush	rushes
massage	massages
watch	watches
judge	judges

6. *Do* and *say* have a change in vowel sound.

do	/du/	does	/dʌz/
say	/seɪ/	says	/sɛz/

1. The regular simple past and past participle always end in the letter **-d**. There are three different pronunciations for the final sound of the regular simple past and past participle.

/t/	/d/	/ɪd/
race**d**	live**d**	attend**ed**

2. The final sound is pronounced /**t**/ after the voiceless sounds /**p**/, /**k**/, /**f**/, /**s**/, /ʃ/, and /tʃ/.

hop	ho**pped**
work	wor**ked**
laugh	laug**hed**
address	addre**ssed**
publish	publi**shed**
watch	wa**tched**

3. The final sound is pronounced /**d**/ after the voiced sounds /**b**/, /**g**/, /**v**/, /**z**/, /ʒ/, /dʒ/, /**m**/, /**n**/, /ŋ/, /**l**/, /**r**/, and /ð/.

rub	ru**bbed**
hug	hu**gged**
live	li**ved**
surprise	surpri**sed**
massage	massa**ged**
change	chan**ged**
rhyme	rhy**med**
return	retur**ned**
bang	ba**nged**
enroll	enro**lled**
appear	appea**red**
bathe	ba**thed**

4. The final sound is pronounced /**d**/ after all **vowel sounds**.

agree	agr**eed**
die	di**ed**
play	pl**ayed**
enjoy	enj**oyed**
snow	sn**owed**

5. The final sound is pronounced /ɪ**d**/ after /**t**/ and /**d**/. /ɪ**d**/ adds a syllable to the verb.

start	star**ted**
decide	deci**ded**

GLOSSARY OF GRAMMAR TERMS

action verb a verb that describes an action.
- *Alicia **ran** home.*

adjective a word that describes a noun or pronoun.
- *That's a **great** idea.*
- *It's **wonderful**.*

adverb a word that describes a verb, an adjective, or another adverb.
- *She drives **carefully**.*
- *She's a **very** good driver.*
- *She drives **really** well.*

adverb of frequency an adverb that describes how often something happens.
- *We **always** watch that program.*

adverb of manner an adverb that describes how someone does something or how something happens. It usually ends in -ly.
- *He sings **beautifully**.*

adverb of time an adverb that describes when something happens.
- *We'll see you **soon**.*

affirmative a statement or answer meaning *Yes*.
- *He **works**.* (affirmative statement)
- ***Yes**, he **does**.* (affirmative short answer)

article a word that goes before a noun.
The indefinite articles are *a* and *an*.
- *I ate **a** sandwich and **an** apple.*
The definite article is *the*.
- *I didn't like **the** sandwich. **The** apple was good.*

auxiliary verb (also called **helping verb**) a verb used with a main verb. *Be, do*, and *have* are often auxiliary verbs. Modals (*can, should, may . . .*) are also auxiliary verbs.
- *I **am** exercising right now.*
- ***Does** he exercise every day?*
- *She **should** exercise every day.*

base form the simple form of a verb without any endings (*-s, -ed, -ing*) or other changes.
- ***be, have, go, drive***

capital letter the large form of a letter. The capital letters are: *A, B, C, D, . . .*
- ***A**licia lives in the **U**nited **S**tates.*

clause a group of words that has a subject and a verb. A sentence can have one or more clauses.
- ***We are leaving now.*** (one clause)
- ***When he calls, we'll leave.*** (two clauses)

common noun a word for a person, place, or thing (but not the name of the person, place, or thing).
- *Teresa lives in a **house** near the **beach**.*

comparative the form of an adjective or adverb that shows the difference between two people, places, or things.
- *Alain is **shorter** than Brendan.* (adjective)
- *Brendan runs **faster** than Alain.* (adverb)

comparison a statement that shows the difference between two people, places, or things. A comparison can use comparative adjectives and comparative adverbs. It can also use *as . . . as*.
- *Alain is **shorter than** Brendan.*
- *Alain isn't **as tall as** Brendan.*
- *He runs **faster than** Brendan.*

consonant a letter of the alphabet. The consonants are:
- ***b, c, d, f, g, h, j, k, l, m, n, p, q, r, s, t, v, w, x, y, z***

continuous See **progressive**.

contraction a short form of a word or words. An apostrophe (') replaces the missing letter or letters.
- ***she's*** = *she is*
- ***hasn't*** = *has not*
- ***can't*** = *cannot*
- ***won't*** = *will not*

count noun a noun that you can count. It has a singular and a plural form.

- one **book**, two **books**

definite article *the*.
This article goes before a noun that refers to a specific person, place, or thing.

- *Please bring me **the book** on the table. I'm almost finished reading it.*

dependent clause (also called **subordinate clause**) a clause that needs a main clause for its meaning.

- ***When I get home**, I'll call you.*

direct object a noun or pronoun that receives the action of a verb.

- *Marta kicked **the ball**. I saw **her**.*

formal language used in business situations or with adults you do not know.

- *Good afternoon, Mr. Rivera. Please have a seat.*

gerund a noun formed with verb + *-ing*.
It can be the subject or object of a sentence.

- ***Swimming** is great exercise.*
- *I enjoy **swimming**.*

helping verb See **auxiliary verb**.

imperative a sentence that gives a command or instructions.

- ***Hurry!***
- ***Don't touch that!***

indefinite article *a* or *an*.
These articles go before a noun that does not refer to a specific person, place, or thing.

- *Can you bring me **a book**? I'm looking for something to read.*

indefinite past past time, but not a specific time. It is often used with the present perfect.

- *I**'ve** already **seen** that movie.*

indefinite pronoun a pronoun such as *someone, something, anyone, anything, anywhere, no one, nothing, everyone,* and *everything.* An indefinite pronoun does not refer to a specific person, place, or thing.

- ***Someone** called you last night.*
- *Did **anything** happen?*

indirect object a noun or pronoun (often a person) that receives something as the result of the action of the verb.

- *I told **John** the story.*
- *He gave **me** some good advice.*

infinitive *to* + base form of the verb.

- *I want **to leave** now.*

infinitive of purpose *(in order) to* + base form. This form gives the reason for an action.

- *I go to school **in order to learn** English.*

informal language used with family, friends, and children.

- *Hi, Pete. Sit down.*

information question See **wh- question**.

inseparable phrasal verb a phrasal verb whose parts must stay together.

- *We **ran into** Tomás at the supermarket.*

intransitive verb a verb that does not have an object.

- *We **fell**.*

irregular a word that does not change its form in the usual way.

- ***good → well***
- ***bad → worse***

irregular verb a verb that does not form its past with *-ed*.

- ***leave → left***

main clause a clause that can stand alone as a sentence.

- *When I get home, **I'll call you**.*

main verb a verb that describes an action or state. It is often used with an auxiliary verb.

- *Jared is **calling**.*
- *He'll **call** again later.*
- *Does he **call** every day?*

modal a type of auxiliary verb. It goes before a main verb and expresses ideas such as ability, advice, obligation, permission, and possibility. *Can, could, will, would, may, might, should,* and *must* are modals.

- ***Can** you swim?*
- *You really **should** learn to swim.*

negative   a statement or answer meaning *No*.

- *He **doesn't** work.* (negative statement)
- ***No**, he **doesn't**.* (negative short answer)

non-action verb (also called **stative verb**) a verb that does not describe an action. It describes such things as thoughts, feelings, and senses.

- *I **remember** that word.*
- *Chris **loves** ice cream.*
- *It **tastes** great.*

non-count noun   a noun that you usually do not count *(air, water, rice, love, . . .)*. It has only a singular form.

- *The **rice** is delicious.*

noun   a word for a person, place, or thing.

- *My **sister**, **Anne**, works in an **office**.*
- *She uses a **computer**.*

object   a noun or pronoun that receives the action of a verb. Sometimes a verb has two objects.

- *She wrote **a letter to Tom**.*
- *She wrote **him a letter**.*

object pronoun   a pronoun *(me, you, him, her, it, us, them)* that receives the action of a verb.

- *I gave **her** a book.*
- *I gave **it** to **her**.*

paragraph   a group of sentences, usually about one topic.

participial adjective   an adjective that ends in *-ing* or *-ed*. It comes from a verb.

- *That's an **interesting** book.*
- *She's **interested** in the book.*

particle   a word that looks like a preposition and combines with a main verb to form a phrasal verb. It often changes the meaning of the main verb.

- *He looked the word **up**.*
  (He looked for the meaning in the dictionary.)
- *I ran **into** my teacher.*
  (I met my teacher accidentally.)

past participle   a verb form (verb + *-ed*). It can also be irregular. It is used to form the present perfect. It can also be an adjective.

- *We've **lived** here since April.*
- *She's **interested** in math.*

phrasal verb   (also called **two-word verb**) a verb that has two parts (verb + particle). The meaning is often different from the meaning of its separate parts.

- *He **grew up** in Texas.* (became an adult)
- *His parents **brought** him **up** to be honest.* (raised)

phrase   a group of words that forms a unit but does not have a main verb. Many phrases give information about time or place.

- ***Last year**, we were living **in Canada**.*

plural   two or more.

- *There **are** three **people** in the restaurant.*
- ***They are** eating dinner.*
- ***We** saw **them**.*

possessive   nouns, pronouns, or adjectives that show a relationship or show that someone owns something.

- *Zach is **Megan's** brother.* (possessive noun)
- *Is that car **his**?* (possessive pronoun)
- *That's **his** car.* (possessive adjective)

predicate   the part of a sentence that has the main verb. It tells what the subject is doing or describes the subject.

- *My sister **works for a travel agency**.*

preposition   a word that goes before a noun or a pronoun to show time, place, or direction.

- *I went **to** the bank **on** Monday. It's **next to** my office.*

Prepositions also go before nouns, pronouns, and gerunds in expressions with verbs and adjectives.

- *We rely **on** him.*
- *She's accustomed **to** getting up early.*

progressive   (also called **continuous**) the verb form *be* + verb + *-ing*. It focuses on the continuation (not the completion) of an action.

- *She**'s reading** the paper.*
- *We **were watching** TV when you called.*

pronoun   a word used in place of a noun.

- *That's my brother. You met **him** at my party.*

proper noun   a noun that is the name of a person, place, or thing. It begins with a capital letter.

- ***Maria** goes to **Central High School**.*
- *It's on **High Street**.*

punctuation marks used in writing (period, comma, . . .). They make the meaning clear. For example, a period (**.**) shows the end of a sentence. It also shows that the sentence is a statement, not a question.

quantifier a word or phrase that shows an amount (but not an exact amount). It often comes before a noun.

- Josh bought **a lot of** books last year, but he only read **a few**.
- He doesn't have **much** time.

question See **yes/no question** and **wh- question**.

question word See **wh- word**.

reciprocal pronoun a pronoun (*each other* or *one another*) that shows that the subject and object of a sentence refer to the same people and that these people have a two-way relationship.

- Megan and Jason have known **each other** since high school.
- All the students worked with **one another** on the project.

reflexive pronoun a pronoun (*myself, yourself, himself, herself, itself, ourselves, yourselves, themselves*) that shows that the subject and the object of the sentence refer to the same people or things.

- He looked at **himself** in the mirror.
- They enjoyed **themselves** at the party.

regular a word that changes its form in the usual way.

- **play** → play**ed**
- **fast** → fast**er**
- **quick** → quick**ly**

sentence a group of words that has a subject and a main verb. It begins with a capital letter and ends with a period (**.**), question mark (**?**), or exclamation point (**!**).

- **Computers are** very useful.

EXCEPTION: In imperative sentences, the subject is *you*. We do not usually say or write the subject in imperative sentences.

- **Call** her now!

separable phrasal verb a phrasal verb whose parts can separate.

- Tom **looked** the word **up** in a dictionary.
- He **looked** it **up**.

short answer an answer to a *yes/no* question.

A: *Did you call me last night?*
B: *No, I didn't.* OR **No.**

singular one.

- They have **a sister**.
- **She** works in **a hospital**.

statement a sentence that gives information. In writing, it ends in a period.

- Today is Monday.

stative verb See **non-action verb**.

subject the person, place, or thing that the sentence is about.

- **Ms. Chen** teaches English.
- **Her class** is interesting.

subject pronoun a pronoun that shows the person or thing (*I, you, he, she, it, we, they*) that the sentence is about.

- **I** read a lot.
- **She** reads a lot too.

subordinate clause See **dependent clause**.

superlative the form of an adjective or adverb that is used to compare a person, place, or thing to a group of people, places, or things.

- Cindi is **the best** dancer in the group. (adjective)
- She dances **the most gracefully**. (adverb)

tense the form of a verb that shows the time of the action.

- **simple present**: Fabio **talks** to his friend every day.
- **simple past**: Fabio **talked** to his teacher yesterday.

third-person singular the pronouns *he, she*, and *it* or a singular noun. In the simple present, the third-person-singular verb ends in *-s*.

- Tomás **works** in an office. (Tomás = he)

time clause a clause that begins with a time word such as *when, before, after, while*, or *as soon as*.

- I'll call you **when I get home**.

time expression a phrase that describes when something happened or will happen.

- We saw Tomás **last week**.
- He'll graduate **next year**.

transitive verb   a verb that has an object.

- She **paints** beautiful pictures.

two-word verb   See **phrasal verb**.

verb   a word that describes what the subject of the sentence does, thinks, feels, senses, or owns.

- They **run** two miles every day.
- She **loved** that movie.
- He **has** a new camera.

vowel   a letter of the alphabet. The vowels are:

- **a, e, i, o, u.**

wh- question   (also called **information question**) a question that begins with a wh- word. You answer a wh- question with information.

A: Where are you going?

B: To the store.

wh- word   (also called **question word**) a word such as who, what, when, where, which, why, how, and how much. It can begin a wh- question.

- **Who** is that?
- **What** did you see?
- **When** does the movie usually start?
- **How** long is it?

yes/no question   a question that begins with a form of be or an auxiliary verb. You can answer a yes/no question with yes or no.

A: Are you a student?

B: Yes, I am. OR **No,** I'm not.

A: Do you come here often?

B: Yes, I do. OR **No,** I don't.

REVIEW TESTS ANSWER KEY

Note: In this answer key, where the contracted verb form is given, it is the preferred form, though the full form is also acceptable. Where the full verb form is given, it is the preferred form, though the contracted form is also acceptable.

PART I

I (Unit 1)
2. breathe
3. 's going
4. goes
5. rains
6. 's raining
7. 're dancing
8. dance

II (Unit 1)
1. c. 'm brushing
   d. Is . . . getting
   e. think
   f. 's looking
2. a. smells
   b. are . . . cooking
   c. do . . . have
   d. don't
   e. Do . . . know
   f. 're keeping OR keep
   g. 'm standing
   h. don't see
3. a. tastes
   b. 'm packing
   c. Is
   d. don't want
   e. 'm not
   f. look
   g. Do . . . feel OR Are . . . feeling
   h. do OR am
   i. hear
   j. 're leaving

III (Unit 2)
2. don't walk
3. lock
4. don't forget
5. Don't put
6. Put
7. Call
8. don't call
9. Have . . . enjoy

IV (Unit 3)
2. moved
3. did . . . live
4. was
5. taught
6. Did . . . like
7. did
8. Did . . . appear
9. did

10. wasn't
11. didn't seem
12. was
13. went
14. Were
15. wasn't
16. began
17. Did . . . expect
18. didn't

V (Units 3 and 5)
2. cook
3. Were
4. used to
5. go
6. went
7. Did
8. didn't have

VI (Unit 4)
2. was mowing
3. rang
4. had
5. wasn't
6. wasn't driving
7. hit
8. did . . . do
9. was trying
10. wasn't paying
11. Did . . . call
12. happened
13. appeared
14. got
15. left
16. called

VII (Unit 6)
2. 'll be
3. 'll
4. does
5. 's going to
6. 'll have
7. 's going to
8. are we going to
9. Will
10. are

VIII (Unit 7)
2. a. get
   b. 'll see
3. a. 'll stay
   b. finish
4. a. graduates
   b. 'll live
5. a. 'll read
   b. eat
6. a. 'll buy
   b. save
7. a. will call
   b. leaves
8. a. turn
   b. 'll be

IX (Unit 8)
1. b. Who went
   c. What did you see
2. a. What happened
   b. What did you get
   c. Who(m) did you study

X **(Units 1–8)**

2. C	7. A	12. D
3. C	8. B	13. B
4. D	9. D	14. C
5. B	10. B	
6. A	11. A	

XI **(Units 1–8)**

2. D	5. B	8. D	11. B
3. C	6. A	9. B	12. D
4. B	7. B	10. D	13. A

PART II

I **(Unit 9)**

2. herself	9. them
3. their	10. yourself
4. themselves	11. yourself
5. yourself	12. you
6. themselves	13. them
7. them	14. each other's
8. one another	

II **(Unit 10)**

2. turned into	8. pass over
3. found out	9. get back
4. set up	10. went on
5. help out	11. get by
6. look up	12. hand . . . over
7. pick out	

III **(Unit 10)**

2. wrote it down	5. help him out
3. pick her up	6. picked it out
4. put it on	7. write them up

IV **(Units 9 and 10)**

2. B	5. A	8. A
3. A	6. C	9. A
4. D	7. C	10. A

V **(Units 9 and 10)**

I have three older brothers, but my role model is my next oldest brother, Orlando. Orlando was

always there for ~~myself~~ [*me*] when we were growing up. I was very small, and he always kept the bullies

away. When I couldn't figure ~~up~~ [*out*] homework

problems by myself, he helped ~~out me~~ [*me out*]. Orlando never gave up when he had problems. Once, in

high school, my baseball team passed ~~myself~~ [*me*] up for pitcher. I wanted to quit the team, but he talked me

~~over~~ [*into*] playing. In fact, he woke [*up*] early every morning ~~up~~ to practice with me. When they chose me for pitcher the following year, we were really

proud of ~~ourselves~~ [*each other*]—he was proud of me for

succeeding, and I was proud of ~~himself~~ [*him*] for being such a great coach.

PART III

I **(Units 11–15)**

2. b	6. a
3. a	7. a
4. a	8. a
5. b	9. a

II **(Units 11–15)**

2. request	9. request
3. suggestion	10. request
4. permission	11. ability
5. ability	12. suggestion
6. permission	13. advice
7. suggestion	14. ability
8. advice	

III **(Units 11–15)**

1. b. should we	2. a. Let's
c. could	b. Could
d. Why not	c. be able to
e. 'd better	d. Do you mind if
f. How about	e. Not at all.
g. should	f. could
h. Let's	g. 'd better
i. We should	3. a. Why don't
	b. Could
	c. could
	d. Would you mind

IV **(Units 11–15)**

2. D	6. D	10. A
3. C	7. D	11. C
4. A	8. A	
5. D	9. B	

V **(Units 11–15)**

2. A: When you were a child, were you able to skate?

   B: Yes. In fact, I once ~~could~~ [*was able to*] win a competition in my school.

3. A: Could ~~please you~~ *you please* help me?
   OR *Could you help me, please?*

   B: Sure. What seems to be the problem?

4. A: Would you mind giving me a ride home?

   Not at all. OR *No, I wouldn't.*
   B: ~~Yes, I would~~. When would you like to leave?

5. A: You really ought ^*to* update your virus protection.

   B: OK. I'll do it today.

6. A: We ~~would~~ *'d* better hurry, or we'll be late.

   B: Don't worry. We can still get there on time.

7. A: Could I borrow the car tonight?

   can't
   B: Sorry, but you ~~couldn't~~. I need it myself.

8. A: Do you mind if my friend *comes* ~~coming~~ to the party with me?

   B: Not at all. There's always room for one more!

PART IV

I (Unit 16)

2. have . . . been	7. have . . . won
3. has . . . gotten	8. haven't told
4. 've . . . paid	9. Has . . . come
5. Have . . . written	10. 've had
6. hasn't read	11. Have . . . chosen

II (Unit 16)

2. Since, for	6. Since
3. for	7. since
4. since	8. for
5. for	

III (Units 17 and 18)

2. C	5. B	8. A
3. D	6. C	9. A
4. A	7. B	10. A

IV (Unit 20)

2. D	6. B	10. C
3. A	7. C	11. D
4. D	8. A	
5. C	9. C	

V (Units 16–20)

1. b. saw
2. a. drank (OR 's drunk)
   b. haven't drunk
   c. 've been drinking
3. a. has written
   b. Did . . . write
   c. wrote
4. a. 've been cooking
   b. cooked (OR 've cooked)
   c. 've cooked
5. a. 've been having (OR 've had)
   b. haven't had
   c. 've had
   d. had
   e. didn't have
6. a. looked
   b. 's been looking
   c. Has . . . looked (OR Did . . . look)
   d. looked

VI (Units 16–20)

2. I have been working as a bookkeeper in
   for OR *since four years ago.*
   this company ~~since~~ four years.

   done
3. I have ~~did~~ a good job.

   gotten
4. I have already ~~been getting~~ a promotion.

   have
5. I ~~has~~ gained a lot of experience in retail sales.

   taken
6. In addition, I have ~~took~~ several accounting courses.

   has liked
7. Since February my boss ~~like~~ my work a lot.

   given
8. She has ~~gave~~ me more and more responsibility.

   shown
9. I have already ~~show~~ my accounting skills.

10. This has been ~~being~~ a very good experience for me.

PART V

I (Unit 21)

1. b. many letters	6. a. it
2. a. it doesn't	7. a. a lot of
3. a. 's	b. many bags
b. several	8. a. much
c. computers	b. some
4. a. It's	9. a. it
5. a. too much salt	
b. It tastes	

II **(Unit 21)**

2. enough
3. a lot of
4. How much
5. a little
6. a few
7. some
8. How many
9. any
10. much
11. a lot of
12. a few

III **(Unit 22)**

2. a, a, an
3. the
4. The
5. the, the
6. the
7. an
8. a
9. the, an

IV **(Unit 22)**

3. the
4. Money
5. Travel, Staying
6. The
7. Vegetables

V **(Unit 22)**

1. b. some
   c. a
   d. an
   e. The
   f. The
2. a. some
   b. some
   c. the
   d. some
   e. The
   f. the

VI **(Units 21 and 22)**

2. B
3. C
4. A
5. A
6. C
7. A

PART VI

I **(Unit 23)**

1. b. cozy
   c. Cheap
   d. perfect
2. a. incredibly
   b. new
   c. hardly
   d. terrific
3. a. good
   b. beautiful
   c. well
   d. obedient
   e. quickly

II **(Units 25 and 26)**

2. A
3. C
4. A
5. B
6. C
7. D
8. B
9. A
10. C
11. D
12. B
13. D

III **(Unit 23)**

2. C
3. D
4. B
5. C
6. B
7. A
8. B
9. B
10. C
11. C
12. B

IV **(Units 25 and 26)**

2. faster, more confused
3. later, sillier
4. harder, more fluently
5. more often, bigger
6. louder, faster
7. more frequently, worse

V **(Units 24 and 26)**

2. is as large as Apartment 22-G.
3. isn't as far (away) as Tony's pizzeria.
4. is as expensive as Tony's pizza.
5. play (OR are playing OR have played) as well as the Shock.
6. doesn't run as fast as (OR isn't as fast as) Jennifer.

VI **(Units 25 and 26)**

1. b. longest
   c. hardest
   d. the
   e. of
   f. best
2. a. big
   b. than
   c. much
   d. exciting
   e. Sooner
   f. as

VII **(Units 23–26)**

I think today has been the ~~bad~~ *worst* day of my life. My car broke down on the expressway during rush hour this morning—~~a~~ *the* busiest time of day. I sat there for an hour waiting for a tow truck. The longer I waited, the *more* ⌃ nervous I became. I was a wreck when I got to work. Of course, this was the day we were closing ⌃ *the* biggest deal of the year. My boss called me five times about one letter. And ⌃ *the* more frequently he called, the worse I typed. My next worry is the repair bill for the car. I hope it isn't as high ⌃ *as* the last time.

I'm going to try to relax now. There's an ~~interested~~ *interesting* movie on cable TV tonight. Jan saw it last week and says it's the ~~better~~ *best* film she's seen in a long time. After the movie, I'll take a ~~hotter~~ *hot* bath and go to bed. I'm looking forward to tomorrow. It can't be as ~~badly~~ *bad* as today!

PART VII

I (Unit 28)

2. to planning
3. for watching
4. about speaking
5. without worrying
6. in learning

II (Unit 31)

2. too messy
3. not cool enough
4. too tough
5. aggressively enough
6. loud enough

III (Units 27 and 30)

2. telling
3. smoking
4. giving up
5. Following
6. to feel
7. To save
8. to read
9. drinking
10. to take
11. eating
12. shopping
13. to reward

IV (Unit 29)

2. It's necessary to join
3. participate enough to meet
4. too busy to call
5. flexible enough for them to have
6. advise them to think about
7. it's important to know about
8. soon enough for them to pay
9. too busy to take
10. encourage you to start

V (Units 27–32)

2. B   5. A   8. D
3. A   6. D   9. C
4. C   7. C   10. C

VI (Units 27–32)

2. to hit
3. having
4. winning
5. playing
6. to become
7. to make
8. becoming
9. doing
10. to go
11. to accept
12. to study
13. studying
14. agreeing
15. answering

VII (Units 27–32)

2. D   4. B   6. D   8. C
3. D   5. D   7. B

PART VIII

I (Units 33–37)

2. b   6. b   9. a   12. a
3. a   7. a   10. b   13. b
4. b   8. a   11. b   14. b
5. a

II (Units 33–37)

2. necessity
3. preference
4. conclusion
5. expectation
6. prohibition
7. future possibility
8. conclusion
9. expectation
10. conclusion
11. necessity
12. prohibition

III (Units 33–37)

2. C   5. B   8. A
3. D   6. B   9. B
4. A   7. C   10. A

IV (Units 33–37)

2. She prefers not to watch science fiction.
3. It must be expensive.
4. She (OR Linda) wasn't supposed to open it in front of him (OR Somchai).
5. He must not be at work today.
6. She (OR Sue) might not like curry.
7. You (OR I) have to arrive at the airport by noon.
8. She (OR His sister) was going to go to his graduation.
9. It couldn't be Carl.
10. It could be very valuable.

V (Units 33–37)

I ^'m supposed to take my road test tomorrow. I'm a little nervous because I heard that there might be a storm. I'd ~~not rather~~ *rather not* drive in the rain! My instructor, John, is supposed to pick me up at 8:00 and drive me to the test area. Then he ~~have~~ *has* to wait for me while I take the test. He ~~doesn't have to~~ *must not* OR *can't* be in the car with me during the test—it's not allowed. I like John. I don't know much about him. He says he's been driving for more than 40 years, so I guess he ^'s got to be at least 60. He ~~maybe~~ *may be* even older than that.

Well, it's getting late, and I should go to bed. I'd rather ~~watching~~ *watch* some TV, but I ~~hafta~~ *have to* get up early tomorrow.

INDEX

This Index is for the full and split editions. All entries are in the full book. Entries for Volume A of the split edition are in black. Entries for Volume B are in color.

Notes

Notes

Notes

Notes

Notes